A Better Me

A story of my weaknesses, strengths, triumphs, and downfalls; and how I made it through in one piece.

Martina Common

A Better Me: A story of my weaknesses, strengths, triumphs, and downfalls; and how I made it through in one piece.

Copyright © 2023 by Martina Common

C.A.B.R.I.N.I. Publishing

DEDICATION

To My Angels in Heaven: My brother: Marvell, my Grandmother Rosie, and childhood friends of Cabrini Green I hope I continue to make you proud. Your legacy and love lives within me, Rest Peacefully.

To the loves of my life: my mother Elaine, my two sisters Ta'Rika and Jada, thank you for walking with me through my happiest moments and most importantly my darkest. You three are the reason why I smile, why I stay motivated, and why I continue to strive for the best. Without you, I wouldn't have the strength and faith to keep on keeping on. I appreciate you three for staying up with me (sometimes for a full 24 hours) when I was sick, working on school projects, creating this book, holding me when I cry, sneaking beautiful cards under my pillow at night, hugging me for no reason at all, being overprotective of me when it came to friendships and relationships downfalls. You never judge, you're always there, loving me for me. Mommy, I applaud you for being able to take care of three girls by yourself molding us into women of intellect. You have instilled the power of strength, faith, love, respect, and a platform to withstand anything. I can honestly say: I'm a lucky woman to have a mom like you: who has made sure I and my sisters live a life we love.

To Joseph: thank you for coming into my life and showing through your actions the definition of what a father is; it means more than words can express. To my professors, teachers, and role models: from Sojourner Truth School Mr. Spicer and Mr. Price, Schiller School: Mrs. Turner, Simeon Career Academy: Coach Chick, and Columbia College Chicago: Jeff Jacobson the lessons you all taught me to intertwine into one jewel: stay true to self. That jewel means a lot because with it I've been able to accomplish, learn, explore, and appreciate many things. To my family, extended family, and friends that have rooted for me, stayed excited about what's to come and supported me since day one. I appreciate you. Thank You. To the almighty above, thank you: especially for the gift of life. I never would have made it without you. The lessons have taught me a lot about life and I pray that I can be of help to a hurting heart.

To My Son: you were inside my tummy getting ready to arrive in the world when this book was in its last stages of being written. And you were finally here laying on my lap, over my shoulder, sleeping close to me when I wrote my last sentence. My motivation: my miracle. I hope that you learn from mommy's journey and instill within you that mommy will be right by your side throughout every walk of life. Never give up and always stay positive. You are my biggest blessing. I do this for you. And even with this being the second edition of A Better Me, you are the reason, I rebirth my dreams and my voice.

A Better Me

Contents

Chapter 1

Not Ashamed

Not Ashamed

On a cold December day of 2009, I was walking through Chicago's Cabrini Green Housing Projects located on the Near North Side, consisting of 23 "red" buildings, 8 "white" buildings, and two-story row houses. While walking through the projects, it brought back memories. From one building to another, vivid memories of snowball fights, making snow angels, and getting lost amongst the piles of slush.

I remember watching workers prepare to plant rose gardens in front of the buildings every Spring, seeing mothers hanging clothes on-ramps to dry as summer chimed in, and listening to Z.Z. Hill: Down Home Blues and B.B. King: The Thrill Is Gone traveling from one house to another. Children would run house to house to get icy cups made from frozen kool-aid, and young men played football on the front lawns.

But on this particular afternoon, everything was quiet. I walked to my old building, 2 out of 8 that were still standing. I pulled my gloves and hood on tighter, remembering the walks to this same building during my favorite time of the year, summer. I would stop by the candy lady stand, which was in the playground on the building's side across from mine.

Mrs. Evans was my favorite candy lady, selling candy ever since my grandmother Rosie was alive. Sometimes I would stay with her for an hour as I waved to my mother in my bedroom window across the way, smiling at me. Mrs. Evans had all the candy you can think of: chews (one of my favorites), cry baby bubble gum (that would have my eyes watery as I jumped up and down, but I still loved eating them), chips with taco meat, and hot cheese (Flamin hots were the best), tootsie rolls (in all flavors), pop rocks, sugar babies, dots, watermelon suckers (which were in the shape of a watermelon, that tasted so good in the raspberry flavor). Her candy was neatly in order on the table, and she made a lot of money.

After my hour sat with her, I walked across the street to my building. When I got to the front of it, I waved up to close friends and elders, calling me off the ramps, and proceeded through the double doors. When I got upstairs to the apartment I lived in (with my mother Elaine, big sister Ta'Rika, and later down the line baby sister Jada), I inhaled dinner outside the door. My mother was cooking macaroni, string beans, garlic bread, and catfish.

I could never eat catfish without mistakenly letting the tiniest piece of bones slip down my throat. So my mom took her time, peeling the skin and meat off the bones for me on a plate. On the other hand, my sister gobbled down her fish with a gallon of hot sauce in about two bites. I'll be on plate one while she was on plate three.

We sat at the kitchen table connected to the living room and discussed our day. My mom talked about the different people who came into her office downstairs in my building. She worked for the management of Cabrini. She'd talk about how people ask the same questions repeatedly as if they didn't hear the person in front of them ask the same problem.

Questions like when is rent due? How much can we put down on our light bill? How can we get a new refrigerator and stove? I chuckled because I knew how my mother was about that; she always said, "pay attention, so neither you nor anyone else would have to keep repeating themselves." And it amazed me how even adults at the time didn't pay attention.

My sister discussed her day at school and how she pinched some boy for blowing kisses at her. And me, just like every night, discussed my drum group trips. Sojourner Truth Elementary School, centered in the middle of Cabrini's white buildings, had a drum team instructed by a woman named Mrs. Hope. Mrs. Hope reminded me so much of my grandmother that she always made sure we were safe, respectful, and bonding with one another.

An ear for sound and creativeness of instruments coming together caused me to join the drum team. Requirements to join were having a G.P.A. 2.6 or higher, good comments from teachers, respecting others and keeping your studies up. Mrs. Hope wanted only people that are serious about the craft and their education on the team.

My sister and I and a few guys and girls made the drum team. Every day after school we practiced for two hours, and only practiced longer when we were getting closer to performances. The girls and I played the cymbals, and the guys played a variety of drums. Mrs. Hope set the platform for us to showcase our talent beyond the school auditorium.

Navy Pier, restaurants holding gatherings, marches, and parades were amongst the places we performed. Navy Pier hosted an event that brought out families, schools, and people of Chicago. The event took place on a stage centered in the middle of the opening entrance. Plays about bullying, peer pressure, depression, and learning not to talk to strangers were amongst the lessons gracing the stage.

Afterward, entertainment: singing, dancing, and drumming were displayed. I talked that night with my family about our drum trip to Navy Pier. "Once you come in, there's no walking out" is all I kept hearing at the performance. The people acted like someone was standing on every sidewalk of Cabrini, with a gun in one hand, pointing at us, while smiling and waving.

The image played in my head while I slammed the cymbals together, putting on a fake smile for the crowd.

"Made you want to throw something at them, huh?" my mom said, shaking her head.

"Yes," I said with a lot of aggression.

Then I went on to tell them how one man with a long leather black jacket on in the middle of the summer had the nerves to say "little lost black kids, huh." We continue to look on with smiles putting our anger into the instruments. Mrs. Hope stood firm, in front, not taking her eyes off the man. In return, the man glanced at Mrs. Hope, stared back at us with disgust, bit on his lip, not uttering another word.

"That's a good thing that you all stood your ground because you have to learn how to ignore the negative comments. If you react, you're only proving to them that they can get under your skin," my mom said, shaking her head once more. My mother was tied up in meetings that day and couldn't make the performance; after telling her what happened, she never missed one again.

Due to the experience at Navy Pier, my mind frame as I got older was to prove people wrong. When someone asks where I'm from, I say, and still say, Cabrini Green. And the looks I got then and now are priceless. Some: eyes want to pop out of their heads, others: smack their lips, while the majority look like they were ready to run away from me and hide.

The response back then was, "Oh yeah, they're about to get torn down" as if it was a relief for them. I hated knowing that the buildings were coming down. Walking to my old building for the last time, I slowly took in the beautiful trees and grass that covered the spots where other buildings once sat. I walked through my old lobby, greeted by guys that attended school with me.

I gave the guys hugs, asked how they were, and kept walking towards the elevators. I leaned against the green walls, stared out the back of the building, down the street, to where the second remaining building stood. It was funny how the two left had the same address, 1230, just different last names: Larrabee and Burling.

As the elevator opened, one of the guys with a black sweater, in his mid 20's, named Jay, stopped in front of me smiling. I smiled back. "You're still dancing, Martina?" he asked with a grin. "No, not anymore," I said as I walked onto the elevator. As the elevator door closed, I could hear him talking to the other guys about how, when I danced, I brought smiles to everyone's faces in the community.

Boy, how I miss those days because dancing used to be a significant part of my life. I would gather up some kids at Stanton Park, the neighborhood park district located in the whites. The kids were younger than me, ages six through eleven, and I remember teaching them how to do the tootsie roll, the clean version.

Jay sat in the bleachers, overlooking the gymnasium, watching. "Squat like you're about to push," the children would giggle upon me saying it. "Then turn your legs inward, moving them in and out, sometimes fast and sometimes slow. There you go, yall get it". I sped up the dance steps if I saw them catching the hang of it.

The little girls, with pigtails, looked adorable out on the gym floor. Even the little guys cracked me up trying to do it but instead looked like they were hurting themselves. Some of my friends and other people my age would come in later. That's when I let myself loose. Footwork and pop-locking moves were the dances we did. Jay would still be up in the balcony, his buddies joining him, bobbing their heads to the tunes, watching every move; they knew how serious I was about dancing.

My dancing started at four years old. I learned how to step to James Brown Big Pay Back, watching New Edition dance moves, mainly

Bobby Brown, because he was always on point. I engaged a lot into the artist's foot movement and the feel of music that gets a person up on their feet. My mom always had ol skool music playing, and when I put the music to the music video, more steps sparked in my thoughts.

I begin envisioning myself on stage inspired by dancers and creating dance moves of my own. My dancing was a hidden talent that came to life, and a talent my community could see. We prepared for the neighborhood talent shows that took place every Spring. There were no first, second place winners. Everyone was winners.

Outside dancers, not from the neighborhood, performed to make the shows more significant and better. You had to pay three dollars to get into the talent show. Silver bleachers spread across the gymnasium, and the balcony that overlooked the gym occupied dancers' families and friends. Balloons hung throughout the gym hanging from bleachers, doorknobs, and chairs with a color theme that fit each year's flavor.

The majority of our families would sit up front in the center, on the bleachers downstairs to get a better view for pictures. What I loved most about Stanton Park talent shows, besides making up the dances with my dance group, was the energy from the crowds shouting, singing, and dancing along with us in

their seats.

Each dance group displayed a unique talent along with stylish clothes: spray paint t-shirts, throwback jerseys, even suits. Jay was always amongst the crowd giving me two thumbs up. I went from dancing in Stanton Park talent shows to also dancing in my elementary school, Friedrich Von Schiller, also located in the center of Cabrini's white buildings, talent shows as well.

At the school shows, I performed routines similar to the Stanton Park show with the dance group. I remember us practicing for hours at my mom's office inside a room filled with brown wall-to-wall boxes of books donated to Cabrini Green children for the upcoming school year. We would perfect the crafts of Missy Elliott's dance routines as well as making up our own.

I was determined to learn as many moves as possible with the vision of being a part-time choreographer when I grew up. Unfortunately, I began to have consistent back pain that made it hard for me to move and walk. I thought it was just the many moves I did while dancing that made me feel this way. So I tried to rest some days, but the pain wouldn't go away.

My mother was worried and decided to take me to the hospital for tests. A few weeks later, I learned my diagnosis was a severe case of Scoliosis, the curving of the spine. When my doctor revealed "any other move could paralyze you,"; I had to make a big decision; risk my life or leave dancing forever.

I chose to leave dancing because I knew I had another craft. I had my life ahead of me to do many things, and I probably wouldn't be able to if I hadn't stopped dancing. So my decision was made. I still have tapes, recorded by my mother, dancing in the shows that I will forever cherish.

I watch the recordings when I'm feeling down; it helps my motivation rekindle. Dancing was a passion that's a reminder that anything is possible if you work hard at it. And if you come across a roadblock, think about what's best for you in the long run. I had to close the chapter on one of my passions. I also ended a chapter on a friendship.

Jay and I had a strong sibling bond. While growing up, we did everything together, such as attending the same school, having movie nights, dinner, and long talks over the phone. I remember when Jay was terrible at school one day, and he came over to my house. Jay was scared to go in because he knew my mom had already talked with his mom about him cursing out a teacher.

He walked through the front door of my house and stood there. You could smell taco meat coming from the kitchen. "Pumpkin is that you," my mom yelled over the sizzling of meat. "Yes, ma," I yelled back. "Hey, Jay," she said firmly. His eyes got bigger as he plopped to the floor by the front door.

"You are not going to come in," I whispered.

I knew my mom was finish cooking because I didn't hear the stirring of the meat anymore. She stuck her head around the corner. "Jay, you need to start doing better in school and respecting your teachers. They are here to help you not be mistreated by you" she still had the silver spoon from cooking covered with grease spots in her hand.

Jay leaned his head over in shame "you two come on in here, wash your hands, eat, and take out your homework so I can go over it with you" my mother disappeared back into the kitchen. Jay looked at me and said, "so glad to have you as my best friend" I just smiled. I remember those words as if he just said them to me.

Our friendship faded as we became teens. Jay soon became mixed up in peer pressure years. He became involved with the streets, hanging with the gang members, and selling drugs. I knew I had to let our friendship go. I saw Jay outside in the playground, secretly passing bags to a man who seems to be out of it.

The man was nodding and scratching his nose repeatedly before handing Jay some money. I stood there watching Jay as he turned to stare me straight in the face. No words exchanged as I walked off, I wave bye to him, and that was it. I stayed in contact with his family because I cared and loved him; their response was always "Martina, he's alive" That's all I needed to hear, praying that he would change one day and do better.

The whites, reds, and row houses of Cabrini housed many guys whose life went in the same direction as Jay's outcome: prison, watching their back all the time, death, or all three. What we had to experience within the community as kids you would've thought would change their actions, but it didn't. Growing up, we heard about other kids dying from crossfire and fighting to get by within the community.

My mother told me about a kid on their way to school and got fatally shot by a sniper. The kid was not the intended target. Our community came together to call for security to be present for our safety. During this time, police brought out metal gates, metal detectors, and scanners, placing them throughout the building lobbies. These safety procedures helped all children of Cabrini get to school unharmed.

I remember looking at a newspaper, trembling, seeing a headline of a child being raped and beaten in causing parents' sense of security and awareness to strengthen. For my friends who didn't have someone to take them to school in the mornings, my mother would let them stay the night and take us before she headed to work.

Those experiences made me more alert to my surroundings. The incidents also encourage us to form a peace march where children throughout the community walk Cabrini grounds while the drum team and I led the way. Parents marched by our side, holding stop the violence signs, while others looked off the ramps clapping.

I had to start using survival techniques such as paying close attention to everything around me, learning who and who not to trust, and walking faster when I felt something wasn't right.

I stepped out of the elevator where I used to stay. I could see Jay waving from in the front of the building at me. I wish things were the same. I missed our apartment.

Our first one was in 1230 N. Larrabee, on the 8th floor consisting of two bedrooms, one bath, a living room, and a kitchen. Due to the 8th floor apartment having bad pipes, we moved down to the 6th floor. The 6th-floor apartment consisted of three bedrooms, one bath, a living room, and a kitchen. The bedrooms in our apartment were right next to each other.

The walls were white with the bottom paint lining black. People in the community painted their apartments all types of colors: tye-dye, polka dot trims, even their kid's hands splattered across the walls. It was pretty interesting to see apartments looking as if they were a portrait of creativity inside an art museum.

In our apartment, it was a must to sit down and have dinner together at the table. The wooden table sat on the left side, seating up to four people. If you were the one sitting in the seat next to the refrigerator, you were lucky. Having access to the kool-aid first was why that was my special seating, even if I was sitting at the table alone.

Behind the kitchen set going towards the apartment's back, three brown sofas brought out the room paint lining's richness. And the television screen centered in the middle of the sofas shined comedy movies such as Nutty Professor, Problem Child, Dennis to Menace, and Home Alone. While my mother was at work, my big sister and I would build tents in the living room with bed sheets making our spooky edition of the horror flick, Scream, a movie based on a killer running around with a hook, black throw gown, and mask.

When mom got home, we played Twister, Connect Four, Candy Land, Shoots & Ladders, or Goldfish. This type of love and quality time in a place where people thought was horrible everyday made it more peaceful, especially Sundays.

We went to Sunday dinner at Granny's house in the next building, 1340 N. Larrabee, across from ours.

My granny use to say "Gimmie dat-air spoon Tina Marie" while I helped her cook cabbage, greens, ham, turkey, candy yams, neck bones, smothered potatoes, and cornbread. She'll ask, "how many of dem cornbread is you et?" as I tried to hide the crumbs behind my back. "Well, you know Tina Marie, your uncle is a-comin, so you gwine have to save him at least two. And I see ima hafta hide that from you".

I giggled as she passed me a bowl of corn that was soaking in water. "Gwine, make sure it's clean for me." My granny's attention went on my cousin, who was coming into the kitchen with his pants hanging down. One stare from her, he quickly pulled his pants up. I greeted him with a hug. "yall go ahead and get washed up" she turned back to me and smiled.

Family members arrived as all the pans of food were being set out on the table by my mother and big sister. We stuffed our mouths with granny soul food while other families in Cabrini had traditions going on as well. You could smell the sweet freshness of buttered cornbread lingering outside through the trees and windows within every building, giving you a taste of southern life.

When southerners arrived at Cabrini in the 1970s, things changed in the community. Cabrini Green became predominantly black; the crime rate had risen, an increasing amount of unemployment and gangs were developing. The young guys were all joining gangs, including one of my cousins, who started going to jail at age 16.

My cousin Curtis as he got older happens to be one of the people Jay was around. And when he was younger, just like Jay, he thought it was cool to hang around the gang members. Curtis felt that they genuinely protected him, could earn cash fast to buy the latest name brand outfit and shoes, and have the reputation as a man about his business, the illegal way.

Even with the family's support surrounding him, he still wanted to be like the next person. Curtis spent most of his time behind bars from his teenage years to thirty. He'll only be out for a month or two then right back in. Curtis walked around with the same clothes on for three days, pants hanging low (had the nerve to have a belt on it), and didn't have shoelaces in his shoes.

I can recall a heart-to-heart conversation we had together before he returned to what we call his second home, jail, a week later. "Curtis, you must like going to jail?" "This is my way to live" "you haven't tried living the right way" "Is there a right way because the way I was living at first didn't keep these stacks of ones in my pocket" we continued to stare each other down as if we were getting ready for a boxing match.

"The way you are living now isn't even keeping the stack of ones in your pocket because you always get it taken when you" Curtis put his head down. "You're very wise to be only 12 years old, Tina Marie. I'm going to try to change for you". After our heart to heart, Curtis walked out the door. I continued to pray that we wouldn't get a collect call in the next hour or worse, a morgue call. I didn't want to see Curtis shot- fighting to survive.

I used to have nightmares of red sirens flashing as I walked towards the ambulance. My family screams, getting louder with an image of my cousin's arms hanging from the sides, stretched out and slumped as if he were a rag doll. I kept him in my prayers like I kept Jay. In the present, Curtis and Jay are still alive.

Curtis lived the same illegal life, and Jay was trying to get his life back on track by putting more time into working a job to support his daughter and going after his dreams: to be a model and in the music industry. I'm proud of Jay but still haven't had the opportunity to reconnect, with it not being through his family, but one day I'm sure we will.

To change the thoughts from running through my mind, I'll watch three of my favorite shows and movies: Cooley High, T.V. sitcom Good Times, or Candy Man, all made in Cabrini. In 1974, the sitcom Good Times, taped in Cabrini Green's "red" projects, became a popular show from the past to the present. Good Times featured glances of the entire Cabrini in the opening and closing credits.

I loved watching Good Times because it showed how life was like for low-income families, painting a picture of what people have to go through from family issues and looking for good-paying jobs to keep a roof over their family heads. In 1975, Cooley High followed high school friends through the highs and lows of their life. The movie depicts how teenagers went about their studies, personal experiences inside and outside of school, and the good and bad friends they kept.

Cooley High is one of my favorite movies because of the message it captured: if you don't make smart decisions, your actions can result in bad influences and adverse outcomes. In 1992, the movie Candy Man Part 1 was released as a horror flick that caused children not to want to say Candy Man in the mirror, or he's going to come after you with bees and a hook. The first Candy Man shot glimpses and action through Cabrini grounds.

Sometimes family members dared me to say Candy Man five times in a mirror at my granny house, but I wouldn't say it for anyone. Movies and T.V. shows captured a community from the view of artistry instead of only been documented for its crime. Watching shows took my mind off a lot when residents were going through hard times.

Even though public housing was for low-income people didn't mean all was able to live there. Some people weren't able to live in Cabrini because of theirs or someone on the lease background. If there are criminal charges and nonpayment of rent, evictions took place. Management and Sheriffs would use master keys to go into an apartment to remove all tenants' belongings to either the ramp or the curb outside the buildings.

I wondered how you could put someone out on the street with small children. How could you put an older person out? Those questions scattered my mind as I got older, witnessing this happen to people. Residents would go to outside sources like a church, alderman office, the YMCA, and catholic charities to pay their rent.

Some were paid in full while others partially paid if they did receive assistance, depending on the amount due. Therefore it's a myth when you hear people say public housing was cheap. It might've been affordable for some but more challenging for others. Outside of living conditions, I took appreciation of education being important throughout the community.

What sticks with me is hearing and reading that children from the projects lacked brains in education. That is incorrect. We worked our butts off in school, attended many after-school programs, and helped each other with weaknesses. My principal at Sojourner Truth School decided to have a contest one year where we had to read a certain amount of books, take a test on the computer for each, and the points that we passed for each test tallied up a dollar amount for a Christmas spree.

Every child in my grade was determined to read as many books as possible and pass the computer tests. The shopping spree was a week before Christmas. From September to December, we remained motivated, earning as many points as possible. On the day of the shopping spree, we piled up in school buses at 4 am, chaperoned by teachers, parents, and our principal.

When we arrived at the mall in Wisconsin, we darted out the buses and ran through the toy stores throwing everything into the shopping carts with the chaperones' help. When we got to the register, the cashiers scanned each item as if we were purchasing with actual cash. Dropping the toys into the bags, the smiles on all of our faces, and the help needed to load the bags onto the buses made me realize that hard work pays off at a young age.

When we arrived back home from the shopping spree, the bags were carrying me. It felt good to accomplish a goal and bring not just ourselves but our families' things back too. Our excellent scores on the ISAT and IOWA, basic skill tests in schools, and reading comprehension reflected what we learned in the classroom, during the contest, and at home.

When I got to the 2nd grade, the teachers and principal came up with the idea to send the top 2nd graders who excel in class and test what they decided to call "a weekend of Truth." The week consisted of staying at a college, located on the south side of Chicago, The University of Chicago. While there, we step into the shoes of a college student: living in the dorms, getting up for class, and seeing the many activities to become involved in around campus.

We also traveled back to many Chicago historical sites such as the Sears Tower, now Willis Tower, Chicago Theatre, Field Museum, and Museum of Science and Industry during our week's stay. We learned why each place is as historic as the people who created them. After our week's visit, it taught us about what lies ahead in the future and that it's up to us to accomplish what we know we could if we just put our minds to it.

What will always stick with me; knowing that the learning process and support start at home. My mother stayed involved with homework assignments, studying, and what was going on in class by keeping in touch with our teachers. By my mother, being so engaged in our education made me motivated.

Unfortunately, some children don't have the same guidance and support at home, which causes them to drift onto negative paths. Many more children would be motivated to do right and follow their dreams if we became more involved and people as parents engaged more in their kids' education.

I believe it would be the start of kids having a positive mindset if they had the support from those who mattered most.

But if you don't have the support, it shouldn't stop you. Many times, friends would come to me for help with reading, writing, and math. And I was willing to guide them because I wanted to see everyone around me do better.

You also have teachers who stay after school to help children out, but you must be willing to work hard and want help.

It's up to no one but you where your life leads. A song I always refer to is the movie Sister Act, with Whoopi Goldberg, "If you want to be somebody if you want to go somewhere, you better wake up and pay attention."

Pay attention to what's taught to you, paying attention to those who are reaching out, don't let what anybody says stop you from achieving goals.

Let whatever living condition you have to motivate you whether you are still living there or have moved out. Although we moved out of Cabrini before the demolition process began, I continued to travel back and forth to Cabrini for school during my elementary days.

After graduating, I still had family and friends that I visited.

My mom still worked for the management of Cabrini, so it was like I never left. The surroundings were different; townhouses raised around the area as part of Cabrini were still up. My relatives and friends were receiving 180-day vouchers to relocate as their building was in the hot seat of being torn down.

Others moved into the community buildings that weren't in demolition yet while many relocated throughout Chicago areas going west and south. It hurt seeing where I was born and raised disappear. But what warms my heart is the memories. Memories of friendships, kids running to the park, talent show days, snow day from school, caps, and gowns flooding Cabrini grounds from graduations, and my favorite time of the year where you could smell barbeque grills cooking burgers, steaks, hot dogs, and ribs, on building ramps.

In 2009, when I walked the grounds of Cabrini for the last time, I shed tears of happiness and pain. I was happy to have gotten so many positives out of a community that the media sheds only the negative aspect. I was delighted to have learned the value of appreciating what you have. The pain of seeing now that the community is gone, people I have grown up with are dying in other neighborhoods.

Pain, of knowing that every time I drive past Cabrini Green grounds, I can visualize the buildings but come to the reality that they are gone, and maybe if they were still standing, more positives could've been brought through the walking grounds. I didn't see myself writing this as just background.

As much talk was on television and the radio about one of the dangerous public housing developments in Chicago known as Cabrini Green, the truth, beyond the violence, deserves to be known. The thoughts, the people, the experiences, good and bad, that help molds me into the person I am today made me realize that no matter where I stay or where I go, Cabrini Green will remain a neighborhood that I'm not afraid to say that I'm from.

Chapter 2

Granny, where are you?

Granny, where are you?

G rowing up, I was granny's spoiled brat. She took me everywhere with her and always made sure I had my bacon bits. Bacon bits were for salads and rice, but for me they were chips. I could eat a jar as quickly as she handed them to me. My granny used to laugh as she put up groceries in her small kitchen. From the cabinets, she watched my pink and yellow barrettes swinging and a jar bigger than me pressing against my face.

The honey syrup scent traveled through my nostrils as I could hear granny say, "Tina Marie, you gwine turn into a bacon bit one of these days," handing me my second jar secretly. My mom would always tell her that the bacon bits were too salty; she should stop giving them to me. But granny would just look at my mom, say okay, hiding another jar in the cabinet behind the seasoning salt, lemon pepper, paprika, and crushed peppers.

If you thought my bacon bit obsession was crazy, my mango one was twice the craziness. Granny would sit on her green love seat couch, as I sat in between her legs, my head pressed gently on her thigh, watching her slice the red streaks with yellow fruit. Her thumb would be centered on the mango as she cut it in circles, putting one in her mouth, and handing me the next slice.

My face squinted up from the reveal of sourness, but I still wanted more pieces, so she waited for the cue of my hand wiggling behind me. Spending time with her was like Dorothy off of Wizard of Oz. Dorothy says, "there is no place like home" I would always say, "there's no place like grandma's house."

My Grandma Rosie treated all of her grandchildren the same, molding us into not just cousins but more like brothers and sisters. If you were in school, you came to her house afterward, showered, ate, did your homework, and relaxed until it was time for you to go home. For dinners, birthday parties, and outings, each family member had to be in attendance.

Granny had her way of going by things regarding how a family operates, especially when stressing respecting one another and getting along. After arguing with a family member, she made you sit down and talk it out. My cousins were always arguing, but they knew to get their act together fast by her raising them.

Granny believed in staying caring, loyal, and lovable. Opening her door to others in Cabrini, cooking, watching over adults, babysitting their kids, and even disciplining them. Being younger than my sister and a few cousins, I was able to see grandma in action showing just how much she cares.

It was a family of four boys that lived a few doors down from granny whose mother worked a lot and wanted to know what her kids were doing at all times. The woman kids had got kicked out of school due to constant fighting, disrupting class, and ditching, so granny had a key to her house and went over to check on them.

Sometimes they would come to my granny's house to eat lunch with granny and me, and she would talk with them about the world's cruelty. They would stay quiet, not taking their eyes off her, and just listened. When they did something terrible, their mother would report it back to my granny. While on punishment, the only outside the boys seen when they looked out their window that faces the building ramp with frowned faces, crust in eyes, with black wave caps on.

I watched Granny talk to them, from the window, about life and what they should want for themselves. When grandma would walk back to her house holding my hand, she'll say, "they aren't hearing me." When the boys became adults, trouble repeatedly knocked at their door. Two got killed, and the other two are doing long bids in prison for attempted murder and kidnapping.

"I don't understand why people just can't do right," granny said one day while washing dishes. "Tina Marie, you betta stay the way you are now alert and smart. Do you hear me? And always listen to your mommy" "yes, grandma," I would say, sucking a mango dry. She'll smile, wiping her dishes with a cloth.

Granny introduced me to financial independence by observing her ice cream and candy store that she ran inside her house. "Just a way to make a little more money; you see, you have your bills money and then the money you can save for a rainy day," she would tell me while counting her earnings at closing.

I quickly learned its value, so I focused on saving and taking care of responsibilities as I got older. I knew not to blow money on things that weren't necessary by remembering the words "there are people who cannot provide and do things for themselves or their children. So cherish what you have".

I witnessed kids coming to my grandma's candy house with little to no money, and my grandma would still give them the candy and ice cream they wanted. But that was only for the small children ages five through seven. As for teenagers, she didn't trust their words so quickly "people like to get over on ya, you'll know if what they are saying is true. You'll feel it", granny would say.

The things that would come out of the teenagers' mouth, as an excuse, didn't make any sense "I sneezed and it fell out my hand and dropped down the stairs" or "my dog swallowed it, pooped it out, and I didn't want to touch it after that." When they saw she wasn't going for it, they walked off.

Her candy spread was the same as Mrs. Evans, but Mrs. Evans didn't sell any ice cream making grandma popular. Ice cream flavors granny sold were vanilla and cookies and cream, the flavors everyone wanted. I remember one day, Granny started laughing at a few customers who were leaving and me.

She sensed my confusion, picked up a napkin, and began wiping off the chocolate on my chin and nose. "You done made yourself a beard there," she would say, laughing even more. The customers and I laughed along as they wiped their chins and noses. In addition to having a store, she babysat.

Granny provided a pallet on the floor and a hot meal for anybody in need. Her reason for babysitting: to give the young mothers in the neighborhood a chance to work and go to school. Granny house was the first preschool for some children. They didn't just sit around all day doing nothing; she taught kids the alphabet, numbers, how to write their name, and trace it.

And the kids colored and were taught how to share. The children's parents appreciated knowing their kids were safe and learning because Granny made sure of it. She kept her focus on us being well advanced when heading to the preschool building. I was mad my time came first.

I wasn't quite sure I was ready. Was I not being able to see granny all day? Was I not being able to run around with bacon bits or mango? I wasn't ready for that. "Could I take it with me to school?" I ask my grandma one day as she was fixing me pancakes with bacon as a smiley face. She laughed, grabbed my cheek, and said, "every time you come here when you get out of school, I will have your bacon bits and mango waiting for you. Or I will just bring it to your house, pinky promise". I held granny to her word.

After school, I would walk past her building every day to her on the ramp in purple pajamas, rollers in her head, with a bacon bit jar in one hand, waving off and squinting her nose around to push her glasses up. I'd scream, "hey granny," and she would yell back, "are you coming up here? Or do I have to bring the treats over?"

It was the same every day looking up seeing grandma on the porch like she was doing an ad campaign for bacon bits and mango. I loved her even more for doing things like that, and I could not ever take her for granted. One day, I was excited to leave school because I would be going straight to grandma's house. I kicked the leaves on the ground, bundled up in my orange knee-length jacket, as I headed in her building's direction.

I glanced up to the 6th floor to see Granny standing on the ramp. "Come on up here; I got your mango cut for you." She was going on a Mississippi trip to see her mother and a few relatives. My mom, sisters, cousins, and I were at my granny's house to help her pack. I stood in the middle of her room door, eating slices of mango. I noticed her suitcase was spilling over in clothes.

My mom leaned on my granny wooden dresser jokingly, saying are you sure you are coming back? Granny laughed, and we did too with my mother, helping her close her suitcase. She was leaving that weekend. "I'm not going to be on the ramp come Friday, Tina Marie. So I sliced up just enough for you throughout the weekend."

Granny Rosie kissed my forehead as she and my mom walked out of the room to join everyone in the living room for charades. I was in her doorway for a minute longer, looking at the suitcase before joining them. Granny slowly sat down on her green love seat couch, observing us, smiling, and chuckling from time to time.

She even cooked a small dinner of string beans, corn, bake potatoes, and bake chicken. We ate well and joked with her about what grandchild had gotten the most spankings. Time was passing on by, and we didn't even know it was going on eleven at night. We gave granny a group hug then headed out the door while my mom talked with her.

The elevator was opening up when my mother came walking out of the house with my baby sister Jada in her car seat. Granny peeked her head out and said, see you all tomorrow. When we made it out the back of her building, we could see her looking at us, waving, till we were out of her sight.

It was chilly that late night in October of 97. I grabbed one hold of Jada's car seat to take some weight off my mom as we walked to our building. Ta'Rika's hands were inside of her jacket arms. My mom called granny as soon as we made it through the door. We went straight to bed after that.

School the next day went quite fast, and I was anxious to see granny before heading on her trip. I wanted her to stay, but she deserved a getaway for a little while, so I kept my mouth closed. While I walked past granny Rosie building the afternoon of October 16th, 1997, a few weeks away from turning 8, a couple of years being in school, the purple satin pajamas and roller set hair were not on the ramp.

Is she sleeping? Is she putting my newborn sister down for a nap? Wait a minute, where was my mother? Why aren't we headed to the granny house? It was quite weird to have my uncle Jim picking my sister and me up from school. I remained silent, walking past Stanton Park and through the car lot towards my building. The elevator ride was quiet as my sister, and I stared at each other.

My uncle kept his face towards the buttons on the elevator. As we opened the door of our home, the house phone immediately rang. I jumped down on the couch to answer it, my sister walked towards the bedroom, and Uncle Jim froze. "Hey, Pumpkin," my mom sounded like she had a sore throat. "Hey, Ma, are you okay?" a weird pause. "Where's your uncle?" "Right here, ma."

I signaled for him to pick up the phone then stared towards the television screen. T.V. sitcom Sister to Sister was on, and it happened to be one of my favorite reruns. In the episode, the family was sitting at the dinner table, eating, laughing, and listening to music. I quickly glanced back at my uncle, observing his face, and noticed it was as stiff as a person having a stormy night of interrupted sleep.

He looked at me, then away, as he hung the phone up. He looked again, this time longer. I just stared at him. Uncle Jim bowed his head, took a deep breath, and whispered "Granny Is" and stopped mid-conversation. My big sister walked into the living room to join me on the couch but instead leaned against the wall.

Her caramel face shined from the lamp sitting on the table. Our attention went back to Uncle Jim, who was beginning to part his lips. "Granny passed away," released his mouth. I remember throwing candles and family pictures off the table, each fixture crashing to the floor, breaking into pieces with a burning sensation piercing my heart. I let out a scream as I felt soft cocoa butter scented hands rubbing my back. My sister tears rolling off her cheek, hitting my cheek. I looked over to see Uncle Jim drowning into his hands. I couldn't console him. My sister cried and constantly tried to pull me up off the floor. Uncle Jim walked over to help while wiping his tears. When they finally pulled me up, we took baby steps out the door. Getting downstairs, out of the building, to the car felt like a race we couldn't win. And for the hospital to be a straight shot up the street, the car ride was even worse. My uncle stared into the rearview mirror, watching my sniffles as I caressed my sister's hand but wouldn't look her way. I could see that we were slowly approaching the hospital. Stepping out of the car, I instantly noticed my mother sitting against the emergency entrance wall with her face in her knees. Family members were surrounding her with sad and stale looks. I got closer, noticing she was shivering, lifting her head slowly, as if she knew her child was standing in front of her. I kneeled but couldn't open my mouth to speak. I just stared, watching as she slowly put her head back down on her knees. I stormed into the hospital while Ta'Rika stayed glued to our mom. I walked through the entrance of the hospital and noticed more family standing inside. As soon as they saw me, they quickly walked over, but I walked past them. I said, "where-is," and they pointed in the double doors ``first room on the left" through a whisper. I kept walking and pressed the button on the side of the doors to enter. I stalled, taking deep breaths as I walked up to the hospital bed. My granny just lay there, rollers in her head, dark skin glowing, and a tube in her mouth and nose. I could hear people outside the door whispering to one another, but they wouldn't come in. I slowly sat in a chair near the bed, pressing my chin against her hand. My grandma's hand was warm, and I could smell mango's sweetness as if she had just cut the slices to eat. She wasn't holding a mango in her hand, and I wasn't sitting in between her legs with my face gently pressed against her knee. My eyes glanced up at the unresponsive body. I whispered, "Granny," waiting for her to respond, but she didn't. I pressed my face harder against her hand and cried. My mind raced with questions that I was expressing verbally without even knowing it, "what happened to my granny?" "Granny, why did you leave?" I said it repeatedly as family members entered the room. I jumped up, stormed out, sliding along the wall on the opposite side of the door, making sure I could still see her. The family turned my way but didn't step out of the room. A burning piercing sensation attacked my heart once more as I tried to block out the reality of my granny eyes, never opening again. I wouldn't hear "Tina Marie" again. I wouldn't see her smile and feel her soft touch as I fell asleep lying on her thigh. No more bacon bit secrets, no more mango time, and no more seeing granny purple satin pajamas. I closed my eyes and didn't remember opening them until I woke up the next day at home in my bed, and my mother told me I had fainted. My seven-year-old body was weary, and the exhaustion got worse as her funeral neared. I couldn't concentrate, so I missed a week of school. My teachers sent their condolences and homework if I was up to doing it. I remember sitting up at night getting homework done and looking at pictures of my granny and me. I'd tiptoe into my mom's room at different times of the night to make sure she was alright. Peeking through her door, around her black dresser, I could see her staring at the wall, rocking my baby sister Jada to sleep. I'd run back into my room when I saw that she was looking at me through her mirror. When I got under my covers and pulled them over my head, I could feel my mother pulling them back down. Suddenly Jada leaned over to blow spit bubbles on my head. I softly giggled while glancing up at my mother, cracking a faint smile. As they left my room, Jada turned her head around, not taking her eyes off me. When they were out of door reach, I dropped my head. Looking at Jada reminded me of the events that took place the day granny passed away. She was in her car seat, on granny's couch, while granny laid on the kitchen floor. My mother worked as a teacher assistant at Schiller School when she got the call over the intercom to come to the principal office. When she arrived at the office, everyone's faces frowned. One of her close male co-workers, Cordero, who grew up in the neighborhood and was watched by my granny as a child, said he would drive her to granny's building. In the front of the building, the paramedics, neighbors of my granny, and family members were outside. The paramedics were bringing my granny out of the building on a stretcher. Cordero quickly pulled my mom out of the car, holding her hand as they hurried to the ambulance. Uncle Jim had stepped in front of my mom to tell her he tried C.P.R.; she came back but then drifted. In the ambulance, they tried again, she came back, struggling to breathe, and drifted again. When they arrived at the hospital and began hooking her up to monitors, she flatlined. My mom remembers screaming until she blacked out. My heart aches from the thoughts as I begin to see the difference in myself and the people around me. My mom was losing weight and her face sunk in. My big sister remained buried under her sheets in silence. My cousins, my granny, raised, were lost in spirit and didn't understand what was happening. It was so sudden for us all and unexpected. That's what hurts the most. The first week of grieving and the years that went by were hard. Our family had a lot of emotional days with thoughts of giving up. I watched my mom battle with depression because of the loss of granny. But she remained encouraging, my sisters and I, and the family strength and spirits up. My mother is like my granny in many ways. So we always feel like granny is still here because of her similarities. We hold many celebrations in her honor, visit her resting place, and have moments of laughter sharing her memories. And we keep her legacy alive by making sure we embrace my granny through quotes, pictures, and keepsakes throughout our home. Still today, I feel like our time was cut short. I have moments when I'm sad, angry, frustrated, or all the above. So don't beat yourself up about feeling heartache because I still long for my granny. It takes me writing my emotions in a diary, talking to my mom, and visiting the cemetery alone for a spiritual closeness to deal with it. Throughout my journey of becoming stronger, I've gained a special appreciation for the importance of grandparents. For one, your grandparents' don't have to watch you let alone take you in. They choose to because they love you, hold a special bond of supporting the family when needed, or want to help your parents out. Grandma Rosie watched my sisters and me when my mother was at work. I remember her giving us exercises such as watching SchoolHouse Rock, a cartoon that teaches History, Science, Math, and English. It strengthens our minds and abilities, leading her to ask what we learned from it. She was an on-call doctor for us when we were sick. Ol Skool remedies she used to cure common colds and illnesses worked better for us than medicine did. Granny had sweet talks with us when we were sad, giving a better understanding of prayer, life, and faith. I'm so glad I have moments and quality time spent with her in my memory bank. Please sit down to remember the things your grandparents have done with and for you. Do it now. Maybe you'll appreciate them more while they're alive. Often grandparents end up raising their grandchildren due to many circumstances. My granny raised some of my cousins because my uncles and aunts were getting their lives back on track. She showered my cousins with love, taught them right from wrong, and stayed on them about being themselves, focusing on education, and wanting positive outcomes. Many who are raised by grandparents or parents don't carry what's taught throughout their life. They erase all manners, respect, and lessons of upbringing at a certain age as if it doesn't represent them anymore. People have in their mind that when they hit grown status, they follow their own rules. If you were taught right from wrong, well-loved, and respected as a child, you should be adding up the lessons as an adult, not subtracting from them. My granny always told my cousins, "just because your parents have a rough patch doesn't mean you're going to have them. You're capable of making a good life for yourself, so you will not have to experience what your parents are, trying to overcome". Some of my cousins took heed to it while others did what they wanted to do. Now they wish they would've listened. I see people with their grandparents today, and I wish I were the one smiling, holding hands, having tea, and going out for walks with mine. It hurts to be one of the individuals who had to experience what losing a grandparent was like early. For me, it hit that she was gone when I saw her in the casket. She rested in a beautiful white dress, glasses, tight curls, a streak of grey hair, and a smile on her face. When we went to view her the night before her funeral, the funeral director wanted to talk with us. He said the hairstylist informed him that granny didn't have a smile on her face at first. We took comfort in knowing that granny was giving us confirmation; she was fine. I stared at her smile as I stood in front of her white casket, decorated in trimming of gold, and prayer hands on each side. I went back to my chair and looked around the funeral home. The seats were full, so the remainder of the people stood up in the back and the funeral parlor's hallway. My big sister and my cousin Dre stayed outside because they couldn't handle seeing her. Family members took turns caressing my mother while Jada was carried around in the arms of Uncle Jim. There were many screams, sniffles, why's, and inspirational words from family and friends. I could see my granny was loved by many who came out from Mississippi to Cabrini. A close friend of the family sung GC Cameron, It's So Hard To Say Goodbye To Yesterday, as the last viewing came to an end. He then repeated the song as pallbearers carried my granny out of the funeral home. My eyes were glued to the casket as they put it into the hearse. When they closed the hearse back door, I got into one of the black limos, occupying my family, keeping quiet as the cars pulled off. The rain was coming down as I listened closely to the wetness of the tires on the street. We stopped in front of Granny building as I took the time to reminisce. I looked up at the 6th floor picturing her throwing plastic jars of bacon bits out the window to me in a brown paper bag. Now the window was empty, with the lights off and curtains still. My mommy screamed, one of my aunts consoled her and wiped her tears. Family members patted their eyes and nose with napkins while Ta'Rika bit on her lip. I slumped down in the chair, zip my coat up to my face, and cried the entire ride to the cemetery. As we entered the cemetery gates, everyone, except my mother and Jada, got out. My mom just stared out the window, rocking back and forth, crying, while Jada slept. I wanted to stay in the limo with her, but something in me said get out; be strong for her. The pallbearers strolled through the rain and mud, with Granny casket, approaching a hole shaped like a rectangle on the ground. As they placed her inside the rectangle for lowering, my sister and I held hands. We looked back towards the limo my mom sat in then back towards the casket. After the last prayer, relatives and friends slowly dropped their roses on top of Granny, dragging their feet back to the cars. Ta'Rika and I stared at the flowers covering the top of the casket. We couldn't believe what was happening; our hearts were drowning in pain and worry. We look back at the limo that our mother occupied; back down at granny, wondering who would protect us from Justice now?

Chapter 3
Justice

Justice

I loved going to kiddie land, an amusement park full of colorful rides, excellent food, and eager kids. I remember waking up early so we could be one of the first families there. The reason: having access to all the rides before the park got too crowded. Kiddie Land was surrounded by its theme railroad tracks, which occupied a red train that we used as a winding down period before we left.

The train took us on an observation of the park and showed us highlights about it. I always looked forward to returning; my mother assuring us that we will. One morning as we headed there, we sang along in the car to hip hop tunes we knew nothing about, the concept that is. I remember us singing rapper Mystikal, "shake it fast, watch yourself, shake it fast, and show me what you are working with."

My mom laughed at us in the driver's seat, looking through her rearview mirror. In the back seat, we chanted what rides to get on mine would be the waterlog. The water log climbed to the top, overlooking the amusement park, and you nestled inside seats of carts designed as a log. If you didn't want to get super soaked, you sat in the front. With no warning, the water log dropped down, splashing you and bystanders with water. I'd always tell people not to eat before they got on there because the food they ate would be coming back up, but of course, they didn't listen.

They would have to buy expensive park t-shirts and spend time standing in line to use the bathroom. After getting off, those who did listen to me would sit in some shade for a while, eating ice cream dots before getting on another ride. I was curious about the little balls of ice cream that made everyone relax, maybe the coldness or the unique tastes of vanilla, cookies & cream, and sherbet melting in your mouth. The flavors had us going back for more.

Looking around at my family, the brightness in everyone's eyes showed they were having a good time. Even my mom was smiling. Her face was not tired, stressed, and she didn't glance at my sister and me with worry. My mom was relaxed, enjoying time with family and us, which didn't come when we were home.

At kiddie land, everyone was able to be kids' even grownups. They didn't have to worry about jobs, put food on the table, or buy clothes. And we didn't have to worry about Justice. He wouldn't come looking for us, making frequent calls, or sending anyone to follow us. It's as if he knew he wasn't in control when we were not at home. So my mom made sure whatever day she had off of work, during vacations from school, or on a lovely weekend, we were out away from pain.

She was determined for us to see life outside of our apartment, four walls. Still, to this day, I appreciate her for that. I remember our car rides home being quiet. I would stare out the window overseeing each street wishing there was traffic. The longer it took to get home, the better. It was those moments that matter when I felt like I was on vacation; I was free.

I would glance at my mom in the front seat, watching her caramel face focus on the road. "Pumpkin and Re Re, would you two like to go over grandma's house tonight?" Every time she said Ta'Rika and I nicknames, it was in the most soothing tone, like listening to a seashell's sounds. My sister quickly responded, "yes." I just smiled at my mom; she knew my response. "Alright to grandma's house, we go." When we got closer to Cabrini, we passed our building straight to Grandma Rosie's, my mother's mom.

I glanced up at my bedroom curtains as we drove past, back down to the parking lot. My mood instantly changed. I froze, became aware again of my surroundings; my mom and big sister did too. I realized why I hated parking lots so much, especially my own. I remember tiptoeing to my side window every night, lifting my head watching as a grey Jeep pulled into reverse, missing a pothole before pulling into its original spot. A man would step out, dusting his pants leg, staring at his shoes, and positioning his hat a little over his eyes. He rubbed an invisible mark off the driver's side door before climbing back in.

I remembered all the times that the car would come to my grandmother's parking lot and honk for hours. My grandma would step on her ramp, with one hand on her hip, purple satin pajamas, and rollers in her head, waiting for him to honk again. He would quietly get back in, speeding off. Grandma didn't care that he stood 5 foot 9, athletically built, mellow yellow (as people called him), and a stale facial gesture. If anyone could put him in check, it would be her.

I remember the first time I noticed her checking him during my kindergarten graduation. I had a black dress filled with roses and my hair tightly curled because I wanted to look like my grandma for the day. I sang loud and proud on stage with a giant smile on my face looking into the audience. I watched my family as they sat in the fourth row towards the front. My mom, along with my granny, snapped pictures yelling Pumpkin, forcing a smile. My big sister repeatedly winked at me.

As my eyes traveled, I looked over to see Justice leaning against the school gym room, monkey bars glancing in my direction. People walked past him, stopping to shake his hand while pointing at me. I imagined them saying congrats she's a bright little girl with him responding, "thanks. I know," I tuned into more people walking by him dropping off gifts for me to find out later, not any was from him.

The only present I got from Justice was seeing my mom afterward hiding behind black shades. After the ceremony, Grandma Rosie had walked out of the school doors, passed graduates who were taking mommy and daddy photos, and grabbed Justice's door before it closed. She put her finger up to his face, and the expression he gave her was a kid in trouble. "One day soon, you're going to realize you are not as powerful as you think" she slowly put her finger down.

Grandma looked around the car at each of us, "you know what? I think it's best if you all came over to my house. I'll put something together; call the family over for dinner". Granny's heels clicked as she walked over to each side of the car, opening doors not taking her eyes off him. Justice didn't say anything back and knew not to try to stop her. Granny grabbed hold of my mom's hand while my sister and I grabbed hold of each of their free ones. "They won't be coming home tonight," granny said as we walked away.

We walked off, hand and hand. I turned back to see Justice sitting with his hands on his face. Grandma Rosie intimidated him, and her stepping in all the time kept us safe. I wished she could still do that. I started hoping she could come to rescue my mother, sisters, and me. I wished she could bring me bacon bits and mango. But wishing wasn't enough. Driving from kiddie land to grandma's, my mom whispered, "Pumpkin is you okay?" staring in the rearview mirror. I imagined feeling my mother next to me, rubbing her hands through my hair. "I'm okay" I gave her a crooked smile that always manages to show one dimple.

As we pulled into my granny parking lot, I could see her standing on her porch, waving at us. We got out of the car, walked into the building, and said our hellos to residents. They knew how much we adored granny Rosie. She was our healer, motivator, heart, and protector. But a few years later, we didn't have that superwoman shield anymore. From when my grandmother passed away due to a heart condition, every night was a crying fest having to hear my mom scream and Justice's voice rise.

I would bite down on my covers hard because I couldn't take it anymore. So I jumped out of bed to help my mother in combat. Our oak entertainment center, fish tank, glass tables, and brown furniture disappeared from my living room vision. All I could see were his hands hitting my mom's face, every hit feeling as if he was hitting me instead, while he stood over her, kneeling to swing more.

Blood dripped down my mother's brown eyes that night as his face tilted towards mine like he was pre-warning me not to come near. But I didn't turn to run; I ran towards the kitchen, grabbing a knife out of the dish rack positioning it behind my back. The blows to her face got stronger. I tensed up from it, sounding like pans clashing together. I ran out of the kitchen, directly into the dining room, getting a good aim at his back, before jumping on him.

I could hear my mother's whimpers, Justice panting, and my sister and I shriek for help as I crawled on his back, digging the silver blade into his shoulder. He went down slowly but not as quick as I thought he would, so I dug more. Through his piercing screams, he began releasing his hands from my mother's face. I twisted the blade around; his knees became weaker, as I kept my free arm around his neck so I wouldn't slip off.

He yelled louder and threw me to the ground. The knife landed inches away from my temple. Dizzy, I glance around, seeing my mom trying to crawl over towards me. She reached her hand out for me; he stepped his black boot with force in between. Lifting my head slowly, I could see him staring at me, holding his right shoulder. As blood trickled down on the side of me, I noticed that the knife just scraped his arm.

Laying my head back on the ground, I turned to see my big sister run from around the corner that leads to the bedroom, taking the same leap towards his back. She punched him repeatedly in the wound I had made. It must've been deeper than I could see because he went down again, twirling around punching her in the face. She hit the ground next to me like a bottle thrown into a garbage can.

My mom cried out for us while my sister rocked back and forth, holding her face screaming, "I hate you." My mom, finally able to get off the floor, had enough and struck back, punching him repeatedly in the nose. He stared with confusion, madder now, grabbing hold of my mother's neck. As my view became clear, I picked the knife up on the side of me, squirmed on the floor towards them, stabbing him in the leg. I could hear the end of the blade break off with him falling.

As he called out for help, my mom, Ta'Rika, and I ran towards the bedroom, locking the door. We turned from the entrance to see my baby sister Jada still asleep in her crib with headphones covering her ears. I was glad she didn't have to hear or witness any of it. One thing my mother didn't want is for his rage to escalate to us. That night was worse than other nights throughout the years and continues to haunt my thoughts because he attacked all three of us.

I believe his aggression became stronger, knowing there was no one to stop him. My sister and I being fourteen and eleven years old, there was only so much we could do. Justice was never nice; he only came around at night and never played his role. Instead of protecting us from the harm, he was causing it. And we went to bed many nights distraught.

I remember my mom pulling a dresser up against the door, afraid that he would knock the door down from all the banging he was doing. He'd slowly stop, and minutes later, we could hear him snoring through the living room walls. We would lay under my mom, one of us occupying each of her legs while she hummed the tunes to Aretha Franklin's amazing grace.

And baby Sister Jada remained occupied by Elmo's voice through her headphones. I could recall the nights my mother called family and friends for help or nights she dialed grandmas' number, stopping after the last digit. It was clear that we were all we had because everyone else thought it would be easier to walk away. I can tell you: it's not.

Justice had ties to higher-ups due to his excellent business position as a lawyer, so everyone looked up to him. They felt he couldn't do any harm; he was all about saving people's lives and firms, and that he was a good role model for all guys. Even the police respected him for his constant contributions to the low-income communities around town, so they gained a brotherly bond.

And when we called the police, nothing was resolved. What was shocking to me is when officers would throw out any order of protections my mom had on him. Some officers even lied for him to cover up disturbances calls from our home. That's when I knew it was such a thing as good cops vs. bad ones. After seeing pictures of my mother's face bruised, with cuts on her mouth, her eyes the color of raccoon eyes; they glanced at it then looked off. No one could see the monster we had to endure. No one wanted to. Fighting for life was becoming more challenging and scarier.

Ta'Rika's anger grew each day, but I felt like my anger was on a more powerful pedestal because I believed I looked just like him while she resembled my mom. I remember always going outside and people saying, "you look just like him" or "oh my god, you have his eyes." I was not too fond of it. My mother thought that my tears were just related to his abuse, but it also had to do with how I looked.

I started running away from mirrors so that I wouldn't see myself. I even went to the extreme of darkening pictures using computer apps so I wouldn't appear light-skinned. My mom assured me that I didn't look like him; she stated, "you resemble my brother, your uncle." I thought she was only trying to make me feel better, so I put what she said in the back of my mind. I didn't realize my uncle is who I resemble, and the thought of me looking like Justice weighed heavily on my mind.

As it consumed my thoughts, it turned my pain into motivation. I began searching the internet while I was at school during lunch breaks.

I knew my mom wouldn't be able to do it because, unfortunately, people around her paid close attention and relayed information back to him. After many attempts at emailing realtors about our situation, getting the same response, "I'm sorry for your circumstances, but I will not be able to assist" I came across the perfect realtor.

When I sent her a message about our situation, I told her everything and that we were looking to start anew. She quickly responded that she agrees to handle our move. Looking back, it amazed me what I, as an eleven-year-old, could do. But I was always told from a young age that I had an old soul. My Grandma Rosie would say that I inherited that from my mom, still having the mindset beyond my years, which could be a blessing and a curse.

Jackie, the realtor, finally sent me listings of places across town. So I sat my mom down later that night, during one of Justice's snoring rituals, to talk about Jackie's findings. We couldn't clap or shed happy tears yet. My mind rambled around how we were going to pull it off. It possibly would take months, years, and we didn't have that long. "Leave that up to me, Pumpkin," my mom said. Even still, I thought about what he would try to do if he found out we were leaving. "We're going to get out; I'm going to make sure you girls are safe even if I have to go down with a fight."

The urge to get out built more from the presence of my little sister Jada who hadn't, thankfully, witnessed or got a chance to experience Justice abusiveness. Jada was getting ready to turn one at the time, full of cooing, and loved Justice. She adored the caring, happy, and sensitive side of Justice we weren't able to get to know, but she and everyone else in town could see. As she got older, we decided not to tell her about the side she didn't know of, but her mind became curious about why we didn't have a relationship with Justice.

And as the questions came, we answered. But we stressed to Jada to not base our experience on how she viewed him. Jada understood and also appreciated our mom for getting us out. Older now, she even remembers when we were packing for our new house and arriving at it. I remember too. We planned our move a year early, packing little by little so Justice wouldn't notice the difference. We went about our lives the same: going to school, mom going to work, and weekends and vacations spending time somewhere fun.

Even when my mom changed the locks, he always managed to gain access to our apartment. She was able to persuade someone to put an additional safety, a deadbolt, that only she, Ta'Rika, and I had a key to so it would be harder for him to get back in. We were relieved the deadbolt kept him out but still had to deal with him seeing us outside, going to school, and seeing my mom head to work, so we survived each day by faith.

In school, my big sister and my academics didn't change; we remained focused, and I believe it was because of the strength instilled within us and wanting to become women of intellect. Our teachers would ask if we were okay when we came to school with exhausted faces. The ones we trusted knew about our situation and stayed determined to keep us safe on school grounds.

They kept in touch with our mom, letting her know if we needed anything or any help, they would jump to it. We never wanted special treatment, though, such as going home early or getting rest in class. What kept us going was focusing on school and engaging as much as possible; our teachers respected us for that. My mother's colleague was a kind-hearted guy who had ties to people who knew martial arts; although she didn't tell him about what we were going through, she felt safe around him because of his connections.

Jada remained going to her babysitter's house while my mom was at work. Her babysitter, Anna Mae, reminded us so much of Granny. Anna Mae didn't have a problem with checking anyone who tried to disrespect her. We knew Jada was safe. As moving day approached, our teachers lightened the homework load, but we still asked for extra assignments just in case we had to miss a few days.

Ta'Rika and I went off to school like usual on moving day while my mom stayed home, getting everything out. I remember sitting in my homeroom class at school, watching the clock. I decided to text my mom during lunch break to make sure everything was alright. She texted back and said, "all was well, and she managed to get everything out before he got off work."

When Justice got off, he heard about seeing moving trucks and my mom. We had already left school for the day, headed to our new house while he was breaking into our old one. I wondered how he reacted; probably ran through the house like a pit bull or screaming out, "he's going to kill us." My mom was able to get everything onto the moving trucks that day with the help from some guys she tutored during her teaching days.

He tried finding out what guys had helped us, but no one would say. The guys believed they had to after always stressing out when hearing the screams and cries come through the walls. They even apologize for not doing anything about it. The same day we moved, Justice called my mom's cell phone to ask if they could talk in person. He wanted to make things work. I didn't trust my mom being by herself with him, so I decided to drive with her.

I didn't question our purpose of going because, for some reason, I knew she wanted to close the chapter face to face. On our way there, I sat thinking about what he would try to pull. I knew I had to pay attention to him, he was sneaky, but I wasn't stupid. I said to my mom, "if he tries anything," with her looking at me saying, "he won't, we're in control now."

When we arrived at his aunt's house, he was sitting in the kitchen drinking a beer. My mom didn't shiver, nor did she cry. I held onto her hand, walking towards him as he stood up with a blank face. He went on to say, "so now you want to leave me; I thought we were supposed to be a happy family." My mom didn't fall for it.

She stood in silence; he stared at her and then looked at me. The only words that released my mother's lips were "Goodbye Justice." Tears covered my face, this time, tears of joy. I felt like he didn't have control over our lives anymore. As we turned to walk out of his aunties house, I turned back to look at him. I could finally see that I didn't look like Justice.

I caught a smile appearing across my mom's face. I was touched because that smile had been a frown for a long time. Mom was finding herself again. We walked towards the door glancing back at him each step we took. I was surprised that he didn't try to stop us. Justice just stood there in his black boots, fitted cap, gazing at the ending of trauma.

We finally could live somewhere that we could call a "full-time" happy home. I remember arriving at our new house, staring out the passenger seat window at the beautiful garden and back porch. No jeep insight. No banging on the doors. The only thing we heard were the crickets outside of our windows. Mom was saying a silent prayer, Ta'Rika closed her eyes to inhale and exhale, Jada continued playing with her Elmo in her car seat, and I took in the peaceful vibes. I look back and say to myself, no wonder Jada remembered that day; it was pure happiness.

One night I got up, opened the door to my big sister's room, and my mom's to see them, including Jada, sleeping peacefully. I then went to my room and whispered, "this is what I call home." Even though our new home life was great, we still had to travel back to our old community for school and for my mom to go to work. She didn't want us to change schools, nor did we want her to leave the job she loved, but we remained aware of our surroundings.

Especially when one night, we noticed that someone was following us as we headed home. We knew his calmness was too good to be true. My mom begins cutting through alleys; the car kept following slowly behind, with the person driving trying to disguise himself by having on a cap and shades. We kept going, stepping on the gas a little more, but the man kept consistent behind us.

As a yellow light was nearing, a loading truck from a docking station tried backing out. We sped through the yellow light as the driver got cut off by the loading truck. We concluded: it was someone that knew Justice following us. Taking different routes and watching all cars became our routine for a year. Thankfully, Justice gave up trying to have someone track us down.

What made him stop, we will never know; we didn't want to know. My mother wasn't hiding behind dark shades or long sleeve turtle necks anymore; she smiled and let her natural beauty show. Ta'Rika's anger had turned into calmness. Jada grew up not having to endure what Ta'Rika and I had to, which humbled us. And I stopped running away from mirrors; I would stand in front of them saying aloud, "I'm a beautiful young woman" with a smile on my face because, in our way, Justice had been served.

And in my way, I begin to see how Justice not being around made me a healthier individual. Justice was supposed to be my first protector, love, pathway, and representation towards what I should look for in men's character traits. Only thing I could take away from Justice and apply it to men: knowing what I don't want in one. There were moments when he would be in my presence into early adulthood, and I would feel like I'm about to catch high blood pressure.

But over time, in my forgiving phase, I cleared a lot of anger from my heart. In the present, we've had mini conversations, a few moments of laughter, and maybe a joke or two that always includes Jada to be the one to start it. She signifies peace. There's still no bond between Justice and me and no request for a sit down from him to just talk, and I haven't asked for one.

I may have forgiven him, for my sanity, but it doesn't change the fact that only my mother has raised my sisters and me. Statistics state children who have only one parent in the household cannot take on a successful path in life. I disagree. Speaking from experience, only you can decide what you want your life path to be.

Even if you had to endure what I went through or worse, there are still options you can turn towards, such as therapy. Also, learning to forgive so it won't hinder you. You can think about the future of what you would want in your household, the man or woman you will not want in your home. Fill the empty part of your heart that misses that parent figure with motivation from your parent that is there, sit and express your frustrations and concerns with the one that is there and appreciate them for raising you on their own.

I'm thankful that my mom put all of her time, energy, and unconditional love into raising my sisters and me. I'm glad I was in a household with just my mom instead of still in a home where the pain was in power. Yes, it would've been great to have both parents, but sometimes things don't work out that way. To me, it's better to be in a healthier situation than an unsafe one.

I honestly don't think I would have made it this far or gone down the road I've traveled of positive accomplishments within goals, my faith, and identity if Justice would have remained close in my life and home. Through my experience with him, I learned, instill, appreciate, and humble myself to keep on going, learn from the lessons, what I had to witness, experience, and, most importantly, forgive for me.

Chapter 4

Picture Perfect

Picture Perfect

On Valentine's Day, 2000, I attended a dance that brought teenagers together for a fun night. Stanton Park gymnasium decor was cupid-shaped balloons, red and white streamers, and backdrops of hearts along the walls for pictures. The girls in attendance wore red spray paint tees displaying the name of their significant others. The guys had on black and white attire, hugging their beau tightly. I couldn't help but notice the hot guy in front of me through all the love in the air. Shad always wore the latest outfits, new shoes, and kept his hair clean cut. He was caramel, with small brown eyes, and had a pointy nose at the tip but a nice size. He stared, smirked, and asked could I be his valentine. I answered with a nod. Shad signaled for me to come closer to take a picture with him. I called for my friend Tory, who was serving a punch, to capture the moment. When Tory saw Shad, you would've thought I was standing next to someone famous. Tory smiled, grabbed the camera from me, and walked with us to one of the backdrops along the walls. He lowered his eyes and moved the camera to an angle for better quality. When he signaled that he was ready, I pressed my head against Shad's chest, as Shad squeezed me tightly. We embraced the moment as Tory snapped the picture then quickly released one another. Shad grabbed my hand and told me to let him know when the photo was available to get. He walked away, waving goodbye as he rejoined his friends, and I returned to mine. I looked back at Shad to see him smiling at me. I couldn't wait to see him again.

I went to get the pictures developed at Walgreens nearby. A lady of customer service stated the photos would be ready later on the same day. I returned to Walgreens with Tory, who was more excited than me to see how the picture came out. The picture captured the essence of Shad, and I was looking as if we were an item. For me to be nervous, I appeared calm. The white spray paint shirts we were wearing and headbands with our nicknames in cursive accented one another. Tory felt like Shad and I should be a couple. I laughed it off but I agreed. I sent Shad a text to let him know the picture was ready. He sent a quick one back, letting me know he will come to get a copy soon. I showed Tory the text as we walked down the street, high-fiving each other, and laughing with joy. I didn't know what this meant for

Shad and me, but I was hoping it led to something special. Thank God it did. Our relationship started with us both being on our best behavior, spending a lot of time together, and getting used to each other's friends. Normally that's what happens in the beginning, the honeymoon phase, everything goes well, and you can't get enough of one another. You get a little more comfortable and slowly reveal more of yourself. You start to see what makes your mate mad, if they snore in their sleep, how they're with their family and friends, what they don't like, what they're afraid of, and if they have the potential to be a long term mate. Thankfully Shad and I grew to love each other even more through that, including our flaws. I remember us taking walks through the park, discussing worries, goals, and dreams. Sometimes we went for bike rides around our community, passing people who smiled and waved at us. We spent time together at each other houses watching movies, cracking jokes, and cooking. Shad didn't make a big deal about me being quiet and shy. I was more of an observer towards people I didn't know before interacting with them. Shad accepted and understood that. He started talking to me about meeting some of his family members. I was nervous, but he assured me that it would be a breeze.

I remember walking down a row of houses to his uncle's house when I came upon a door a woman was standing in. "You must be the girl we always hear about," the petite woman, a cousin of his, said with a smile. She pulled me inside to meet the rest of the family. I felt accepted. I looked over at Shad to see him taking in the atmosphere. I knew he was happy that they like me, and I was relieved too. Going into two years of the relationship Shad and I begin to talk about marriage, kids in the future, and possible career interests. I like that our communication expanded beyond just that moment and that our wants were similar. Although everything was going well, I wondered if Shad was ready to be committed. I knew many girls throughout the community like, crushed on, and claimed to be with him before becoming an item. So I kept hoping that we wouldn't have problems with people liking him too much, and he fed into it. But for the most part, he ignored girls' advances. He always said in his past if he wanted to see a girl, she would jump up and head straight to him. I couldn't understand why but I knew I wasn't having that; school came first, and I was glad Shad respected me. He would always say I'm full of determination, intelligence, and passion. Shad consumed a great acceptance of me, including my moments of stubbornness. I loved knowing that because it's hard for people to accept you for who you are. We attended many events together during the holiday season, from museum's tree exhibits to see how other cultures celebrate Christmas, July 4th firework display on the lake, summer movies in the park, and family barbeques. Shad and I also were in attendance regularly at an event in Cabrini throughout the late Spring until the end of summer called ol skool Mondays. The Temptations, Isley Brothers, and Ojays exit through the sound system in the neighborhood park's grass. You could catch us stepping along with the ol skool members as they watch us with smiles. I enjoyed exploring the city and positive things in the neighborhood, but I couldn't hide my true homebody. I could stay in and watch classical movies, comedy shows, and cartoons for days. I thought it would become a problem for Shad since he loved to be outdoors. But he joined me, with no nagging, on days I would lounge around the house. We brought up topics about the no's in a relationship. No's was a game we played to discuss what couldn't fly in a commitment to each other. My two were abuse and cheating. I trusted Shad, so I went into detail from Justice's experiences to shed light on what I meant. He assured me he would never cheat or put his hands on me. I believed him. Shad no's were a woman who wanted to change herself to keep a man and a person who could not overlook flaws. I could agree with him on both and told him no one is perfect, so he didn't have to worry about me sweating over small things. Shad was relieved to hear me say that, so he showed appreciation with a warm hug. When it came to being family-oriented, we both were on the same page. Shad knew how much my mom and sisters meant to me. He also knew that he was, for sure, an important person I saw myself expanding with if he met them. I was happy that when he met them, he got along well with them. They enjoyed his jokes, gifts, and his one-on -one talks with my mom about where he could see himself with me. I told my mom that I could get used to being treated like a Queen. She smiled while my sisters teased me about being so mushy.

Chapter 5

Shake Up

Shake Up

S had was my first serious relationship, and because it was going well, I never thought about the worse or another guy. But I learned although it's a beautiful thing to be in love, don't get blindsided. A shift can happen at any time to test real loyalty and trust. I didn't think a shift would happen so fast for us. Shad started making fewer calls, shorter visits, and began hanging out more at functions with his friends. I was feeling kind of weird about his change. I begin to wonder if he would be present for me through thick and thin. When I called his phone to see if he would stop by, it was always an excuse from him about already making plans or him shooting a text saying he was pretty busy with no time on his hands. My thoughts towards believing that lasted up until she approached me at school.

Schiller School held many dances throughout the school year for students, one being a sock hop where you came, danced, and played in your socks. If you were hungry or thirsty, the teachers directed you to the cafeteria for refreshments. During the sock hop, I worked up a hunger from all the dancing I was doing, so my friend Tiffany, I, and a few more people went to the cafeteria. While sitting at the cafeteria table, a girl walked up to me, with a picture in hand, pointing, asking was I dating Shad. I looked up at her, confused, responded yes, and asked her who she was. She said her name was Ivory and then began twirling up her nose, smacking her lips, and leaning on my chair's edge. I put my cup of fruit punch down and turned towards her. I stared at the picture of Shad in her hand. Then I glanced at her two friends, one on each side of her, looking me up and down. Still confused, I asked her, "Is there a problem?" While waiting for Ivory to respond, my friend Tiffany and the others stood up. She hesitated then said, "I used to date him; we still talk from time to time; we hung out last night" she put a strong emphasis on the words last night, smacking her lips again. My other friends slowly sat down while Tiffany remained standing. Back then, I had a non tolerance level towards a person when I felt like they approached me in an uncivilized way. I spent a few moments inhaling and exhaling, so I could keep my composure, not get loud, or make a fool of myself. Ivory friends were still staring at me and were starting to make me feel uncomfortable. I got up, moved around them, and walked towards the bathroom with Tiffany following close behind. I looked back to see Ivory and her friends walking with their arms crossed to a table of people as Ivory patted the top of her head. I started dialing Shad's number while walking through the bathroom door. Tiffany paced back and forth, pounding her fist into the other. I became a detective at heart. Shad picked up after the second ring. "Shad a girl by the name of Ivory, you dated her?" "Yes" "Are you still dating her" "no" "do you hang around her" he seems like he was thinking of an answer to say by the way he stopped then began talking again. "Yes, because we have mutual friends" is what he ended up saying. I begin explaining how she approached me in the cafeteria as if something was still going on between the two. He assured me that it wasn't and stated that he was in the middle of a conversation with his aunt and needed to call me back. I told him alright and that we will talk later. When I hung up, calmed Tiffany down, walked back into the cafeteria where my friends sat with curious faces, glanced over to the table Ivory was sitting at with her friends looking me up and down; I had a gut feeling that he was lying. To not get the rest of my friends worked up, I return to the table with a smile. They didn't ask any questions. I took another look in Ivory's direction as she turned her head the opposite way. After the sock hop, I found out that Cheryl, whom I had classes with, was her big sister. Cheryl would tell everyone how her little sister liked to party, did horrible in school, and chase any man willing to catch her. The demeanor Ivory had was similar to the girl's Shad said he was involved with before us. But since Shad so far didn't give me a reason to believe he was doing anything behind my back, I couldn't make a big deal about what he says she says. But the pep talk I was giving myself didn't change the intuition in me. What Ivory said kept playing in my head, causing me to toss and turn at night, questions Shad constantly about it, with my questions resulting in arguments. We went from this happy couple to a war zone. I didn't like what we were turning into with arguing nonstop about an ex of his. I questioned, was this what I had to look forward to? After a week went by, I bumped into Ivory again. This time she approached me with a disgusted look on her face and said, "Well, I guess you made a pretty boy into a good man." Ivory walked off, staring me up and down. Shad knew the situation with Ivory bothered me. So he worked on trying to gain back my patience and understanding by coming around more often. When he saw that I was finally moving on from it, he insisted on addressing the issue for one last time by saying nothing new was going on between them. I took his word for it and was glad we were getting back to our normal, loving, routine. I passed by Ivory in school a lot more than I ever did, but no more weird feelings developed. I didn't hear anything else about Ivory and Shad after that.

Chapter 6

Detour

. . . .

Detour

I started to enter a period of constant detours. You know when you're detouring through construction, and no matter how far you try to get away from the construction site, you still come near roadblocks? Shad and I ran into one in our relationship stopping all communication. For a few days, I didn't receive calls or texts from him. And when I tried reaching out, his phone went straight to voicemail. It threw me off, but the voicemail I received the next day started putting the pieces together. "My brother will be away for a while." The voicemail was from his sister Nikki. I didn't know what she meant, so I called her back, leaving a message letting her know to reach back out when she had a chance. Ironically the same day she phoned me, I received a letter in the mail from Shad. Inside was a green ticket with the date of his next court appearance. My mother gazed at me with concerned eyes, and I read the letter out loud.

Ima get to the point, love.

I got into a fight; this guy continued to run his mouth in front of his friends. His friends kept egging him on as we stood in the parking lot of my homie building. He continued to talk harshly to me. I got mad (you know, my temper towards stupid stuff), and I smacked him in his mouth one good time, told him to stop playing with me, and I walked off. He came up behind me with a kitchen knife; please tell me who carries around a kitchen knife in their right mind. My best friend came rushing towards me, yelling out, "watch your back." People hanging out their windows yelled the same thing. I thought he had a gun. All I remember is me turning around to see a sharp object nearing me. I blanked out after that. When I came to, he was lying on the floor with the knife sticking a little in his side. That's why I'm in jail. You know I didn't mean to do it. I even apologize to him over the phone. Now we just got to wait it out. He didn't press charges against me. But they still got me locked up. I'll keep you posted. Keep your head up for me.

My mom and I sat in silence; I didn't know if I should be hurt, angry, worried, or all the above. I asked my mom if she would call the phone company to start receiving collect calls for him to reach out. The phone company said it would take a week for collect calls to start coming in. I quickly wrote Shad back, added our house number in the letter, and informed him to call within the time period. Two weeks had passed by, and our third anniversary was approaching. Shad friends thought it would be a good time for us to bond since school was out for the summer. His friends were a valuable part of his life, more like family, so I knew bonding with them would make him happy. Our short conversations when Shad was present would be about how good we were as a couple. Now it was, "Why are you sticking around for?" "You just don't get it; you're the other woman." Why were they coming to me like this? And what was this other woman stuff? Days later, I was sitting in the neighborhood playground, giving them a tutorial on how to play a card game of spades. Shad's three friends caught on quickly, so we decided to team up.

Keith and I were on one team while Mitchell and Gerald on the other. We wanted to raise the stakes a bit, so whichever team won, they had to buy everyone a pizza puff, fries, and mild sauce. I knew Keith, and I was going to kick their butts. Mitchell was sure we wouldn't. As I shuffled the cards, the sun was setting. Keith said, "I wonder if Stacey has been to see Shad" out of nowhere. They instantly looked like a group of deer in front of headlights. I stared at Keith, waiting to hear more. But Mitchell quickly changed the subject to some random topic about getting dreads when he didn't even have hair.

Gerald hung his head low, shaking it with shame. I handed the cards to Mitchell to pass out; he slowly grabbed them. My phone rang, and their eyes froze. It was only my mother calling to ask if I was ready to head home. But I didn't let them know that. I told her yeah and quickly hung up. "Not Shad," I said, tracing all three with my eyes. Mitchell, Gerald, and Keith's faces relaxed a little. I threw my hand of cards down, strapped my fanny pack on, and said a dry goodbye to the guys as they watched me walk off. I was sure I heard Shad talking on the phone with someone by the name of Stacey before. I thought it was his female friend I hadn't got the chance to meet yet. But from the way they were acting in the playground, I needed to find Stacey. Ivory words, I guess you turned him into a good guy now came back to haunt me. I had heard stories of how men can have a good girlfriend but still do whatever. Shad and I had many good memories, overpowering the bad ones, so I hoped they wouldn't reverse.

Weeks later, I was standing in the grocery store when my cell phone rang; I quickly said hello. "Martina, it's Paul, Shad's cousin, I got him on the line." I never picked up the phone for numbers I didn't know. Shad had Paul three-way me so he could ask why I wasn't accepting his collect calls. I could hear Paul lay the phone down. "I've been busy," I lied. "That's all you had to say. I can understand that." I was getting ready to ask Shad about Stacey, but I stopped myself; Paul could still listen. And I didn't want my business across town because I knew how people could talk and switch your words or issues around. Shad was about to say something, but I couldn't make it out because the phone reception was starting to mess up. Then the line went dead.

I waited for him to call back. But he didn't. My attention went back to the steaks, chicken wings, and burger patties but all of a sudden, I wasn't hungry anymore. I left the store, still glancing at my phone; there still was no return call. I decided to accept a few of his calls after the drop call in the grocery store. He said he missed me and hoped to finish where we left off when he got out. It was sweet to hear, but I still wanted to know about Stacey.

Although I had him on the phone alone, I didn't bring her up. I thought that I was probably putting too much thought into it. I know his friends could've been just trying to be messy. I tried forgetting about the topic of Stacey so I could enjoy our talks. The conversations were reminding me of how intriguing they were at the beginning of the relationship. He even brought up a conversation about me meeting his mom. I had heard good things about her and was anxious to meet her in person. Shad said his two favorite girls had to know each other, so we would meet when he got out. During a collect call conversation with Shad one night, he asked me to call his mom three-way. I asked him was he sure as he laughed, telling me not to be nervous; she's cool. I clicked over, dialed her number, and switched over fast so Shad would be on the phone when she answered. When she picked up her southern accent was the first thing I noticed. It gave me comfort reminding me of my Granny Rosie. They laughed, said I miss you, and then Shad said to his mom that his girl was on the phone. "Hey, Stacey," came out of her mouth. I was sure I had swallowed my tongue. Shad tried playing it off by laughing, jokingly saying, you playing right, mom. I wanted to curse him out. He then introduced me by my name, but his end of the phone hung up because his time on the collect call had run out. Shad's mother stayed on the line saying hello; I stared at the phone, wanting to say something, but instead, I hung up. I had never been as upset as I was then. I was too mad to cry. First, it was Ivory, which I instantly moved on from because nothing else happened. But when his mother directly called a woman's name out, that's not even close to mine; it let me know two things. He never told his mom about me, and two, Stacey was a lot more than a friend. Shad called back an hour later, but I didn't answer. He had his sister Nikki call my cell phone to leave a voicemail stating his mom didn't mean to say that name, it was an accident, and that Stacey was nobody important, just a female he messed around with before we got together. It was suspicious to me that it was always a female who was supposedly before us. I decided to ignore Shad's calls for the remainder of the summer. I was going to focus on myself. I hosted slumber parties at my house with friends, volunteered to work at Stanton Park as a junior counselor during summer camp, and went away to resorts with my mom and sisters. Although I had an excellent time, Shad was still in the back of my mind. I didn't talk about how I felt to my family or friends because I just wanted to breathe. I had received numerous voicemails from Shad's cousin, his sister, and his best friend's phones. Shad on the voicemails, let me know how upset he was because he didn't understand my reason for ignoring him when he hasn't done anything wrong. He even said he thought I was cheating. Every voicemail I deleted and the letters he sent, I sat to the side, sending no response. I figured he would at least give in, due to my ignoring him, and open up about who Stacey was. Knowing how his friends like to run their mouths, I was sure they had opened up to him about them speaking on it. I didn't care because my intuition was still bothering me. All signs were pointing to him, keeping something hidden. I finally felt like it was time to confide in one of my closest friends, Tory, about it. He insisted on a male opinion that Shad had to be lying about something. I took into consideration what Tory was saying. But before I made any decisions, I had to find out for myself. It was up in the air of how long Shad would be away. He was still going back and forth to court. To get to the bottom of Stacey's mystery quicker, I had some research to do.

Chapter 7

Bryant

Bryant

As the days passed, I continued to ignore Shad, but I kept tabs on what was going on with him through his cousins, and he updated me in the letters he sent. Unfortunately, I still wasn't able to gather any information on Stacey. So I left it alone. I wanted to enjoy the remaining of the summer without thinking about any of it. I had already taken up too much time stressing and going back and forth with myself. And it wasn't doing any good. Summer was in its last month, I needed to focus on the upcoming school year since orientation was approaching. At orientation, I gained new bonds, made better friends, and met Bryant. He was athletic, tall, with clear mocha skin, and intelligent. Bryant and I talked like we hadn't just met and had gained this solid bond fast. We would spend weekends of the last month of summer together going out to the movies, bowling, and the zoo. My phone would continuously ring while out with him. Bryant would say, "Shad," then I would give him a nod putting my phone back in my purse on silent. I only told Bryant that Shad was away, and we were having communication problems. I avoided deep conversations about the real reason for me ignoring him or issues about his absence. Bryant didn't pressure me to know either; I like that about him. The following night I was on the phone with Tory, and he asked me out of the blue did I like Bryant. I quickly said, "no, you know I love Shad, and regardless of what he and we as a couple got going on, I will remain loyal and faithful." Ever had that moment of knowing you said something out of your mouth that your mind tells you to rethink? I should've listened to my better judgment. Tory went into detective mode, "Do you know if Bryant likes you?" I hadn't even thought of that. I looked at Bryant the way I looked at Tory. I always had better bonds and connections with male friends' more than female ones. One thing about Tory; he didn't sugarcoat anything. "You should rethink this relationship with Shad. Maybe Bryant is the sign". I laughed it off. But if anyone knew me, Tory did. I went to bed thinking about whether Bryant liked me more than a friend and would it be silly to ask him. As I was dozing off, I got a text from Bryant asking could we hang out the next day. I told him that's fine. I turned my attention to my dresser to look at a picture of Shad and me; Valentine's Day one. I missed him. And I knew I wanted it to work out. I figured that maybe we need to have another conversation about what we both wanted from the relationship when he returned home. I sent Bryant a text back, letting him know that I will rest up tomorrow for school the next day. He said okay with a sad face. I didn't respond.

On the first day of classes, I returned to my locker during lunchtime to a card sticking out with a letter inside; it was from Bryant. On the front of the card were two teddy bears hugging with hearts surrounding them. The message inside was Bryant opening up to me about how he liked me but respected my relationship with Shad. I hate knowing when Tory was right. I put the card and letter inside my Science book to head to class. Before heading to class, I dropped my bookbag on the ground to put my notebooks inside. I noticed four pictures had slid off the top of my bookbag. The photos were of Bryant and me, making silly faces, after a movie. I realized Bryant must've walked past as I was reading the letter. I looked down the hallway from my locker to see Bryant leaning against a wall watching me. We both knew we couldn't be more than friends. And we had to accept I loved and was with Shad. But a part of me knew if Bryant were aware of what I was going through with Shad, our glances at one another would've been different. I glanced back to see if Bryant was still standing there, but he was gone. I had hoped we could remain the way we were, just friends.

Chapter 8
Rollercoaster

Rollercoaster

I came home from school tired and irritated by the cold weather. I opened the screen door with the mail falling to my feet, noticing a brown envelope reading Shad Dickerson. I gathered the mail and proceeded into the house. I threw my coat in a nearby chair, kicked off my boots, and walked into my mother's room, handing her the mail. She glanced down. "I see Shad has written to you." An unwanted smile appeared on my face. I knew she could see through it. My mother knew when something was wrong. I open the envelope to read silently.

I hope you know you got me up in here, stressing. I can't eat or sleep without thinking about you. I go through this every day, and sometimes I will be crying, and you know that isn't me. One of my homies says it's love, but I say it's pain. Because that's all it does is hurt me. If I'm not crying, I'm stressing, and if it's not that I'm thinking about you. I know you think it's a game I'm trying to run on you but little do you know how I feel; it hurts. It seems like every time a month goes past, you forget about me more; Tina, I need you to be here for me. I don't have much else to say. So I'm going to end my letter. Love you. P.S You know I care about you and love you, right. But it's something weighing on my mind, so I got to come out and say it. I was cheating on you with Stacey. I'm sorry. I broke up with her, and if you want to know why it's because I didn't know what you were on at first. But now I see you're going to be here when times are good and bad. So I hope you want to be with me still, and I hope you are not mad.

I tried hard to keep my composure together in front of my mother. "Is everything okay Pumpkin, he's hanging in there." I quickly said yes and that I was going to head upstairs to get my homework done. My mother looked at me, paused, and then said okay. I walked out of her room, up the stairs, slowly shutting my bedroom door, and screamed into my pillows. I cried and fell asleep. When a person lies one time, they have to keep making up a lie to cover up the last one. But it will soon catch up. And it did for Shad. I spent my remaining first week at school trying to stay focused, but you could always tell when something was bothering me since my face showed it. I got asked in my classes by students and teachers if I were okay. I responded with a quick smirk and was relieved they didn't nudge me for the truth. Afterward, I went to the library later on that day to study. It seems like all eyes went straight to my table when Bryant walked over. He looked worried.

"Tina, are you okay." I couldn't hide it from him anymore. I had felt bad enough about staying my distance. Bryant had never crossed me, lied, or took my kindness for granted. He was a good friend and gentleman. I stared Bryant in his face and, in a whisper, told him everything. He sighed in between the conversation and moved a little closer to rub my back while his free one held mine. I was so embarrassed to be telling him that the man I've been faithful and fighting so hard to work it out with was cheating on me. Bryant listened and comforted me. The eyes of everyone around the circular tables went back into their books. After our heart-to-heart session, I respected Bryant much more for not giving me a pep talk. He realized a shoulder and ear were what I needed most. Sometimes that's all we want people to do is listen, with no judgments and no words. Our bell rang for the next class; we both got up as he embraced me with a kiss on my cheek. I whispered thank you into his ear with him rubbing my chin as we parted ways. People around us smiled. I went home that day, realizing two things, good and bad. The good: I had people in my life that cared about me after having to experience friends who didn't. The bad: I was running from the truth all summer. The signs were there, the evidence was there, yet I still didn't accept it. When your intuition is talking, listen closely to it, especially if it keeps you up at night. It's for a reason. So don't let it go unnoticed like I was trying to because it will slap you in your face when you at least expect it. Although I was hurting, I made my mind up; Shad needed to see my face's disgust. So I decided to visit him the following weekend. It was my first time having to visit someone in jail. The whole experience was terrifying; being checked like you did something, asking for someone by a jail number instead of their name, and seeing them have restricted contact to live. It makes me want to stay on a positive road the best I can. During the car ride with my mom to the jail, she talked with me about knowing my worth. I hadn't even told her what he revealed to me, but she put two and two together. I listened to her explain the importance of not settling for less and that I deserve the same love I give. I was teary-eyed a bit because I knew she had been through similar, so the inspiration she was speaking was truly from the heart. She held my hand and told me to take deep breaths and pray on it. I did just that. When I arrived at the visitation, he stared at me through the glass with a grin on his face. I sat down and shook my head. Shad stared at my expression, his grin disappeared, and he went on to say, "I'm sorry for not telling the truth." I remained silent. I wanted to bust the glass open, grab him by the neck, and strangle him until I felt better. But I insisted on him suffering more from my silence. Shad started to realize he wasn't going to get any words out of me, so he kept talking." I didn't mean to hurt you." When he said that I could see my reflection through the glass, it looked like someone had let out a wet fart. I wasn't buying the story, though; I couldn't. I laughed, got up, signaled for my mom, who was standing along the wall. My mother looked at Shad with disappointment, and we walked out. Shad's mouth was wide open until I was out of his sight. I felt humiliated but happy he could see in person that I wasn't moving on from this. The car ride home with my mom was silent. My mother didn't try to pressure me to say anything. And I appreciated that. My mother blasted Mary J Bilge's song, not going to cry on the ride home. I nodded my head with the beat. I always had hope of never having to experience that type of pain. But thanks to Shad, I knew about it now. After our visit, he called my house phone constantly. I informed my mom to call the phone company to put the block back on the phone line. When he realized it was back on, he started sending two letters a week with the envelope reading. I'm sorry, I just threw them on my dresser. I took down all of the pictures around my room, and I placed them in a shoebox on my closet shelf. Each one I placed in the box I glanced at for a second. All good memories of times we shared throughout the city, events, and at home. Not once did I think he was doing something behind my back. But it explained a lot behind his distant act. I ignored Bryant and Tory's phone calls, and I felt bad about it, but I knew I would end up crying on the phone if I talked with them. Bryant and Tory both hated to see or hear me cry. They sent constant text messages, letting me know they were thinking of me and wanted me to call if I just needed to scream or vent. My only response to the text messages was hearts. They accepted that. It was a good thing Tory was attending school across town, so I didn't have to worry about bumping into him. And I believe Bryant tried his best not to bump into me because he wanted to give me my space. I had received a text from Bryant at the end of the month, telling me I deserve better. I knew he was right. When we love a person who has done us wrong, we try to dodge around all the problems, hold on to them as long as possible, and even make excuses. We never want to accept the person they're showing us because we're still holding on to what we hope it could be. But sometimes, hoping what it could be if it's not what the individual wants will not change a thing. I loved him, but it was obvious he didn't love me. I didn't know what decision I would make. Until I figured the decision out, I continued to stay focused on myself and ignored Shad. A month later, my phone rang while I was painting my room with Bryant, and I noticed it read Shad's mother's name. I had programmed her number in my phone just in case I wanted to contact her after the crazy first interaction. Instead of the country accent, I was hoping for; it was Shad's voice on the line. He won his case, the judge ruled it as self-defense, and he was home. I thought I would be excited; I wasn't. I still ached from his betrayal and lies. And I made him aware of it. He promised me that he would change now that he was home. Bryant looked on with worry. I got off the phone with Shad to Bryant, embracing me with a hug. "Be careful, Tina," he said, hugging me once more. Bryant left my house that day with our friendship lingering in the air. Tory called me after I texted him the news of Shad to say, "he doesn't deserve a second chance." When our family and friends tell us the truth about some things, we refuse to listen. I learned quickly second chances are not for everyone. I could understand if you alls' communication wasn't right or long-distance made you unable to connect in the way you'd like, then I could see why a second chance is possible. If a person constantly hurts you in the form of cheating over and over again and causes you to forget who you are, a second chance needs prayer before going forth with it. When Shad came home, we started on good terms. I even met his mother, Gloria, who automatically bonded with me.She talked with me about his poor choice in a few friends and Shad needing to redirect his life. Gloria also apologized for Shad not telling her about me and for her calling me another woman name. I like his mother due to her honesty and compassion towards her son. Shad started spending a lot of time with me at my home and reconnected with my mom. I was glad my mother was a forgiving woman, but she still let him know he was walking on thin ice with her. Shad and I revisit landmarks and holiday traditions we shared before he went away. He even apologized to Tory for the way he was treating me and hoped they could be cool again. Just like my mom Tory accepted the apology but let Shad know he was watching him. Shad was back to caring and loving me for who I am. I didn't realize it was the calm before the storm. I begin stressing out about Shad returning to partying a lot, not answering my calls, and not seeing me unless he wanted to. I felt stupid for him, and I knew I should've let go before I started to lose myself. But it was too late.

Chapter 9

Reality Check

Reality Check

Losing yourself to someone is when you invest so much into them that you stop investing anything into yourself. You're not your own identity anymore; you're theirs. You're breaking into pieces, giving up on yourself, not listening to the ones who love you, and continue holding on to something that's not there. I remember holding on until there was no fight in me left.

It was two in the morning, and my body was physically tired with constant chest pains. I called Shad's phone numerous times, catching on to him, ignoring my call because it went straight to his voicemail. I stared around my room at the tweety birds that would typically change my frown into a smile, but not now.

I wanted to dial Tory's number but couldn't. I even wanted to reach out to Bryant but couldn't. I wanted to scream downstairs for my mother or sisters to come up to hold me, but I couldn't. I quickly developed thoughts of taking numerous pills but couldn't get out of the bed to do it. My stomach knotted as I curled up under my covers and fell asleep.

My mother prayed over me, but I couldn't pray for myself. Being young in a serious relationship was something I dreaded at that moment. I should've been running around playing a hopscotch game or red rover. Instead, I took on issues that people in their twenties and up were enduring. Here I was at fifteen, driven into a mental state that wasn't safe.

I begin to question why I have such a broad personality and being wise beyond my years. I learned that I inherited my old soul from my mom. When she was young, she was more outspoken and adventurous than a child of her age. Her first relationship was at the age of 12, the same age that I started. My mom has a close-knit relationship with my grandmother; the same close-knit relationship I have with her made it easier for her to help me because she understood what I was going through.

I believe that my mother may have handled her emotions a little bit better than me at that age. My mother tells me, "she wishes she would've waited till she was older, mature, and able to cope better with what relationships bring" I wished I would've waited too, for the same reasons as my mom, I notice the fragileness occurring in myself.

I wouldn't wish that pain, heartache, and frustration on anybody. But I was glad my mother's prayer kept me safe that night. I woke up to my phone playing Jennifer Lopez featuring Fat Joe: Ima hold you down. I knew it was Shad. "I've been calling you all morning." I had no missed calls or voicemails. I hate knowing when he was lying.

"Let's meet up," he said as the wind blew through the phone. I threw on some clothes, not looking towards the mirror to see if my appearance was okay; I didn't care. I met up with him at the gymnasium, where I practiced for the talent shows every spring and took our first pictures together. I sat on the balcony staring down at the basketball courts until I felt warm hands on my back.

"Did you have a long night?" he said, massaging my shoulders. I remained silent, continuing to stare off the balcony of the gymnasium. As he talked, I chose not to hear any of the words released from his mouth; anything he would say, I would take as a lie. "It's over," I said. I glanced over my shoulder. "Get. Wait, what do you say?" his eyes widened.

"It's over, Shad." He looked at me, puzzled, lifted his hands off my shoulders a bit, with his fingertips still touching them. "Nah, you don't mean that," he said while starting to rub my shoulders. I removed his hands, got up, and walked down the stairs. Shad came behind me, gently grabbing my arm. I went off. "Don't call me. Act like you never met me. And every memory we had, keep it here, Bye." He slowly let go of my arms as tears blurred his vision.

"It's over, Shad," I said one last time before turning away, leaving him standing on the stairs. I walked out crying, but the weight lifted. It was time to live truly, breathe, and not care about anyone for the moment but for me. Where did the strength come from to make me say those words to him? I knew my mother's prayer played a part in it.

I was at rock bottom. It couldn't get any worse than that. If you find yourself feeling like this or getting to the point I was at night in my bedroom; please reach out to someone you trust. Confide in a person who is not going to judge you but wants to help you. I tried to block everyone out from helping me and soon learn by doing that cause me to spiral into a deeper depression.

Having to go through an emotional breakdown experience is one reason I don't judge people. You never know what someone is going through. I was hurting behind closed doors. When I let my loved ones in, I finally gained the courage to do something different because making the same mistake wasn't going to change my train of thought, sanity, or life.

I begin turning all of my focus into being a teenager, concentrating on dancing and my studies. I also resumed hanging out with old friends at the movies, dinners, and sleepovers. We'd all smile, embracing our friendships and reminiscing about what was before all the boy problems came into the picture. I felt whole again and enjoyed the actual feeling of being happy. It was a feeling I wanted to keep conjoined with forever. Now take a breather before reading the next line:

I didn't want to break up with Shad.

I wanted to teach him a lesson. I wanted him to realize that having more than one girl was not cool. I wanted him to feel how the person you thought would always be there can quickly give up on you. Simultaneously, while thinking about these things, I remain upset with myself because I knew I deserved better. I wanted him to love me. He had to want to love me; it wasn't something I could force. I turned to my mother for advice. She flat out stated she didn't believe I was ready to get back into a relationship. My mother saw how much it affected me emotionally and didn't want to see me like that again. She discussed more experiences that she went through as a teenager, dealing with cheating, emotional and physical abuse, to shed light on what she did to make a better life for herself again. I knew my mother wouldn't steer me wrong. But that old soul of mines was like I got this. I had kept in contact with Shad's mother the whole time I was focusing on myself. She would tell me how he stayed locked in his room, wondering who I was seeing and what I was doing. Gloria let me know he was even branching off from his friends and spending more time with his sisters. Before our anniversary, I decided to go to his mother's house to talk with him. As I approached, he was sitting on the porch listening to music. You would've thought I was a ghost the way his eyes widened.

He jumped from the top stair, stumbling a bit, pulling me into his arms. I was ready for Shad to hear me out. "The first time you mess up, I'm gone," I said with a firm voice. He promised that he wouldn't do anything else. How many more promises he would break? How many more times would I believe him? Should I've just listened to what my mother was saying to me? Had he gotten used to me just taking his word? I knew what real love should have felt like by a man from the unconditional love I received from my uncle, males cousins, and grandfather through the support they gave me, communication, trust, and loyalty. What Shad and I had didn't even compare to it. When someone says I love you, it could just be their way of keeping you around. I told Shad how I didn't feel loved by him. He sat in silence, listened, and said he would make things better. After meditating on the relationship and Shad, I realized his biggest problem was everyone catering to his needs. It rubbed against, negatively, his relationships with people. His family used to fix his mistakes and believe his every word even if they knew he was wrong. Therefore in a relationship, he wanted that same layout because he knew how to get away with it. I always brought to his attention what I was feeling or the doubts, so he steered towards the direction of girls who wouldn't ask the things I was bringing to him. Although it is not a good excuse for the way he treated me, sitting down, and looking into his lifestyle and the journey, I was able to figure out where his attitude and actions started. Shad's actions led us to where we were: a bigger problem than a solution. Whenever I tried to talk to Shad about the things he wanted out of life to better himself, it was as if he gave up believing anything good would happen. And he questioned what was there to look forward to accomplishing. What I loved, though, no matter how defeated he felt in figuring out his life, going to the street was never an option. He said it wasn't in his character to do so, especially seeing some of his own family going down that route with harder consequences. I was glad he thought that way because I wasn't attracted to those types of guys and wasn't going to start. After our discussion and soul searching, I left Shad's house, taking a leap of faith in the relationship. He discusses how he wanted to get his GED, equivalent to a diploma, by taking math, reading, social science, English, and history classes. I supported him with the decision, told him I was proud and that he had my full support. Shad stated that whether I realize it or not, I motivated him because no matter what I was experiencing with my health, social life, family life, and what he had put me through, my focus never went off my studies. He feared I would soon get tired of him if he didn't get himself together and leave for good. Shad was tired of letting life pass by. That conversation was the first time I believed Shad wanted better for himself. He was ready to change his direction in life, what he brought to the relationship, etc. I had already missed being with Bryant, who showed what better could be through his actions and loyalty as a friend. So Shad had a full 360 to complete. Ending our fourth year on a good note and heading into our fifth year felt like a dream come true. Things were going well, we communicated better, and no new girl's name was released from anyone's mouth. Even my mother, sisters, Tory, and new friends I filled in on our journey, Shad's mom, family, and friends were rooting for us. I was so happy to witness that. Shad was now twenty, I was seventeen, and I could honestly say he had become a better person. He received his GED, was working a full-time job, and getting ready to get his place. There was no more run-in with girls eyeing me, no more friends blurting hidden things, and no more Shad staying out all night at parties. In 2005, in our free time, we were glued to one another. We graced our neighborhood grounds as if we were Barack Obama and Michelle. We continue to enjoy the holidays, the summer, and memorable moments attending events as well. I realized when you're having a good time, the days fly by, so take in every moment. We cherished our love, plans, how to stay happy with one another, how to trust, and how to stay committed. Due to things working out so well, what happened next, changed everything.

Chapter 10

Loved, Learned, and Loss

Loved, Learned, and Loss

September 16th, 2005 was my last time walking through the community where I was born and raised. I couldn't take the sad stares from everyone or the hugs that felt like an embrace; you would give a child heading to school for the day. The constant "it's going to get better" when no one could understand my chest's tightness, and my heart closed off from the remainder of reality. The thought of walking past a restaurant that simmered a nightmare that left me sleepless for weeks, months, with constant trips to the hospital. I wasn't eating or sleeping, causing my mind, body, and soul to shut down. I couldn't accept the heart shape charm dangling from my neck, a picture I didn't have the strength to look at, with rest peacefully engraved on the back of it. I remember on the night of September 16th, my house phone ring twice, and I could hear my mother's voice. She said hello enthusiastically then shifted to a concerned tone. I peeked at her, wrapping the telephone cord around her finger as she leaned against the small dining room wall. Curious but wanting to dry off, I disappeared from the crack in the door. When I begin to pat my face, she appeared saying call Nikki. I waited for the reason behind it; instead, she repeated call Nikki closing the door quickly. I grabbed my cell phone from the violet toilet cover, dialed Nikki's number; her phone went straight to voicemail. I peeked back through the crack of the door to get my mother's attention. She was on the phone again, expressionless, secretly looking at me then back to the wall. "Ma, Nikki didn't pick up" "call again," she said. I sat on the toilet cover, with a rose towel shielding me, hearing Nikki voicemail again. I hung up, sat, wondering if my mother's phone conversation had ended, but her voice was hard to make out. Looking at my phone, I notice Shad still hadn't call back from earlier. Was the restaurant that crowded? Becoming impatient, I strolled down my contacts to call him when my mom appeared at the door looking at me, moving her lips, but no words coming out. Horizontal lines made way to her forehead; lips moved again; no words came out. I stepped out of the shower, not even knowing that a part of me had stayed behind in it. In a quick instance, my life became a movie plot. A girl falls in love with a handsome guy who lives happily ever after, isn't it. The words that revealed themselves through my mother's lips could have stayed sealed if Shad and I were in each other's arms. Instead, something more powerful was standing in between that ever happening. "Shad was shot," was my mother's hesitant words to me as she stared with glossy eyes. She leaned her head on top of mines and slowly revealed more, "he died." I remember screaming as my mother caressed me tightly. I felt like a toddler who had fallen off a bike or had gotten lost through an amusement park's busy crowds. I heard her whimpers as she prayed over me. I pressed harder against my mom, releasing my tears onto her chest. My sisters stood in the middle of the bathroom door as my pain took over them with a repeatable phrase exiting my mouth "he was supposed to call right back." Shad was in the busy restaurant during the time I was cleaning up my room. He called twice, but I didn't hear the phone through the romantic verses of R&B group Jagged Edge songs. But when I walked over to the radio to pop in another cd of theirs, I saw Shad's name blinking on my phone screen. "Well, finally, you come to the phone," he said in a joking manner. "I had the music loud while cleaning up; that's why I didn't hear it the first time you called," I said. "Don't you mean the first couple of times," he coughed as if he was trying to hold back the giggles. He went on to say, "Okay, I'm sorry, but how much more cleaning do you have to do?" Before answering, I looked around to see the progress. The only thing that had been touched so far was the seating area transformed into a tweety collage. Shad broke the silence in laughter. "I just bet you are still on that tweety section" he knew me well. "You're going to be thirty with tweety birds everywhere." I couldn't deny that he was right. Shad continued to talk, but I couldn't hear him because of the noise from customers and registers beeping. Then finally, it sounded like he made his way towards a quiet zone. "I'm going to call you right back as soon as I leave out of here" his voice was a little lower now. "Are you coming over in the morning?" I asked. He quickly said, "Yes." I smiled at his answer. "Okay, make sure you call me right back" as I started to hang up, I could hear him going back into the crowd. I walked over to my radio; it read 8:25 pm. Scratching my head, I returned to the tweety birds and picked one of the big-headed fellows up off the floor. I picked up the tweety with a tight red and white fitted shirt that read in bold letters: beep. I smiled because Shad had just bought me that tweety as a thinking of you present. I turned to position my eyes back toward the radio clock, now reading 8:35 pm. No return call from Shad yet, so I decided to escape the large, pink, and rose-filled tweety room for a dive into the shower before he called back. At the moment my screams were growing louder, I could feel the vibration of my phone. Every second a different name popped up. I sat the phone on the bathroom sink, closed my eyes, and bit down on my lip to ease the screams. I started to make out my mother putting clothes on me. I thought about the last conversation, the last hug, the last kiss, and the new beginning we had. I kept my eyes shut, not accepting the realization of a part of me being gone forever. My eyes reopened in my mom's car as we headed downtown to Shad and his family. I could see the number of missed calls and voicemails changing on my phone. I looked out the window, then down again, seeing Tory's name blink on my screen. I answered, but my sniffles were the only thing leaving me. "I love you" was the words of my friend coming through the phone. I took the phone from my ear and pressed the end button. Tory sent a text afterward, reading, "I love you, Tina, I'm here." I bit down on my lip once more while my face, shirt, and pants were covered with tears. My mom grabbed my hand tighter. Justin Timberlake's, Until The End Of Time, played on the radio. I started shaking my head back and forth, panting. My mother turned the radio off. I looked at myself through the side-view mirror; I could already see a change. My face appeared distressed. Once more, I whispered, "he was going to call right back, ma." When we arrived at the hospital, my mom and I drove up to the hospital entrance. My mom continued to lead the way clasping tight onto my arm. She kept her emotions from showing to be strong for me. When the doors opened, I could see Shad's sister, Nikki, a family friend, and one of his sister's boyfriends filling the chairs leading towards the back. The other seats throughout the emergency room were empty but recently occupied from the way they were positioned and scattered over the place. I glanced at the receptionist's desk, but the older woman did not look up. She knew my reason for being there. I turned to Shad's sister, studying my movements, while my mom held me close. I grabbed onto a nearby chair, stumbling, and my mother slowly tilting me to sit. I raised my head to see Nikki standing in front of me. She wiped her wet face then rubbed my hand. I parted my lips but was interrupted when the doors leading to the back opened. Shad's family members came out, heading towards the exit of the hospital. My mom helped me up; we followed behind them, coming up on a slender woman who was shaking and pressing her face into someone's chest. I couldn't take the pain away from Gloria, and I didn't know what words to say. I always had given her hugs, but this one was different. Still, a hug of compassion and love, but the broken hearts intertwine, causing dampness. As I inched away, I stared into her eyes, and her words to me were, "why my baby?" Gloria wept as Nikki grabbed hold of her. As I walked back to my mother's car, I kept turning around to look at his mother. She's a beautiful lady that treated me like her own and said I was a good lady for her son. I took one look back to see Gloria and family members looking at me with their faces filled with pain. I was more concerned for them than I was for myself. Losing my grandmother, I knew what loss was, and it took a long time to develop the strength to carry on. Now here I was again lost, confused, angry, and hurt, leading me into a hospital bed. Four days had gone by since Shad was killed, and I was still trying to wrap my mind around why him? Who would shoot him? He didn't do anything, nor did he hang out in the streets, so what's the reason? I glanced around my small hospital room filled with tweety bird balloons, roses, and get well soon cards. I watched visitors come in and out, squeezing my cheeks, kissing my forehead, and telling me how sorry they were for my loss. My mom, sisters, and Tory never left my side during my hospital stay.

Even Bryant had stopped by to spend time with me and joke about the good days. My friend Tiffany from elementary school came to express her gratitude and ended her one-sided beef. Shad's family and friends called my mom to check on me. I was relieved they didn't come up to the hospital because I knew seeing his family would make things worse for me. Friends from high school sent cards by Bryant, telling me they loved me and apologized. I sat, trying to get my blood pressure under control, and wept. I wondered how I could become stronger. I started to block out thoughts of having my own family and being married. Can I love again? Go back to regular routines? I needed the guidance, support, and strength from my family to help me find my way. Once again, I was experiencing a sudden loss. I didn't know how to grasp it, and I felt like I had died with him that day. A death that happens unexpectedly is one of the worse things to endure. When

I return home after my three-day hospital stay, nothing could get me out of bed. I had headaches, sleep deprivation, and no appetite. I didn't want phone calls and couldn't play slow jams, it was even hard to look at Shad's pictures, and all my daily activities and being present in school came to a halt. I was in what I call the danger zone of grieving.

All I had were memories, and even those I didn't want to remember. I believe nights during that period were the hardest for me. I would sit up when everyone went to sleep and cry. I played the last voicemail Shad left me on repeat to hear his voice. I held the previous tweety bird he bought, watching it soak from my tears. Some nights were worse than others. My mom would come into my room to lie with close friends, and me, one being a close friend named Cassata, came by to keep me company. In the mornings, I sat quietly, staring at the television, lying in my mom's bed. She would fix me the only thing I would eat is rice, cheese, mixed with broccoli, with ginger ale.

My mom didn't force me to talk; instead, rub my back from time to time. We believed that a week off from school could help me, so Coach, an assistant at my school, made sure I received homework. When I was up to it, I completed the assignment. My mother returned to work after a few days, so my sisters, Tory, and my dear friends, Cassata and Bryant, watched over me. Jada was a toddler and couldn't understand what was happening. What she did know was that Shad wasn't coming back. She would draw pictures of Shad and me; sneak them into my bedroom while I was sleeping. I could hear her little feet hurrying out the door.

Shad's family kept my mother up to date on funeral arrangements and how his mother was doing. My mother would inform me she was holding on the best she can; I understood. During this period in my life, a lesson I learned was who would be there through thick and thin; I didn't have the energy to invest a reaction in the individuals that weren't. My mother received a phone call from Nikki, letting us know about the funeral arrangements. When my mother told me, I panicked. I wasn't ready to see Shad. My mother said it was my decision if I wanted to go or not. But I knew I had to find some strength to attend because I had to see him. On the Day of Shad's funeral, I remember driving in my mother's passenger seat to the funeral home. As we got close, my body went numb. My mother helped me out of the car, holding my hand tightly, as we crossed the busy street of familiar faces and their stares.

We walked into the funeral home, went down a long hallway, and came upon doors where a royal blue casket sat. The night before, my mother went for the viewing of Shad's body. When she arrived back home, the front door opened, and shut slowly. I was sitting in the dining room as she approached me then turned away to walk towards her room. "Ma," I whispered out because I could see the hurt in her face. She stopped and leaned against the wall. "Oh my god," she said, and she burst into tears. During Shad and I new beginning, my mom and Shad had gotten closer. She started calling him a son, and he adored it. So I knew she was hurting just as much as I was. When I saw the royal blue casket, I didn't look towards the opening; I looked at who stood in front. It was Keith, crying and being consoled by Mitchell. I turned to my mom, "I can't do it." She walked me towards where Shad's family sat. I slowly took my seat, and I could see a caramel face peeking from underneath a seat in front of me. It was Shad's nephew, Ivan. I bit my lip while watching his handsome face cover in tears. Ivan's face wasn't capturing the smile I would normally see. And he wasn't holding Shad and I hands to cross a busy street. I could tell Ivan's little face of fear was confused about why his uncle was asleep in a casket. I started directing my attention to the podium as people got up to speak about Shad. I didn't want to make out their words, so I closed my eyes, put the tissue in my ears until the end to block out the screams and tears. While the last viewing of Shad started, I stayed in my seat as his family went up. Tory walked by and rubbed my shoulder with his fingers trembling. When I glanced up again, my mother was standing on the side of Tory with Cassata joining them. I whispered I was ready to see him. They helped me up and held my hand as we approached the casket. Everyone had already left out to get in their cars for the funeral procession to the cemetery. Two of his friends and Nikki stuck behind watching over me as I walked up to the casket. I remember seeing that he had on his favorite color, royal blue, and looked like he was sleeping. The next thing I know, I opened up my eyes in Tory's arms, who carried me to a seat outside of the room, with Nikki and Shad, two friends running towards me. I couldn't get the image of Shad with his eyes closed out of my head. I closed my eyes as they carried me to my mother's car to drive to the cemetery. When we got there, I remember strolling to his casket the same way I walked to my grandmother's. The pastor said words that I couldn't make out as I looked down at the casket. I could feel myself falling as they lowered it. My mother caught my fall with my attention going to Gloria and Shad's sisters. They looked at me in tears; I looked away. When everyone walked back to their cars, I stayed a little longer looking at the casket. I whispered to my mom, "he said he would call back ma, right back." She held me close. We walked to the car in silence, watching people glance my way with saddened faces. As we drove off, my eyes stayed glued to the rectangle hole occupying Shad until it was out of my sight. I didn't know what the future had in store for me? I became closed up, guarded, and my trust in others deteriorated. I went into confinement mode: school back home, that's it. I would go to bed, hoping I felt better; I didn't. When my grandmother had passed, I remember learning that you don't get over grieving in one day, three weeks, or a month. I also learned that everyone grieves differently. Valentine's day rolled around; I was not too fond of it. Our anniversary date came and went; I was not too fond of it. I saw couples at school, and I tried to tune them out. I had to give myself time. As time passed, Shad's birthday was around the corner, and I was at the end of my junior year of high school. I knew that there would be festivities for his birthday, but I wouldn't attend. It was just too soon for me. At least, I wanted to take a trip back to where I was born and raised to see his family.

A day before his birthday, I drove through the row of houses to his uncle's house. As I approached, I could see Gloria standing on the porch; a smile appeared on her face. She yanked me and held on tight. "We missed you," she said. I missed them too. She didn't ask how I was, but I knew it's what Gloria wanted to say next. I had gained my weight back, the complexion around my eyes softened, and my mouth didn't look like a permanent frown. I told her, "I'm taking it a day at a time," with Gloria saying likewise. His uncle, sisters, and a few cousins came to the door, hugging me when they heard my voice. You could sense the hurt still was within us all. As they let me go, I slowly step back to walk away. I could feel their eyes staring at me, but I didn't turn around. I walked back to the car, passing his buddies; Mitchell, Gerald, and Keith, who hesitantly stopped me. I gave them warm hugs. "We missed you, lady," they all said. I gave them a warm smile, climbed in the car, and waved goodbye until I was out of sight. Then I let the tears fall. Within my first serious relationship, I had loved, learned, and lost.

Chapter 11
Mystery Diagnosis

Mystery Diagnosis

I remember three years of my life feeling like I was in a tunnel with no escape route, opening my eyes always in a hospital bed, not understanding what led me to it or suggestions releasing doctors' mouths. Waking up and not getting back to sleep due to pains, aches, worries, and troublesome thoughts. People revealing their true colors, discovering my body was thinner than usual, feeling like I wasn't myself, trying to hold on to faith, but even that was a stretch, and some nights wondering if I was better off dead. I hated that my mom, sisters, and I witnessed, endured, and lived through it. No one knew how to help me, heal me, or get to the root of what was damaging my health and sanity. It got worse before it got better. I was crying out for better answers.

I felt like my doctors were opening up a dictionary rambling around words, ideas, and phrases instead of just saying they didn't know how to resolve it. My hidden strength, family observations, research, and faith kept me on the path of remaining here. But I couldn't stop wondering if I would ever get answers to what had been happening physically and mentally for such a long period. One of my first symptoms was panic attacks. My chest would tighten up, and airwaves clogged, I became hot, drenched in sweat, lose balance, blackout, waking up in a hospital bed. My doctors would run numerous tests concluding that I could be a borderline diabetic. I agreed it could be signs of diabetes because the trait ran through my family. So the doctors instructed me to lay off sugar-sweetened beverages, eat more fruit, drink more water, and get plenty of rest; until they tested me again.

Directly after the hospital visit, another attack came. I was at school in French class, looking up and down at the chalkboard taking notes on how to greet someone in France. The chalkboard looked as if it wasn't directly in front of me, my vision started getting blurry, followed by a migraine, and then sweats came. I asked my teacher if I could be excused for a sip of water. She stated that I could. I tried to stand up to walk out of the classroom, but I went sideways towards a closet. I started panting, blacked out, with me awakening in the hospital. My friend Tory had come to see me and told me how afraid he was. He said when I fell; I hit my head against the closet metal pole. Our teacher had tried to wake me up, but I wouldn't move.

"Tina, I thought you were gone."

Tory hands began shivering as he looked down at the floor. "What's wrong, what's happening to you?" he grabbed my hand. I whispered, "I don't know. "He was getting worked up, so I insisted that he go home. Tory was hesitant about leaving, but my mom told him she'd keep him updated. After he left, my doctors returned, looking more clueless than before. They opened up a vanilla folder and looked over towards my mom. "We still don't know what's causing these panic attacks and fainting spells. But we found that she has scoliosis. And although her hitting her head wasn't a good thing, we could spot the spine because of it. The curving of the spine will cause a lot of discomfort issues towards her back. And if not properly taken care of, she can become paralyzed. So we will prescribe muscle relaxers as well as a referral to a back specialist. And for the fainting, we firmly believe she could still be a borderline diabetic, although it's not popping up that she is."

I wasn't satisfied, and I could tell by my mother's expression she wasn't either. The panic attacks and fainting spells continued on and off for two years. The same results occurred; my mother was getting very impatient, and I no longer felt like I had control over my body. I changed my eating habits frequently due to doctor's requests, drank plenty of water, Gatorade, and got more rest with still no progress. I was stressed by this but didn't want it to start damaging other areas of my life, especially school. My teachers always assured me that my grades were still the same, in good standing. It was a relief to hear the teachers' words as I kept telling myself it had to stay that way.

Unfortunately, I missed a few days from school due to being in and out of the hospital, but I developed a study and work ethic during those periods. My teachers kept me up to speed on what was going on in the classroom and my assignments. Thankfully a swift of hope came into existence when the attacks out of nowhere seized through 6th, 7th, 8th grade. I was happy, relieved, and grateful. I continue to see a back specialist for scoliosis. As for the panic attacks and fainting spells, we concluded that my body was probably going through a puberty phase and left it at that. I graduated from 8th grade in better health, excited about the summer, and anxious to start high school. I wanted to spend my break relaxing and enjoying the fun of slumber parties, skating trips, visits to KiddieLand amusement park, and the zoo. But I woke up one morning with my vibe feeling awkward and off.

This feeling extended for weeks, turning me from wanting to explore the city into barricading myself under the sheets. I didn't want to go outside, talk with friends, have movie nights with my family, or eat. I stayed in my bed with the return of aches, sweats, along with crying and fearful thoughts. My mother wanted to keep a closer eye on me, so she insisted I sleep in my little sister's room across from hers. When I usually walked into Jada's room, I would gain energy from her Scooby-Doo pictures, but it was like they didn't exist during that time. The pain and misery I was feeling were blocking happy vibes from them. Many nights Jada would peek into her room concern because I wasn't my goofy self. She would lean her toddler-size body against mine, staring me in the face, as if she was hoping I would smile. I couldn't even fake a smile for her, and that hurt me more.

A doctor I was going to prescribe a multivitamin that would help boost my appetite and energy. I started eating Popeye's wings, KFC honey barbecue wings, or broccoli rice with cheese. The change in my appetite was a good sign, but my emotional state stayed the same. And after a while, my appetite changed again. I felt like my body was overpowering anything I was trying to do to help myself. Even doctors became frustrated because they couldn't figure out what was wrong or what to do to ease our stresses. My mom would tell the doctors, "I think it's hormonal." Their response, "I don't think so, I think it's depression."

I didn't believe it, but they insisted it was while my mom began her quest to prove them wrong. My mom made bathwater with lavender body wash every day because it was the only thing that would relax me. Jada would come into the bathroom with her toys to sit on the floor with a face of curiosity. The eyes that would typically get bigger when I tickled her now stared through me. She'll whisper to my mom, "what's wrong with my sister?" My mom whispered back, "she's sick but will get better soon." For the rest of the summer, my mother, sisters, and I went outside to take in peaceful scenery, hoping to redirect my thoughts.

When I went outside, I was quiet but observing. I enjoyed seeing my little sister playing and my big sister snapping pictures of nature. I loved seeing the different flowers, colorful trees, sunlight, and happy people's atmosphere. Once my mind had a chance to become idol, I'd shut down as if nothing was going on around me. Ta'Rika and Jada's faces were filled with worry while my mother tried to remain positive. My friend Tory would call to check on me, often telling my mom how he was hurting because he didn't know how to help. She informed him that checking on me let us know he cared for me, so he helped in his way.

It's funny how you begin to see who will be there through thick and thin when you're going through things. I learned pretty fast that Tory, during that time, was my only friend. I wouldn't let Tory see me in person because I started to notice my appearance was different. My clothes were falling off me, my face had a permanent frown, and my skin around my eyes was so black showing I barely slept. I didn't even want to look in the mirror at myself. It was getting closer to high school starting; things still weren't getting any better, so we decided I should try out therapy. We thought it was time to see if a professional who works with emotions could give us insight into what was going on.

Mrs. Parker, the therapist, was a dark-skinned woman who wore unique scarves, and her hair in a 1960's bun. She calmly introduced herself. We instantly connected, and I thought Mrs. Parker could be someone I could trust. She seemed very concerned with trying to figure out what was going on with me. In our sessions, we talked about my life growing up, the things I love to do, and what I was going through. She focused on looking for clues that may identify hormonal issues with my mother's thoughts.

I continued to see Mrs. Parker, multiple doctors and ran more tests. We still didn't have the answers we were looking for, but I began noticing my physical appearance and sleep pattern were getting back to a normal level when High School started. I went to school, bonded quickly with people, engaged fully in class, attended freshman events, and felt like a teenager again. Things were back to normal until the feeling of being punched in the chest and sweats I felt back in 4th and 5th grade returned.

It became clear I needed more help besides the sessions I had with Mrs. Parker once a week. I reached out to my school counselor Mrs. Davis, a short, concerned, motherly tone, a woman who made me feel safe. She would sit with me during my lunch period and talk about my concerns at hand. She listened, never judged, and offered kind-hearted assistance. Mrs. Davis then introduced me to one of the school assistants by the name of Coach. He was around my grandfather's age, wore only suits, a spiritual person, always smiling, with a positive attitude.

She believed he could be of help with getting my mind in a more peaceful state. They invited my mother to sit down to talk about what path they were trying to help me take. Their goals and my teachers were to be there and get me through my freshman year. My mother showed her appreciation for that. I made new friends in high school. I wouldn't open up to my new friends about my situation because I didn't think they would understand. It would take time to trust people in friendships because of the old ones' bad intentions.

Even though they didn't know what was going on, they always offered hugs and sweet words. While everyone was supportive, Mrs. Parker changed. It was as if she second-guessed me now and tried to add her diagnosis to my pain. I would sit with her and started to feel like I was talking to myself. I told my mom about it, and she decided to come into one or two of our sessions.

During my mom's visits, Mrs. Parker told her about some medicine she wanted me to try out. She stated that medication would help me relax so that I could sleep at night. Instead, it took a different route. The medicine caused sleep deprivation resulting in my body shutting down, leading to absences from school. Concerned, Coach, Mrs. Davis, and a few of my teachers called my mom to see what was going on.

She briefs them on the medication given and informs them that she was weaning me off to see if it will help my physical state return to school. They agreed to take turns bringing my homework to my home. I knew what work needed to get done from the syllabus detailing themes, examples, quick notes, detailed notes, and my memory of what I learned in class.

My mom set up a homework environment in our living room that included a desk, chair, computer, laptop, pencils, pens, erasers, stapler, and a calculator. She also balanced it out with relaxation by purchasing a stress reliever wrap for my neck and putting on soothing ocean music. She began to second guess Mrs. Parker, so my sessions went from once a week to none. My mother even threw away the medicine prescriptions, stating it was adding to my stressful downfall.

My sisters would come into the living room to sit and talk; I could see that they were still worried and afraid but trying to remain positive in their faces. Two weeks passed, and my absence from school didn't count against me. They labeled it as medical leave. I was relieved to know Coach, Mrs. Davis, and my teachers remained supportive and understanding. I was strong enough to return to school as freshman year was coming to a closure. My friends were happy to see me; I was glad to be back, passed my finals, and ended my freshman year on the honor roll.

Coach and Mrs. Davis said they would keep in touch with my mom and me throughout the summer. My mom was motivated to get to the bottom of my health scares before summer was over. After school ended, we received a phone call from Mrs. Parker. She stated to my mom, "I understand why you were hesitant about the medication and wanted to be more involved in therapy sessions. I wanted to see how things were and also if I can see Martina".

I felt like it couldn't hurt to see her; I was gaining control back over my life, the passing out hadn't returned, the aches went away, and my mother's meditation techniques helped a lot. I was hoping Mrs. Parker would be surprised. The morning we were getting ready to see Mrs. Parker, I woke up to numb legs. I shouted for my mom to come into the room; she was shocked to see them swollen, red, and blistery.

Sharp pains raced up my spine like needles were sticking me. My mother slowly massaged my legs as I tensed up from back pain. I tried putting my feet on the carpet but ended up hitting the carpet face first instead. My face was uncomfortable from the rug burns. My mother pulled me closer to her. "I don't know what's wrong," I sobbed. She yelled for my sister to bring her the phone to call Mrs. Parker to cancel.

She wanted to get me to the emergency room, but Mrs. Parker insisted that we still come in to see a specialist on-site. It took my mother, big sister, and a close friend of the family to carry me to the car. Jada looked on, trying to fight back the tears. When we arrived, Mrs. Parker made the call, gave us the information on where to go, wrote out a referral, and then handed my mother a sealed envelope.

She gave us directions, led us to an elevator, said her goodbyes, and walked away. My mother and I arrived at a building adjacent to Mrs. Parkers, passing for a clinic with security personnel outside. We entered the lobby, were directed to go through double doors, onto an elevator, dropping us off on a floor with a long hallway. We came upon another set of double doors down the hallway, we had to get buzzed into, and when the doors opened, a nurse-led us to a conference room.

She put the wheelchair I was occupying in park and told us that a Dr. would be in shortly. Once the doctor came in, my mother handed him the sealed envelope. He read it, looked hesitantly, and gave it back to my mom. She read it and stared at me. The doctor went on to say, "you're being admitted for psychological evaluation." Having individual family members that went away to places involved with what came from his mouth, I knew I was at a mental institution, and there was nothing that my mom could do about it.

I started shouting, "why would I be here? My legs are numb". The doctor couldn't give me an answer and went on to ask me if I could stand up. My mother and I looked at him in disgust. We pass closed doors leading to an open room. I noticed the gated windows and turned to my mom and cried harder. I could feel her hands shivering on my back. There was no way out; it hurt seeing my mother leave without me.

Mrs. Parker had a hidden agenda to make it appear as if I was a threat to myself and others, so I had to stay by law. I was there for three days, although it felt longer than that. The medicine Mrs. Parker had given me; they ended up giving as well. So I stayed awake at night, staring through the gated windows thinking about where my life ended and questioning why bad things happen to good people.

I taught myself how to walk again by practicing through the halls, stumbling a few times, finding my balance. I also did stretches with my lower half and massaged my legs. The process of trying to walk again was complicated, but the determination in me kept me going until I perfect it. Every morning, I woke up using breathing techniques and positive thinking, telling myself, "I will get through this," and I went to sleep feeling a little better knowing I was trying to help myself.

My mother and Jada came to visit every day; Jada was curious about the place and kept questioning when I would go home. I had to keep my composure together while she was present. She always left me with a drawing of us that now as an adult, I have as a keepsake. Under my pillow at the facility, I kept a family picture of my mom, sisters, and me that we had taken on Mother's Day. We all had on red with smiles on our faces. The picture made me feel like they were always near.

During visits, you could see the anger in my mother's face as her forehead wrinkled, and the atmosphere felt as if someone lit a match. She felt misled by Mrs. Parker and was more motivated to find out what was going on within me. My big sister wouldn't visit because she didn't understand and couldn't accept that I was there. She also stated it would've been too painful to see me and not do anything; I could understand that.

I was able to make thirty-minute phone calls home to them but hated the process because it made me feel like a prisoner who had been away for years. The thought of never being able to leave kept my focus on getting out of there. To be eligible to go home was based on the progress you made daily within your actions, activities, and scheduled, sit-down sessions with a therapist.

Our activities consisted of peer builders directed towards strengths and weaknesses. We colored, wrote letters to our childhood selves, and paired with team leaders who did exercises involving ways to connect with our inner selves. At the end of each day, the team leaders wrote an essay to the therapist, letting her know each peer's progress. The therapist added their thoughts to making her final decision of who would be released as well.

Am I eligible to go home, a session with the therapist arrived. I was anxious to hear my verdict. The therapist, Dr. Jane, didn't waste any time getting to the results. "Martina, I have seen you show lots of improvement, you're back walking, you smile a little, and you react well and engage in all sessions and activities. So I made my decision, you are free to go home tomorrow morning. I already called your mom to give her the news".

I stared at the therapist, who had a rose flower pinned to her hair. I didn't know how to take in everything, but what she said next swept me off my feet. "Before you go back to your room Martina, I want you to know that I honestly don't understand why you were here. I wanted to have you go home the day you walked in, but laws don't work like that. I watched the support and love you have from your family come in through visits and overheard through phone calls. I even broke down reading the letter Mrs. Parker sent here because everything she said didn't add up. Are you crazy and delusional? Where that's from because I don't see it? I see a young girl fighting with an illness that no one can pinpoint. When you return home, Martina, continue to keep the faith. I can see that's not difficult for you to do, but I know it can be challenging.

And one more thing no more visits with Mrs. Parker". Jane stood up, catching the rose as it fell out of her hair. She hugged me and said, look around. You don't belong here. Get well on the outside. I walked back to the room I occupied with a sense of reconnection with myself. I took the time to reminisce on just three days before being broken, lost, and in a wheelchair. Now I was given a second chance to walk out without it, in better faith, and stronger than I thought I was.

I said my goodbyes to the team leaders and peers as they told me how I inspired them. I told them no, they inspired me. We exchanged smiles as I headed back to the room, packed my stuff to leave, and breathe a sigh of relief. My mother and sisters entered the room, embracing me with a hug. I quickly gathered my stuff, took one look back at the gated windows, the wheelchair alongside the bed, and exited the room.

We walked fast through the double doors, letting out a huge exhale, as they closed with us on the side of freedom. When we left the building, I waved at the familiar security personnel and promised myself I wouldn't return. And I never did. A few days made me realize its individuals enduring illnesses and situations that they have no control over. I witnessed many teenagers in the facility, not having a support system, phone calls, or anyone's visits.

I saw the unhappiness in their faces in a place of solitude with no one to lean on. To better my purpose; my sense of love, support for others, and trying to stay clear from judgmental opinions and assumptions strengthen from that. When I returned home, I searched with my mom for the answers to my health. Mrs. Parker tried reaching out a few times, always sent to voicemail.

I started back doing meditation techniques and read inspirational books that helped me understand I wasn't alone and that people were going through similar things. Calls to doctors and research continued as we stumbled upon a doctor by the name of Mrs. Ruth. She was a gynecologist who specializes in hormonal cases. We told Mrs. Ruth my story over the phone with her wanting us to come the following day.

When we entered Dr. Ruth's clinic, the receptionist greeted us in a friendly manner. A few moments later, a brown eye, freckle face, and petite woman appeared from the rooms' entranceway's examination rooms. "Good morning, come on in," she said. It was Dr. Ruth. We entered a medium-size examination room occupied with a recliner, weight stand, and counter cabinets filled with packaged equipment for exams. My mother pulled out documents, letters, notes, hospital records, and school paperwork dated back to when the panic attacks first started.

Dr. Ruth listened, took notes, and glanced over all the paperwork. My mom handed over a copy of the letter from Mrs. Parker. She started to read it with her face quickly frowning up. Dr. Ruth glanced over to me and back to my mom as I lay on the recliner, observing them. She stood up and began taking blood work from me. "I'm going to run a rapid test, Mrs. Common. I have to agree with you; this seems to all point to hormones".

My mother froze with paper in hand, looked at me, then leaned back in her chair, letting out deep exhales. Before Mrs. Ruth left the room, she patted my mom's shoulder and said: "Mothers who know their kids know best." My mom sat up in her chair, facing me as I gave her a slight smile. Dr. Ruth returned forty minutes later, with a file in her hand, closing the door quickly. My mother and I slowly stood up. Dr. Ruth looked at me, smiled, then back at my mom "it's been a long three years, and Mrs. Common, you were right, it's her hormones.

Martina has a hormonal imbalance, a severe case of it, which is why her body and emotions turned against her.

The illness she has is called **Polycystic Ovarian Syndrome**. I fell into my mother's arms after hearing the name. Dr. Ruth sat the folder down and rubbed our backs. She then passed us brochures and printed paperwork to educate us on what the condition is. PCOS is when women's hormones are out of balance. It causes issues with a woman's menstrual cycle, emotions, and changes in her look from hair growth to acne issues.

When not treated, it could result in emotions and body functions, shutting down for some. The reason is still not understood, and doctors are trying to figure out ways to improve the chances of catching it quicker. To help manage my hormones, Dr. Ruth started me on hormonal pills, meditation, documenting my menstrual cycle, and changing the way I eat. She made me come in once a week to check my hormone levels to make sure what she had me doing was working; thank god it was.

Each time I leave, I receive better results. Ruth was, for sure, an angel in disguise. The three-year battle was finally subsiding. I started my sophomore year of high school, relieved of the progression, and feeling like myself. My studies and work ethic were still adequate, everyone remained supportive, and I started opening up to my new friends more. I embraced myself for making it through something challenging, heartbreaking, and out of my control. It was indeed a defining moment for me.

Although, as an adult, I still have PCOS, the symptoms have not resurfaced, making life more manageable for me with the help of hormonal pills, my faith, strength, love, meditation, and support. I'm thankful everyday for my second chance and most appreciative of my mom, sisters, Coach, Mrs. Davis, Tory, my teachers, and Dr. Ruth.

If you are going through a difficult time: talk to someone about it. Talk to a relative, close friend, someone at school, anyone that has your best interest. And if it is an illness, do research, remain prayerful, and open-minded. And to the parents, please don't give up on your beautiful children. When you see signs that something has changed in them, such as their health, behavior, grades, and everyday routines, please pay close attention, and take action. A child and even an adult could be crying out for help: don't let it go unnoticed.

Chapter 12

What About Your Friends?

What About Your Friends?

"**F**riendships are not a fairytale" I remember saying the statement above and understanding what it meant. False accusations, rumors, tantrums, daggers, and slandering of my name came from people I thought I could trust, who I had much love for, and whom I considered more like family than a friend. I ended up blocking out the people who were true because I was investing all my time, energy, and love into individuals who played me like a fool. Especially the ones that didn't take the time out to see what I was going through but constantly rolled their eyes and whispered lies. I asked myself why to hold on to people and things that hurt me. It's because I wouldn't accept the truth of what was staring me in the face. Someone who tells you they got your back, but they are nowhere to be found, when all fails, is not a friend. Someone who can speak highly of you in your face but behind closed doors talk about you as if you were mud at the bottom of their shoe is not a friend. I treated all my friends like family: help through life issues, drove in the wee hours of the morning if something was wrong, and be that shoulder they could lean on. It hurt me, knowing that some of the friendships had come to an end. But as of today, I'm glad that they did. It gave me space and peace in my heart for people who express what a real friend is. But I couldn't take the realness in until I accepted and let go of what real friends were not.

I walked up to a window and could hear my friends inside talking about me. "She isn't going to make it nowhere, why does she think she knows everything, why is she conceited? I like hanging around her all the time because she has money; we all could use a little, right?" laughter followed right after. The crew was at Katie's house, our meet-up spot before going outside. The elevators weren't working, so I walked up the stairs of her complex. It was crazy how getting on the elevator took longer than walking up the stairs. I wished the elevator was working; maybe I would've missed out on hearing what else they had to say. "What if one day we all just took her money and made a run for it," the laughter grew louder. I bit down on my lip, hurried down the stairs, out of the building, to my phone vibrating. It was a text from Katie saying, "where are you? Let us know when you're almost there". I deleted the text and flagged down a cab to my mom's office, fighting back the tears. When I made it to the office, she was on the phone, getting ready to end a conference call. She looked up and asked, "Is everything alright?" I quickly sat down to discuss what happened and how I felt. My mom didn't waste any time responding, "Pumpkin, I think you need to leave them alone and start new friendships because if they talked about you once, there's no telling how many times they have talked about you before." She was right, but I didn't want to dwell on it anymore, so I took out a notebook, sat at a long white desk for conferences, and turned to my notes to study for a spelling exam.

A week later, one of my friends, Tory, wanted to meet up at the zoo. I didn't hear his voice through the window that day, so I decided to come. I didn't waste any time bringing my concerns to his attention. "Tory, I want you to be honest with me." He had a mouth full of skittles smacking hard, but he swallowed them when I said that. "When you guys were waiting on me the other day, I was standing by the window." Tory eyes got big, and he froze up before responding. "Tina, I swear I didn't say anything" I took in his words, letting it sink in for a moment, while we sat on a bench in front of infant cows watching the toddlers feed them. I said, "I know. I believe you because your voice was the only one I couldn't make out". He put the remaining skittles in his pocket, glanced over at the cows, then back at me. "Tina, they have been talking about you a lot lately," he looked ashamed. I dropped my head. They said to me, "I bet you are going to run back and tell her. But I never would respond. My last straw was hearing them talk about you at Katie's house that day. So I decided to go home, vent to my mom, and questioned if I should call you or not." I shook my head, and Tory frowned. You can call my mom to ask, he said, lifting his phone. I had a special bond with Tory's mom; she liked how I carry myself, and always considered me a good friend. I didn't bother calling; I knew Tory was telling the truth. "I'm sorry I didn't tell you, does that make me a bad friend?" Tory put his phone in his pocket. Before answering, I pulled some napkins out of my jacket. "No, Tory, it doesn't; if the shoe were on the other foot, I would've had to figure out how to approach you as well. But I'm glad you came out and told me". I leaned towards him to wipe the cherry skittle from his lip. Tory smiled as we got up to walk over to the adult horses' residence in silence.

Our crew consisted of nine people; five girls, including me, and four boys. Some of us grew up together since diapers while others came in along the way. We spent a lot of time together inside and outside of school. I was the go-to person for the crew when they needed an ear or shoulder to lean on. They would confide in me; emotionally, mentally, and spiritually knowing I wouldn't ask for anything in return. I always wanted to be there, but I couldn't anymore. As I continued to think of ways to approach them in school, they approached me after ignoring them for a week or two. They were noticing I wasn't sitting by them in class anymore, and when hellos exchanged, I would ignore their advances. We were a week away from Spring break, and I canceled all of my plans that included them. The bell was getting ready to ring after class one day. Katie walked up to me and asked if everything was alright. The others stared while Tory glanced off. I was glad I could finally address the situation. "You remember when we were supposed to hang out" they nodded their heads. "I was standing on the front porch near your window" I stared directly at Katie. She tried to speak, but my hand went up for her to stop. "This has been an ongoing thing from all of you for years. No matter how I felt towards some of your actions, or the snickers and remarks; I still ignored it. I didn't think friends I've been there for could do this to me". My voice sounded like a soprano singer; I knew I was getting emotional. Everyone was looking at their shoes except Tory. I grabbed my bookbag, walked out of the classroom, down the hall, and towards the stairs. I looked back, I could see Tory standing outside the classroom door looking at me. I smiled at him; he was relieved. I knew who my real friends were. I spent my entire spring break with family and Tory. Every day my mom made the drive to pick him up so we could hang out. We went to amusement parks and caught up on our favorite family show Full House. While sitting in front of the television Tory asked, "Am I upset that he still hangs with them?" I told him no; just because I was not associating with them anymore didn't mean he had to stop, and I knew he would learn their true colors on his own. Tory appreciated my approach and honesty regarding his continuing friendship with them. And we made a promise not to bring them or the situation up for the rest of spring break. It didn't take long to recognize how much damage a person can do to someone. Spring break was over, and I was sitting in my computer class doing a typing workshop when I heard my email chime. I opened my email to a message that wasn't made by me, sent to Katie. The emails read bashful words towards her and were really out of character. Katie's response back was hurtful, including harmful threats, and that she didn't regret anything she and the others have said about me. I decided that I wouldn't approach Katie or others yet. I tried to get back to my typing workshop but couldn't. I was desperate to know who hacked into my email and why. After school, I went straight to my mother's office. When I came through the door, my big sister and mother were reading the emails. Being a computer whiz, my sister noticed how the emails sent to Katie were in a fancy font. And everyone knew I only sent out emails to people in normal font. We printed out the emails, including a recent email sent to me from one of the crew members, Sandy, over Spring break. Sandy always wrote emails to people in a fancy font matching the exact font of the emails sent to Katie. While my sister was discovering this, it dawned on me. A few months before, Sandy helped me set up the email account at school and kept my password because I never changed it. My sister and mom looked at each other in shock. My mother quickly picked up her office phone to call Katie's mom. She discussed with her what happened and forwarded the emails so she could see the evidence. Katie apologized for her threats. After hanging up from them, my mom contacted Sandy's mother; there was no answer, so she left a message. Sandy's mom never returned the call. During the remaining months of school, I kept my distance. Although Katie apologized for her threats, I couldn't trust them. I felt like they would always be up to something. I shouldn't have to be worrying about watching my back. Pre-teen years are supposed to be full of fun, adventure, school, excitement, and great memories with friends. But my thoughts were consumed with worrying about who was going to cross me next.

One weekend I was curled up in my bed watching All That, a show that came on nickelodeon when my phone rang. The number was blocked, but I still answered. A degrading outburst of foul language traveled out the phone then the caller hung up. The person called back every few minutes, saying more, and then hung up again. I sat with my mouth open, feeling the tears fall onto my neck. Disgusted, I let the next call go to voicemail. When a voice message alert popped on the screen, I picked up to listen. I could hear people screaming foul language into the phone as the caller continued on a distasteful I hate you rant before ending the call. I screamed, and my mom came storming into my room. While crying, I explained to her what had happened and let her listen to the voicemail. My mother was fed up and decided it was time to sit down with all of their parents. She took my phone away to wait for one of them to call back, but they didn't. The next morning I stayed in bed wondering how it ended up like this. I could make new friends easily because of the type of person I am. But would I be able to let new people into my life after the ones I've grown to love turned on me? I didn't know. I just knew I had to forgive and accept people for who they are. I handled it by reminding myself who I was and not letting others change that. For the talk with the crew and their parents, we decided to meet at a pizza spot. Even after hearing their voices on the voice message, the ones present wouldn't admit to anything. Fingers were pointed at people that weren't present. I found it interesting that only a few bother to show up, but it made me realize that people with a guilty conscience will stay clear from being exposed. Every parent was aware of what was going on, so hopefully, the constant torturing me would stop: and it did. I didn't receive any apologies at the meeting, and I didn't expect to. The crew's actions had proven to me that an apology would be a lie. But I forgave them for my well-being because I didn't want them to control my emotions and train of thought. When I left the restaurant, I left with a clearer understanding of people and myself. No matter how long we've been friends, there was no way of making up and putting a bandage on what happened. I had to move on with Tory and me remaining close. The rest of the crew tried reaching out numerous times to reconnect and pick up where we left off. But some doors need to stay close. I went to High School with a clean slate and a hopeful attitude for better friends. My freshman year consisted of me working on my health, adjusting to my studies while wondering if I should let people in. I closely observed anyone who wanted to be friends. I began letting my guard down for a few that stayed supportive, inspiring, and kind-hearted while I battled an illness. It proved to me everyone is not the same. I introduce them to my fun personality and adventures of going to concerts, movies, hosting pajama parties, dinners, and ladies nights.

I helped with homework, studying, and was a person they could come to if in need of advice. The crew started to become a distant memory, I trusted people again, and my friendship ties were stronger. I didn't want to put all my guards down at once; protect yourself. We all want to see the good in people yet never really pay attention to the signs of bad. Going through the phase with the crew I was able to quickly pick up the signs from a few individuals in high school.

One sign was from a girl named Nevada whom I was close with since freshman year. She was the first person to approach me during high school orientation. I adored the uniqueness of her. She had her style, outgoing personality, and a laugh that made others cheer up in a room. But peer pressure to fit in with the popular kids started to get the best of Nevada. I remember her saying she wanted to start being approached by specific boys and to get them she would need to start hanging around one of the popular cliques. The group she was referring to was The Divas who were linked to the athletic guys. She became infatuated with the clique, the attention from the guys, and being well-liked by people who at first acted as if she was invisible. I started to sense a cold shoulder from her. Nevada went from spending time with the Divas, me, to just them. I was hurt that she ditched me for people who didn't care about her but she didn't see it that way. She felt like I was over exaggerating and was jealous of her newfound friends. I took offense to that because I opened up to her about the things I had to experience with my old crew and how it impacted me. So for her to take my worry and try to warn her as jealousy; she wasn't getting to know me.

When I voiced to her how I felt about her assumptions she shrugged it off like it was nothing. I realized I had to let her see for herself what I meant. I remember when she approached me at my locker to see how I was doing with me asking the same. She told me about her new lifestyle and the names of athletic boys who took interest in her. And before walking away she leaned in closer to say "you were right, I can't trust the divas". So I asked if she didn't trust the divas why to keep hanging with them. Nevada stayed quiet, buried her head into a math book, and walked away without a goodbye. I stared down the hall watching her link up with the Divas. They glanced at me, waved, and placed a sign on Nevada back that read freebies to all. The divas laughed so hard at the sign to the point where their hair shook, with them continuing to walk down the hall, and Nevada leading the way. I kept staring till they were out of sight. She was aware they judged her but said they did it only as a joke; I knew better.

That same day a class we had together she missed. Our professor called Nevada name twice for attendance then looked at me. I shook my head, he shrugged and went back to roll call. How could someone give up the important things just for acceptance? I went home that night and took down the pictures of Nevada and me. As she got in deeper with The Divas she stopped calling, coming to my lunch table, and my locker. The last time I crossed paths with Nevada was when she was making out in the hallway with two of our sport team captains. I was surprised by her face not showing fear or shock when she saw me passing; instead, she was smiling. Lost by her reaction I realized I couldn't keep trying to save someone who didn't want my help. She had to help herself.

I became friends with Keisha, a talented instrument player, who I also met during orientation. What made us bond was the similarities we had from both growing up in a single-parent household, being labeled as book nerds, having an ear for music, and a passion for getting somewhere in life. Our conversations were never dull; we both took a liking in poetry slams as well as plays, and always had each other back. We didn't have any classes together but managed to have the same lunch period for all four years. Things were going very well in our friendship that it took awhile for me to see Keisha's true intentions. When I did; it felt like my past was coming back. Peyton, who I had all my classes with, was a sweet girl, and we instantly clicked. Our days at school consist of working together in class to help one another with subject weaknesses. Outside of school, we stayed up late nights on the phone sharing our deepest secrets and dedicating all of our free time to seeing the rap and R&B sensations bow wow, B2K, Chris Brown, and Pretty Ricky live in concert. Just like with Keisha; Peyton and I main goal were to remain intelligent women on a mission.

Then there was my lucky 5 Elise, Rachel, Kim, Terry, and Cory. The lucky 5 and I are still friends as adults. From high school to now they remained loyal, humble, sweet, and down to earth. I'm thankful to call them my lifetime friends who always have my best interest at heart. Especially when they help me see how blind I was to Keisha and Peyton's true intentions. I loved bringing all of my friends together for a night out on the town. So I decided, as we were ending senior year, it was the perfect timing to celebrate our accomplishments, friendships, and the years to come. I invited Keisha and Peyton to hang out for one last night with me, Rachel, Kim, Elise, and Terry. Peyton had a family emergency so she couldn't attend. Cory was hanging out with his guys and Keisha finally decided to attend at the last minute. We booked a hotel room near a bowling alley, surrounded by downtown Chicago attractions, where we could relax. The ladies and I were full of laughs, jokes, and entertainment at the bowling alley with Keisha deciding to sit off to the side. Kim, Rachel, Terry, and Elise kept looking at me to see what my reaction towards Keisha's awkwardness was; but I paid it no mind. I was set on having a fun night and if Keisha wanted to be a party pooper she would do it alone. Whenever my other friends were around Keisha became distant and had an attitude with everyone. She turned into a kid that doesn't want to depart from their favorite toy. No matter how much I called her out on it; she wouldn't stop. I was on my last straw with her. When we left the bowling alley we decided to go to Mcdonald's to eat. Keisha, Rachel, Elise, Terry, and I got in line while Kim stood to the side deciding she would get a sandwich on the walk back to the hotel. As the rest of us ordered our food Keisha let out a loud sigh that caught everyone's attention including the workers. Elise and Rachel looked stunned, Terry shook her head, and Kim looked annoyed. Everyone was waiting for me to respond, but I didn't. We grabbed our food and noticed Keisha didn't order anything. I was anxious to get back to the room to approach her. When we left McDonald's, everyone noticed Keisha was trailing behind. Kim broke the silence by asking me why Keisha was acting so childish. I shrugged because I knew she was waiting for me to purchase some food and was upset. After all, I didn't. Keisha's flaw was acting like she didn't have any money so that she could spend yours. Then, later on, you would see her pulling out her own for something else. I knew how being used felt, and although all the signs were pointing to it, I still ignored them. I wasn't the type to address a situation in public or in front of anyone. I'd rather wait for us to have a one on one in the hotel to figure out the issue. When we made it to our hotel room, the girls wanted to stay up. We had two couches, a desk, bathroom, sitting area, two beds in the suite, and windows overlooking the Chicago skyline. The idea was to push the beds together for a night of girl talk. We all jumped on the beds except for Keisha. She sat at the seating area, arms crossed, in silence, playing with her phone. Keisha noticed me looking at her and quickly said she didn't want to talk about it. I would normally keep pushing her to talk, but I shrugged it off. I could see Keisha glancing at us and rolling her eyes. The girls noticed it too but smiled because they honored me for not giving Keisha what she wanted, which was my full attention.

The next morning when we woke up, showered, and departed, Keisha didn't say a word to anybody. That was the last time we spoke. I didn't try to call her or blame myself for what happened; I couldn't. I realize it was not my fault, so why carry the stress as if it was. I start looking at it like this; I shouldn't feel guilty for a friendship ending if there are hidden intentions. And if people with bad intentions were walking out of my life, they were doing me a favor. I had to become stronger by letting them go and accepting what was. I remember going home and taking down pictures of Keisha and me putting them inside the same box that included the crew and Nevada. I look back around my room to see the lucky five and Peyton occupying my walls. I walked up to a picture of Peyton and me attending a concert. Our cheeks touched; we held up peace signs and smiled. You could see the love for our friendship, but even pictures can hide the truth. I remember helping Peyton fill out her college applications. She wanted me to look over essay questions she didn't understand. While doing so, she blurted out that she was sick of me and slammed her hand on a desk. The entire room got quiet, and our senior exit counselor chalk stopped moving across the board. I just looked at her. I didn't even ask what she meant. Sometimes we try to figure out why a person would say certain things, not realizing how they were feeling all along. My friend Cory had asked before did I think Peyton was jealous of me. Of course, I said no, didn't even give it a second thought. But when Peyton said she was sick of me, a few memories came to the surface. I was well-liked around my high school for being smart, myself, and how caring I was. And my words came from the heart when I spoke. When Shad passed, it was in the headlines of the newspaper. People from my high school had seen Shad and me together when he would meet me to walk me home. If I weren't outside, they would let him know I was on my way to the door. So when I returned to school from my week of grieving, people greeted me with hugs, cards, and thoughtful words. All the love came from people who just knew me by name or my act of kindness when I saw people. Peyton and Cory were sitting on each side of me. Peyton kept saying she wishes that everyone who approached me would go away. I took it as her feeling like I needed my space. Peyton started looking at people crazy, saying it's not that serious and left the table to sit with her other friends. Cory stayed by my side, collecting the cards from everyone who stopped by and put them in my bookbag. I realize Peyton was being inconsiderate, mean, selfish, and appeared to be a little jealous. Cory words and the memory played back in my head while I tried to take in Peyton's expression. I put my folders inside my bookbag and removed myself from the seat next to her as she struggled to figure out the college essays. Losing Shad, my up and down health, finding out more individuals who weren't real friends; I just couldn't put up with it anymore. Peyton spent the rest of her senior year wishing she could take back what she said. She left gifts at my locker, sent notes by her friends, and left text messages talking about all the fun times. I could sense she was hoping for reconciliation, but I knew that would not take place. I was tired of my kindness being taken for granted. I was tired of letting people into my life, my circle, and my world to find a way to sabotage it. I loved our friendship and the sisterhood, but I had to let go. Although I was done with the friendships, I would go back inside the box to reminisce on how far I've come to appreciate the real friendships I have. From middle-age, pre-teen, to teenager, I learned a valuable lesson. I could hear my granny now, "Chile, you got to let people who mean no good go. Don't let people keep misusing your time, energy, and love." I started to understand what she meant. I also learned that having a few real friends was better than having a lot with devious agendas. So I took what I learned and carried it throughout life with a better outlook on what I would accept, and settling for less than I deserve from a friend, was not it.

Chapter 13

Mirror

Mirror

I love me. I don't care what anyone thinks. I don't care how you would like for me to wear my hair, dress, talk, walk, and smile, eat, or the complexion you rather I am. I'm beautiful, smart, strong, stubborn, god fearing, love to communicate with family and friends, so sometimes I'm glued to my phone. I'm creative, talented, difficult too, and can quickly catch an attitude if you're not listening but want me to listen to you. I'm sweet, emotional, and shy. I am quiet around everyone until I get to know them. I'm family-oriented and love to explore the world. It will take time to let you in due to my experiences; I have to be smart and cautious. I'm more than what you will hear or judge. I'm a forgiver, supporter, and a hopeless romantic. I'm a secret keeper, motivator, and determined to live my dreams. I'm someone who could stand in the mirror and tell myself how much I love myself. How proud I am of myself. And how beautiful I am and mean it, but it was a time that I didn't.

It was a time I couldn't look at myself; I would change something about me to accommodate someone else, cry about people judging my flaws, and not believing I was beautiful. It was a journey that started from my first challenge: my complexion. I grew up as the light bright of my family. What bothered me were the comments people made about me looking like justice and not my mom. It took a toll on my mental process because of the abuse we dealt with from justice. I felt like he was a monster, so I had made up my mind I would become one since I resembled him.

I tried to ignore people, but they made it obvious by saying, "Ta'Rika and Jada you two are your mom twins. Martina on the other hand", and then go to the extreme to say, "Martina where your twin at." I would cringe, cry, or feel sick from hearing it. I went home one day and just stared at my mother's face. She kept asking what's wrong, but I studied her complexion, face structure, and eyes that I didn't give her an immediate answer. Her forehead wrinkled up as she took the words from my mouth "I know you think you look like justice. But you don't. I felt like my mom was trying to make me feel better. "Ma, I don't look like you or my sisters" I kept studying her face. "Yes, you do. You are just a different complexion, but you have my facial features and attitude", she smiled. I giggled at her attitude joke but still felt bad on the inside. I left my mom sitting in the living room while I went to my room. My dresser mirror was draped in posters of rapper bow wow. I stood in the mirror, wanting to peel a poster back to reveal myself but couldn't. So I sat in my computer chair and moved in front of the desktop. I logged in to see my screen saver was a family picture we had just taken. I changed it up by using computer applications to darken my face. Doing this took off the pressure of anyone noticing I didn't look like my mom and sisters. I would end up in my computer settings looking at the original picture, studying my nose, head shape, and smile. Although I could point out the resemblance in our faces, I still found a way to program in my head that I couldn't. Scooting back from the computer, resting my head on the seat cushion, I could hear footsteps behind me and make out a shadow glare. It was my mother staring at the computer screen. She said, "You're not him pumpkin," closing my door slowly. Staring at the closed door, I whispered to myself, "I'm not him." I started chanting, "I'm not him" when a thought came into my head. I chanted, "I'm not him" when I wanted to darken more pictures. I chanted, "I'm not him" when more people said they could see the resemblance. I chanted, "I'm not him" when I looked justice in his face after surviving the abuse and getting away. I peeled my posters off my mirror to look at my face in its entirety. I was a beautiful girl. I was not him. I started leaving pictures of their original color, laughing at people who made remarks about who I looked like and spent more time seeing myself. I was smiling and embracing my beauty. Chanting the words "I'm not him" for months helped direct my thoughts from negative to positive ones.

I had developed a mantra and many others that helped me stay focused on who I was instead of everyone else's opinion. I grew to love my skin, face, freckles that come out of hiding, my eyes' squinting, pinkish lips, and dimpled chin. In the middle of my progression, my mother came to me with a picture, "There's a saying that when someone is around you a lot while pregnant, the child could look like them. I couldn't get rid of your uncle. You resemble him." She left me with the picture and my thoughts. Uncle Jim and I were standing in front of my grandmother Rosie's house. I was a toddler and could tell by the coats we were wearing it was winter. Uncle Jim and I were of the same complexion, had the same eyes, lips, and face structure. I always spent time with him but never studied his face enough to notice. My mother didn't have to tell me the picture was an expression of noticing my skin color and the love, resemblance, and bond with my uncle that I didn't have with justice. I realized it on my own when I accepted I wasn't him.

People tend to make your flaws known but act as if there's don't exist. It could make you feel less than you are. I've gotten nitpicked about two flaws: how quiet I am and how I stayed glued to my phone. I have always been a quiet person. I rather observe the people and things around me before opening up. My family understood and close friends, but Travis would always question it when I started dating him. Travis had known me all of his life, knew I was quiet, but when our friendship became more, he had an issue. He would take me around his friends for the first time, and I would speak, they spoke back, with me just observing them. When I went around his family, I did the same thing. I wasn't anti-social; I just had to get a person's vibe, but I would talk if someone brought up a conversation. Travis was aware of this but still made it a problem. He wasn't so talkative himself, but I didn't nag him about it. I accepted people who needed time to warm up to others. Nothing was wrong with that. For Travis, it was a lot wrong with it. His vibe came off like he was forcing me to become something I wasn't. I needed to ask someone who wasn't very close to me if my quietness offended them. So I asked a male co-worker of mine, Jesse, who worked part-time and saw me twice a week when our schedules were similar. Jesse stated, "No, it doesn't offend me. We went from a few months of hello, I hope all is well, see you later, or conversations about work to television shows, media, jokes, and music updates. I always took it as if you wanted to feel my vibe out. And I could understand that. There's nothing wrong with you not talking often. It's good to be that way, especially nowadays with the way the world and people are". I respected Jesse's response and couldn't wait to tell Travis about it. I decided to get a new female co-worker, Linda's opinion. I asked what the first thing she noticed about me was. Linda responds, "You were quiet." I sighed. She went on to say, "That's not a bad thing. I realized you're just a shy and quiet person who takes time to let people get close. And I accept it. Our conversations gradually get deeper as we are around each other more. We talk about life, friendships, relationships, and schooling. And to be honest, you are easier to talk to than people I've known for years". I thanked Linda for her comments and started to feel better. No one felt like Travis did. I was relieved and ready to discuss with Travis what my co-workers said. When I did, Travis laughed about it and said, "They are not around you all the time to notice that you get on your phone and talk to everyone else, but you're silent when in person with me and my people. And I don't like it". Before answering, I took a minute to take in what he said. Travis made me upset because the people I would talk to on the phone knew me well and got the same reaction from me that his family and friends were getting when I first met them. And as for my co-workers not being around me all the time, he wasn't either. I told Travis this, and he still made it seem like I wasn't trying to open up to him or his loved ones. Then he brought up my phone habits. "Tina, you're on the phone so much to the point I feel like I'm getting to know you through overheard conversations." I could admit I was on the phone if we were driving in the car to a destination. Someone happens to call or text to see how I was doing, in a restaurant waiting for our food, at the house when he left to cook or when he went to the bathroom, when I just needed an ear from someone who I trusted, or if they needed me. But this day in age, who doesn't have those moments. Travis made it seem like I would wake up out of my sleep to answer my phone; during movie nights, I would interrupt by talking on it, cuddling at home my attention went to it, I showered with it, checked it every second; when that was never the case. I started to see when a person believes that they are always right; they don't want to hear their wrongs. Travis would sit in silence on his laptop browsing social media during our quality times; he would excuse himself to answer or return a call. His phone would vibrate, leading him to check it when we were going to bed, and he would look through his phone during dinner at restaurants or in the car as well. Even on our days away from one another, he had moments when he wouldn't return my calls, say he was busy, but on social media, he's responding to everyone else or at events. I never nitpicked him about it. But if what I was doing weren't up to his standards, he called me out for it. I couldn't be myself around him. The vibe, reaction, and response I was getting from Travis made me hate my flaws. I remember one night, after getting overwhelmed,

I decided to have a moment to myself. I thought about when I asked my family and friends the same question I brought to my co-workers, their responses were the same. When I asked my best friend Tory about being glued to my phone, he said, "you are not on your phone like that. Travis has to realize that everyone wants to check on you because of the things you had to experience with your health. " Tory was livid. "And another thing, you have been a quiet person for as long as I've known you. So he needs to drop it. He has to be the one with the bigger issues to be putting it all on you like that". Reaching out for advice to the people who knew me best was hard when hurting because I knew how they would react. So sometimes I hid how I was feeling about a situation or handled it myself. I was trying to make sure Travis was happy. Causing me to fall into a stressful state and think if I didn't change my quietness and phone habits, he would leave. It took crying and being in deep thought to notice he wouldn't ever accept me for who I am. Can I live with that? Could I continue heading in the direction of a relationship with someone who would keep trying to make me their way? Travis took my flaws to the extreme as if I was flirting with people, breaking promises, not answering my phone for him, canceling quality time, being untruthful. My flaws didn't amount to any of that. It's a good thing to try to work on your flaws but do it for you, not someone else. I decided not to hide or beat myself up about them. If I could accept his flaws, he should accept mine. Since I wasn't trying to change for his needs anymore, he left. It hurt seeing him go, but I was happy to see my true self stay.

I adore the love in me to be different. Creating my hairstyles is one of them. I like to switch my hair from braids, wigs, sew-in extensions, and my natural hair. It's part of my personality just to be one with myself and to feel free. I had dealt with someone who didn't feel the same. I remember a guy who was interested in me was consoling me after a stressful day. He rubbed my head out of nowhere and said, "I don't understand why you wear this. I don't care how your hair looks underneath, take it off "in a distasteful tone. I was mad, confused, and thrown off guard. How do we go from talking about my stressful day to my hair? When I started talking to him until his comment, I had my hair in different styles. He never questioned it or said it offended him. I didn't respond to his comment, nor did I remove my hair. I left wondering where we may lead after he brought this to my attention. I didn't want this to jeopardize our chance of being together. I had some thinking to do. My friend Elise reached out to me about a similar situation. She said her family wanted to know why she wore extensions and not the family tradition of natural hair. They gave her talks about why extensions weren't good and that it made her someone else. She was overwhelmed with trying to explain to them her true reason. Elise was dealing with losing hair. The doctors couldn't figure out why but gave her tons of medicine for hair growth. She tried medicine but ended up losing more. She decided she would wear extensions and wigs until she got answers from doctors. Elise didn't tell her family because she believed they wouldn't understand. I informed her I would be here if she needed to talk but to know that she is beautiful. And when she was ready to approach them with her reason, let it be in her time. After a long inner talk with myself, I decided the guy, and I would not work. I didn't bother reaching out to go into the deeper reason behind his comment. But I let him know that we couldn't be, and he agreed. His tone told a lot, and I could tell the topic of my hair would be an ongoing dispute. I took the situation with this fellow as a learning experience. I started addressing the topic of my hair in the beginning stages of dating. If I would've come across someone with the same opinion as him, I'd have addressed it, if it wasn't accepted; my only option would be to leave. I felt it wasn't kind for others to focus on little things they don't like in a person. It's so much more to a person than what you see on the outside. Feeling misunderstood, unappreciated, and misled was my mindset during these times. I was a witness to being wrapped up in someone else's world that I forgot about my own and the path I was trying to take. But the lessons I was learning from the reaction of others and the response I gave them showed my true strength. I overcame the battle of my complexion, worked on my flaws if I believed they needed to be, and did not try to please others. I started telling myself if it wasn't beneficial to any areas of my life; I was going to let it come in one ear and out the other. People's opinions, assumptions, and attitudes directed towards things were going to be around forever. I realized it was not what they're saying that mattered; it's how I responded to them. I had to start believing in myself a little more and release myself from people who weren't.

Overtime looking in the mirror became an honor for a person who experiences, witnesses, and endured what people's views can do to you. I told myself I will not second guess my internal and external presence based on others anymore. I would smile, be beautiful, and breathe. If I kept trying to spend my life living up to others then I wouldn't be living. I invested more time in making myself better and capable of living a life I love. There's a saying you should never judge a book by its cover. There's also a saying that you should think twice before judging someone because you never know what they're going through. I hear teenagers say they aren't pretty, handsome, or smart, and wish they could change something about them. Please do it for the rights reasons; most importantly for you. There were a few things I didn't like about myself and wished I could improve. Acne was one of them. I didn't understand the reason for zits popping up. When I looked at my face I felt like I was playing connect the dots. I would receive school pictures in the mail and just stare into the zits. On numerous occasions, I thought the zits were turning into more. I did not feel beautiful and was anxious to find out ways to make the zits go. I told my mom how I felt and she insisted we see a dermatologist who helps with acne issues. The dermatologist informed me that my case of acne is genetic, from stress, hormonal issues, and diet. I increased my water intake for healthier skin and to fight against breakouts. I eased off sweetened beverages and when I did I felt more alive instead of run down. I consumed less candy helping control my sugar intake. For my stress and hormones, I tried getting rid of negativity, finding ways to relax through listening to uplifting music, and working more sleep into my routine. Gradually I begin seeing a change in my face. The dermatologist informed me to wash my face with sensitive soaps and continue doing what works. It felt good to see the acne disappearing. The change made it easier for me to smile for a picture, look closely at one, and develop confidence within. Once my acne was under control I took notice of a problem with my scalp. My scalp was red, itchy, with scaly patches, and made the top of my forehead blistery. For a while, I used shampoo for dandruff but that didn't help and the problem became noticeable. I couldn't scratch my forehead or rub my hair without the flakes falling on me. I returned to my dermatologist with her telling me to try different shampoos, conditioners, and scalp treatments. None of that was helping so I started to hide under hats. When I went outside, to school, or at events I thought people were looking at my hair. I became frustrated and embarrassed causing me to shy away from crowds. My dermatologist decided to examine my scalp again, keying in on my symptoms, and diagnosed me with having psoriasis. Psoriasis is a skin condition, non-contagious, that causes the problems I was having as well as the possibility of affecting other areas such as the feet, legs, and arms. My dermatologist felt like the appropriate way for me to deal with it, is to use certain greases, shampoos, and conditioners that were for psoriasis patients. She informed me the condition is long-term but if properly treated can become more manageable within weeks or months. My scalp was a severe case so I had to work out ways of handling it to still feel confident. I wore my natural hair and braids when I had moments of clear up; while wigs and extensions helped on a flare-up stage. Changing my hair, to accommodate the condition, made me feel better about myself. I stressed less, wasn't embarrassed anymore, and kept to treatments. When the moments of a guy I was dating, who cringed at the thought of weave, replay back in my mind I say to myself if he only took the time to get to know me. I could've shared one of the reasons why I do wear weave. I could've shared how wearing my different hairstyles made me feel in control of my condition. Even stepping away from psoriasis; I still loved wearing many hairstyles based on my mood, personality, or how I was feeling. Psoriasis taught me I could still be beautiful with a condition. Although there are times I roll my eyes on having to wash my hair daily, scratch my scalp behind closed doors so no one would see, and not wear my hair; I check myself. I realize people are going through much worse with their hair and don't have the same outlet as I do. I learned to be appreciative of myself, have faith that psoriasis will not overpower me, while other things did.

I had an issue with being a sponge meaning I absorbed people's feelings and problems making them my own. This caused a rift in my emotional stability. There is a difference between being there for someone and becoming their fixer. A family friend, Angie, was going through a time in life when she needed assistance with food and clothing. I helped her out but not as much or quickly as she wanted. Angie would call my phone with shouting matches about how I was like the rest, if she doesn't eat then I wouldn't either, and I should give her half of my work checks. She was being absurd and should be thankful someone was trying to help; she would get angrier and hang up. After being hung up on I would feel bad, think about her situation, and how I could juggle bills that are due to pitch in more. I didn't realize I was on the road of sucking my mental state and pockets dry. I turned into the one needing assistance while Angie was relieved of her stresses. When I helped, Angie calls stopped, then resumed when she needed me again. I started to feel used and realized it was alright to be there but I shouldn't be losing myself or earnings for her. I questioned where this path would lead me. I decided to reach out to Angie's mother, who was a close friend of my mother. She said "Tina; my daughter and I have been on bad terms with one another for a while. I found out she was misusing her finances to support a man instead of her children. She would use what I gave her to still support him. Angie lost her job because of him. She was caught on camera stealing merchandise and taking it out the back door to a car with him in it. I decided I wasn't giving her anything else and if she wanted a place to stay she should move in with me. Angie disagreed, said she hates me, and I haven't heard from her since". I was in disbelief. Angie told me the guy her mother was referring to had ended the relationship with her. She even told me they cut her hours at work so that was the reason she was having struggles financially. I felt sick after I got off the phone with Angie's mother. I called Angie's cousin, one of her close friends, and a god-sister with them all saying the same thing. After numerous nights feeling down, second-guessing myself, and working out the words I wanted to say; I was ready to approach Angie. When I called her to speak about my findings, she cut me off, said she hated me, I wasn't a real friend, and then hung up. I was so stuck on consuming myself with her issues and what she was telling me. I sat with my mother and talked with her about how I felt regarding Angie's distrust and behavior. She told me "start being mindful of how you look at people's situations and demeanors. You'll be surprised what you learn from them when you observe closely." Angie did an incredible job deceiving me. I took a step back from being someone people could turn to for anything whether it was emotional or financial. I started learning how to say no. One thing I quickly learned from the word no: if you say no to someone and they become furious then there's your answer to how they feel or what their purpose is. It is always hidden within their reaction. The experience with Angie made me realize I had to get out of being a sponge, look more into myself, and realize everyone is not meant to be in my life. When I started taking heed to that I could feel peace within myself. Self-esteem, image, and our feelings are a part of us. If we are having difficulties with any of the three then making changes to better us should be our option. A lot of situations, experiences, things, and people can make us start seeing ourselves differently for the good and bad. We may even make the wrong decisions off of what's said. The experiences I had to endure made me aware of where I was headed. Everything I endured gave me the platform to believe in myself. As I stared into the mirror in the morning, afternoon while working, at school, at a friend's house, driving, looking through the rearview, and before bed, I would question other's opinions. But then I realized; there's only one person I saw looking back at me whose opinion mattered most: and that was me.

Chapter 14
Guard Down

Guard Down

Craig was an all-around good guy. We met through mutual friends, became close, and developed our friendship. We would run into one another during our childhood, saying a few words, crack a couple of jokes, and carry on. He was a talented painter, basketball player, and kept one entertained with impersonations. My woman instincts could tell how many women smiled when he walked into a room that he was a ladies' man. But during the time we were friends, he was in a relationship with a girl who attended the same high school as him. To me, they seemed to be in love, but everyone else felt like they were acting like it. I wasn't around him enough to know if what they were saying were true. But occasionally, I observed Craig and his girlfriend at events our mutual friend hosted, saw them off to prom, and even cuddled up in my neighborhood park. Their vibe and togetherness seemed real, but I learned years later, it wasn't. Craig and I lost contact when he went away to college, but we reconnected online through a tagged teenage chat site when Shad was killed. I saw Craig's online page and immediately sent him a friend request.

I had a message from him.

It read Tina I went through everyone for a phone number on you. I was worried about you; I knew you and Shad were head over heels for one another. And I know I can't say much to ease the pain. You have always been real. And I love that about you. Here's my number; call me as soon as you get time. I'm in town on winter break from college. I would love to see you so we can catch up. And I want you to know I am sorry for your loss.

I logged off the internet site feeling good to have a friend who kept me in his thoughts and prayers. I phoned him the same day, and we caught up on memories. I asked if he was a ladies' man in college, he quickly said no and laughed right after. Craig asked when I would be free; I told him I didn't have anything going on. Craig came over to my house for dinner and to hang out. The next day ended up turning into weekends he visited from college, holidays, to every other day when he moved back home. I was grieving over Shad still, and having company from someone I had a bond with helped me take my mind off the reality of the situation.

Craig was one of my friends, one of my boys, and didn't see the signs showing that we were becoming more. Over time, I ignored our childhood days of seeing ladies flock to him; I ignored others' remarks on his past exes saying he cheated on them, and I ignored all the signals telling me to stop while I could. If I left us as friends, I wouldn't have to regret my decision to say the words I love you. Craig was very attentive to my grieving of Shad. If I had moments when I just wanted to talk about the pain, he would listen and explain his experiences with grief. I would see his face turn from concern for me to a frown, with my face developing a concern for him. Craig would assure me that he was okay and that the moment wasn't about him. I appreciated knowing he would put his feelings to the side to tend to my needs. After dealing with unworthy friends, it was a relief to have someone around who genuinely cared about me. Craig would nod his head to agree and say he understands. To get my mind off things; he would invite me out to dinner, a night on the town, to the movies, bring DVDs and VHS of random movies for nights at the house, and even bought hallmark cards with messages of documenting my strength and how in due time I will be able to form a smile.

I had never experienced a guy, other than Tory and Bryant, who went over and beyond to make me happy. I made sure Craig realized his gestures and acts of kindness were appreciated by cooking him dinner. He enjoyed my recipes for baked chicken, cornbread, rice, pasta, and turkey slices. Craig was delighted by my food and let it be known he never ate someone's food, other than the women in his family, that was so good. I would tell him I learned from the best with him giving me thumbs up while he licked the last of the food off his hands. Craig started opening up about his personal life issues from struggles, downfalls, and hopeful dreams as we spent more time together. He even trusted me with secrets. From his conversations, I started to see beyond what others had said. Craig told me I didn't have to tell him because he already knew what others were saying. Our similarities of being misunderstood by others brought me to a relaxed state. Craig gave me insightful responses towards what I would reveal by letting me know he would always be there. We spent a year hanging around one another, building our friendship, and taking in one another's likes and differences. I felt like I could consider him my brother, best friend, and someone I could lean on. I didn't have to question his trust, loyalty, and word. Our time spent together went from hanging out to holding hands and kissing. I can honestly say nothing felt forced. I could tell we were enjoying one another company, but I wanted to take it slow. But I did feel like overtime our friendship could transition into something serious, and Craig agreed.

I finished off my two years left of high school, handling Shad's passing, continuing my studies, spending time with family, and wondering where things would lead with Craig. I decided to wait to tell my loved ones about my interest in taking things with Craig to the next level when we both see fit. I didn't want them worrying about me getting hurt again. Craig made it clear that he wouldn't hurt me as a friend or partner, and I trusted his word. My feelings were getting wrapped up in Craig and me, but emotionally I still wasn't ready for a relationship. I sat Craig down to let him know this. He told me he wasn't ready yet either because he had an ugly breakup with the girl I saw him with during his prom before going away to college. Since it hadn't been that long, he wanted to get over it before deciding to make us more. I understood because I still needed time to heal from Shad. As we both worked on healing, we continued to spend our free time with one another. During one of our quality times at home, browsing the internet, he introduced me to a social media site with a broader audience called MySpace. I joined after seeing how one could design a page to their liking, connect with friends outside of school, and catch up with family you weren't able to see regularly. After designing my page, finding family and friends, I received a request from Craig. I notice how Craig had many women friends who left smiley faces, phone numbers, and hearts under his comment section. I even looked through poems he wrote in the journal sections with women leaving the same comments there. Craig's page had pictures of him, his family, and friends. It also displayed a music player with songs of his liking. I noticed how one song was rapper Bow Wow featuring Ciara titled like you. Craig had said when he would listen to the lyrics, it reminded him of us. I smiled upon hearing it and felt like he was blessing my presence on his page. Then I glanced towards the bottom to the section about your state, schooling, and relationship status. I stared for a moment, blinking my eyes, looking away, and then back again. Craig's relationship status said in a relationship. We didn't talk about us being a couple now, so I became excited because I felt like maybe he took it into his own hands and requested me so I could see. I glanced at his top friend's section, where you could put a few people who mattered most. I noticed his sister's picture, a few cousins, close friends, our mutual friend, and then a picture of a woman with him in it. I clicked the picture bringing me to her page. Instead of her name across the top, she had Mrs. with his last name. I sat my phone down and glanced around her page. When I got to her comment section, I noticed a message from him reading. I love you. I clicked on her photos to a full album of them. I instantly clicked off her page, back to his, glancing back down to see if she had a comment in response. When I glance back over to the section that read in a relationship, I notice it disappeared. I could see Craig was online because the online symbol blinked off and on. I logged out, pulled away from my computer, and looked up at my ceiling. I couldn't cry, get mad, or say anything. My phone started playing the like you song, signaling a call or a text from Craig. He sent me a heart I didn't send one back.

I started ignoring Craig's calls, text messages, and inboxes on MySpace. I didn't understand why he would not tell me he was seeing someone. I felt like we would eventually become a couple after we both healed from our situations. Craig had a lot of explaining to do. After a few days of ignoring him and getting my thoughts in order, I decided to invite him over for dinner. When he arrived, he wanted to get right into the conversation. As I tried to speak, he asked if he could talk first, so I listened. Craig said, "Tina, I don't want you to feel like I deceived you anyway. Although it may seem like I did". I gave him the heard it all before facial expression with him saying more, "Danita, the girl from my top friend section on MySpace. We are in a relationship". I was two seconds from tilting his plate in his face when he decided to continue. "Before you let me have it, hear me out. Danita and I haven't been happy for a while. I've been trying to find ways of letting her know that we have to come to an end. The picture you saw as her profile picture is an old one" he reached for his phone, pulled it out, to log onto his MySpace page mobile. Craig clicked on her page, pulled up the picture, and let me look at the date. The picture was dated four months before I reached out to him on Tagged. "Danita is still holding on to good memories, from over a year ago, to hold on to what we had." He told me he wasn't in a relationship when a year later, it's revealed that all along he was. Not to mention he still manages to find the time, if not working, to be around me when I know he has to be still around her. I let him know it hurt me because I would have appreciated it if he would've told me this before I had thoughts of us, down the line, being in a relationship. Craig seemed hurt by my words from how he dropped his head at the kitchen table, but I wasn't moved by it. My feelings were growing for him, and I was juggling with not knowing if I was ready to be back in a relationship or just like the thought of one to get past Shad's pain. Craig was aware of my juggling emotions, and I started to feel like he was taking advantage of it. When I asked him about my feeling towards being taken advantage of, he stated, "Tina, I will never take advantage of you. You have been so open and truthful". I stared into his face and said, "Craig, due to this news, our friendship is important to me, and I want to save it; I believe we should leave us as just friends."

He dropped his fork into his plate, looked up at me, and said, "over the past year, you have shown me what a friend is and what I would want in a relationship with a woman who cared. There is no way I'm letting the thought of us becoming more than friends go. If you need more time, fine, I could understand. I kept Danita a secret from you, so I get why you're mad". I reacted to my emotions and ignored my intuition because I was still getting used to my new normal after losing Shad. I wasn't thinking clearly or making the right choices when it came to what was best for me in Craig's situation. I accepted Craig's apology too quickly and too soon. After our dinner that night, Craig continued to come over. He was happy I was giving him a chance to prove he wanted more between us. But I wasn't so happy when I came to terms with what my woman instincts gave me during our earlier childhood years. Craig was a ladies' man, and there was no way I could change him from being that. Craig came over to see me one afternoon because I was feeling under the weather. After eating soup, tea, and taking cough medicine, I drifted off to sleep. I had thought Craig left since I wasn't awake anymore, but I glanced at him on my computer when I opened my eyes. My computer was turned sideways, facing my direction as usual to avoid the sunlight glare. He didn't notice I was awake, but I took notice of the picture on the computer screen. He was staring closely at a picture of Danita. Something didn't feel right, so I logged onto my page mobile to take in closer observation of what he was doing. Thankfully my phone was sitting on the side of me, so I didn't have to make any sudden moves and mistakenly catch his attention. Craig began typing on my keypad with his eyes glancing up at the dark-skinned, petite woman, with a pretty smile, on the computer screen. I took my attention off him, logged into my account, clicked on his page, headed to Danita's page, bringing myself to staring at the same picture he was observing. I glance at the comments on the picture reading, "Danita, you look beautiful, I miss you, and I would see you later on." She responded, okay, I miss you to Craig, with smiles. I threw my phone down and coughed, startling Craig. He clicked the screen off, walked over to me, and bent down to touch my forehead for a fever's sign. I smacked his hand away, making his eyes grow bigger. Before he could speak, I told him to let himself out. Craig stood confused as I said, let yourself out again in a more angry tone. He strolled away from me, grabbed his coat, glanced back my way, and watched the words Danita looks nice in her beige blouse exit my mouth. Craig stood at the door, staring at me as I told him to have a good time with her later. When he left my house, I received a text from him stating he was sorry. I deleted the message and fell back to sleep. I spent weeks trying to clear Craig out of my system. I deactivated my MySpace page so I wouldn't attempt to look at him or them. I deleted his cell phone number so I wouldn't get the urge to call or text him. I was glad I hadn't told my loved ones how I was starting to feel about him, or my findings would've crushed them. I turned my attention back on healing, studying, and finishing up my senior year. I was already fragile because of what I had to endure and couldn't be adding more to it. Although prom was nearing, I was content with not having anyone to take. My friend Tory would've been nice to take, but he was attending another high school across town, and his prom just so happened to be the same day as mine. Two months had passed since I heard from or seen Craig when I received a text from a number I didn't recognize. It was Craig asking if we could meet up. I decided to address how I felt, moving past my anger towards him. He said he had some things to get off his chest as well. Craig and I agreed to meet at my old neighboring park to talk. He had brought a strawberry slushy and brownie for me to snack on. I had to make sure that he knew and understood we could return as friends; nothing more. You ever had a moment when your words are saying one thing, but your heart and mind are saying another. I realized during our talk; I was a lot more into Craig than I had expected. And I also realized I was into giving second chances. Craig told me that he and Danita finally had broken things off. He pulled his phone out, went to her page, and clicked to show me that she was in a new relationship. I had forgotten about my frustrations towards Craig and went into consoling him. He said he had found out she was seeing a close friend of his while they were together. He stated it had happened right after the day he left my house. As much as I saw it as karma because of how he did me, I felt that it wasn't the time to be addressing it. But if he had approached me two months before with this, I probably would've laughed at him and walked off. Craig said he wanted to know if we could finish where we left off. All the signs so far had revealed Craig was untruthful, so I shouldn't get myself mixed up with him on any other level than a friendship, but I went against my word. I told him that we could start slow, patch things up, but there could be no more secrets and lies. We left with a smile, and I went from not having a prom date to having one. I wanted so bad to believe Craig would be better, but my intuition started sensing things. Craig's actions in the months forward left me feeling clueless and puzzled about his plan at hand. After our reconciliation session in the park, he came to my house a few weeks later to get a piece of my dress material to look at suits. I was excited to have Craig as my prom date. Two weeks before prom, Craig delivered the bad news to me that he wouldn't attend. He had been reminded of an engagement to be a part of his old high school basketball assembly. The time and date of the prom fell into the same slot as the event. Craig had promised his old basketball coach, months before, that he would attend to give newcomers a speech on achieving their dreams. I knew he wasn't dishonest because soon after he called, I saw emails and news articles listing the speakers for the event, with Craig's name being one of them. Although I was back to having to go to prom alone, I wasn't sad about it. If anything, it would give me more time to bond with friends before departing after graduation. When I made it home from prom, Craig called to tell me to keep on my dress. He showed up with flowers and singer Tyrese cd. We danced to Tyrese's song Sweet Lady. I told Craig, thank you for making my night more memorable. He whispered, no problem swinging me around for one last dance, and I whispered I could get used to this. The months after prom and graduation consisted of me preparing for my first semester at Columbia College Chicago. I was eager to see how college life would be like, making new friends, working on my passion, and giving Craig a second shot. We still were in the dating stages and didn't want to make any necessary changes until we agreed. After more quality time, getting to know one another, and realizing it had been two years since we first reconnected, I was ready to begin a relationship. I felt like I had given myself time to heal, regroup, and get settled into school, so why not start a new relationship chapter with him. Craig and I were in a better place, and I trusted him again after the Danita incident. I decided on our dinner date that I would ask where we go from here. We had dinner at my favorite Italian restaurant, Olive Garden, surrounded by couples in their happy moods. My first college classes just ended and I felt pretty good about my grades and performance, so he decided to take me out to celebrate. I ordered my normal spaghetti with meat sauce, a salad, and a lemonade glass while Craig ordered soup. It was a silence amongst us that wasn't normal, but I didn't pay close attention. I took it as if we both were having a long day and just wanted to enjoy the food. But I wanted to talk about us becoming more, so I weasel a conversation that would lead to it. I told him I appreciated him for bringing me out on a night on the town. Then I went into how finals were for me. Craig would normally talk in between my pauses, but he kept silent this time and just looked at me. I asked was he enjoying himself; he quickly said, yeah. I figured it was time to start revealing the real conversation at hand. I brought up how the past couple of months had been good between us, where I wanted it to head, and how I was ready to become more. Craig stared at me as if I asked him an algebra problem that he needed to break down. I asked was he ready to transition from friendship, dating, into a relationship? He responded, let's talk about it later. I left it alone, taking it as if he just wanted to enjoy the time, scenery, and food but our car ride home was silent. When he left my house, he was silent. Craig didn't even give me the normal thirty-second hug when I would normally wiggle and laughed for him to let go. I figured he was tired and left it at that. As I got ready for bed that night, I sent him a text to see if he had made it home. He responded that he did and was sorry for not letting me know. I texted him back that I understood and how I felt like he was quieter than normal. Craig responded, saying it was because he was giving what I said at dinner some thought. While I was sending a text back about how I was interested in knowing how he felt, he ended up sending one before I could send mine, stating he wasn't ready for a relationship. He also revealed that he didn't feel like he would be in any for a few years. I became angry because that was not what he kept saying to me. The whole time Craig made me feel like we were on the same page of waiting a few months to ease out of the dating stages, now it was years. I forced myself to text him back to ask if he was up for talking more. He replied no, he didn't have anything else to say, that was how he felt. I waited a moment before I replied again with him, sending a quick response back, saying goodnight, and seeing me soon. I didn't know how to take in his change of attitude and plans. Especially since a few months before, Craig was the one who approached me, asking for a second chance. My gut feeling said something was up. I decided to confide in our mutual friend who knew from our actions that Craig and I wanted to become more. I could hear that he knew more in my friend's voice, but I didn't try to work a confession out of him. I reached out to Craig instead. I asked if I did something wrong. I wasn't expecting an answer back, but to my surprise, he replied. Craig said he couldn't see himself hurting me and that I deserve better than him. I was still receiving half-answers that I couldn't understand. I felt like it was a line of excuses leading to the real reason. I don't know what made me re-open my MySpace page, but I found my answer there. I was relieved to know it wasn't Danita, but it didn't take me long to figure out he saw someone else. Craig was not trying to make me his partner; he used me as comfort until he found another. The person I had grown to love, adore, and appreciate led another lifestyle. I was caught up in the friendship, the bond, and the memories we were making together. And all along, he was seeing someone under my nose. The woman had a picture of them together with the caption; he's the one. Everything started to make sense, from the restaurant's expression, giving me the cold shoulder, fewer visits, and less quality time. After two years of putting my time and energy into Craig and me, I finally shed my first tear. It would be years before I tried seeing someone else. I logged out of my page, deleting it permanently, and gave Craig a call to tell him how I felt. Craig said he was sorry and gave me more excuses. I hung up, deleted saved messages from Craig, and decided our friendship was doomed. I no longer trusted him, and his promise to not put me through what I had to already experience; was completely a lie. I had to recover from Craig. I drowned myself in my studies and kept busy. He had promised me many things, said I love you and led me to believe that we would have a relationship. But it was obvious he was just telling me what I wanted to hear. I believed him from the whole situation with Danita to his new significant other; the signs were there that we would never be. I just didn't want to see it for what it was. I also realized, if I paid attention to it, I was his side chick. Coming to terms with that made me feel bad about myself. I knew I deserved to be with someone who wanted me and only me, and until someone was able to bring that to the table, I would remain single. Craig tried reaching out to me a few times, but I ignored his calls. I knew we wouldn't run into one another as we did in our childhood years because we stayed on separate sides of towns. We also frequent different areas and hang out with different friends. I kept trying to hide how I felt from the people who love me, but they started sensing something was wrong. My mother approached me while I was doing homework and asked if everything was okay. She stated she thought it had to do with still healing from Shad's death, but something in her felt like it had to do with Craig. She noticed he wasn't coming around anymore, and I wasn't talking about all the fun times. I listened to her tell me exactly what I had been thinking, and I didn't realize tears were falling from my eyes. My mother took notice and pulled a chair up next to me. She gathered both of my hands closer to hers and asked what was wrong. I told her the truth about Craig and I was going from friends to stronger feelings, Danita, to me forgiving him, dating, wanting to have a relationship, second-guessing it, and finding out he was seeing someone else. My mother didn't give me a response, she listened, and that is all I wanted. After I was done revealing to her what had been taking place for two years, she told me to pray for strength. Before leaving the room, she revealed that she didn't want me going backward. My mother felt like my health and grieving had taken me through enough. When she left my room, I got down on my knees, cried, and prayed. I prayed for strength to get through another heartbreak, I prayed for strength to stay focused on my studies and plans for my future, and I prayed for strength to help me forgive Craig for what he did. I went to bed restless but woke up refreshed. I felt like my spirit had released the hurt overnight. I knew I wouldn't be in any shape to concentrate in class if I didn't relieve myself of the hurt and guilt of being a side chick. I hated the concept of it and was not cool with being in that position. Craig ended up texting again, apologizing, saying he hopes that we could squash our differences and remain friends. It couldn't happen. I wasn't going to accept or let it happen. I thought about if our friendship could be saved. But I had concluded that during that moment, it couldn't because the wounds were still fresh. I told him to give me time. I didn't want to open the door for him, possibly thinking we could return to the way things were. I wished him well in his relationship and left it at that. Craig didn't text me back because I didn't give him the answer or reaction he wanted. I was alright with that. I realized that becoming a little stronger in the love department would take a lot longer to accomplish, but I wasn't looking for anyone or being in a relationship until then. I just wanted to breathe. Shad's passing and Craig's true colors were enough to make me fall into a state of depression. Thankfully it didn't happen. But as the saying goes, sometimes when you're not looking, someone can pop up. I didn't know if that was a good thing but what I did know is I thought I would be prepared whenever it happened, but I wasn't.

Chapter 15

Fast Lane

Fast Lane

Ronald was a gentleman, smart, and full of surprises. He attended Roosevelt University, located in the same school district as mines. Sometimes a nearby park district would get together with professors and students from our schools to showcase awareness events. My professor brought to my attention an upcoming event that Ronald was hosting; honoring bullying and suicidal survivors. Students from both of our schools, kids invited from elementary schools, and Jones College Prep high school were in attendance. My professor believed I would be a good candidate to speak on the podium from my nonfiction readings in class. She made sure I was aware that all I had to talk about is a brief moment of my experience and what I learned from it. When I got there, I was scheduled to be the last person to speak. I had to wrap up the assembly by setting an example and making a difference; the weight of ending with a strong impression fell in my hands. The creators behind the event, including Ronald, sat in the front row listening to everyone's testimony. The crowd took in what all the speakers said by how they nodded their heads and wiped tears away. I stepped to the podium, stated my name, and gave a visual presentation through what I experienced. I could see people moving closer to the front to listen, clapping their hands, and yelling; I was strong. I was the younger of the panel, so I felt more connected with the audience. Ronald didn't take his eyes off me. When I left the stage, I was greeted by teenagers, young adults, and elders who believe I made a difference. The last in line to speak to me was Ronald. As he approached, he clapped and said how emotionally moved he was. He asked what I was majoring in at Columbia, what year I was, and how often I was at school. I could tell by his business-like attire he was someone I would be interested in getting to know. Ronald and I started bumping into each other at places students often met before class, in between classes, or headed home. We would run into one another at Dunkin Doughnuts and Starbucks, discussing our favorite coffee and dessert. After class, depending on the season, I would try to go to Harold's Chicken for a catfish special or get a six-piece wing with fries and mild sauce. Ronald would end up getting the same thing. He would approach me in each establishment, make small talk, or sit beside me as I waited on my order. It turned into a daily thing. Ronald wanted me to know that he wasn't stalking me; he just adjusted to my schedule of coming into these places and wanted to get to know me better. We decided to exchange numbers. We both were busy in classes and our personal lives, so we didn't talk much via phone. We just waited until we saw one another, in person, during the morning or afternoon. I started to catch on to Ronald wanting me to notice how he was secretly ordering the food I wanted, paying for it, and then leaving. He also stopped showing up at the restaurant when I did, but the cashier would give me a gift he left. The gifts Ronald would leave would be journals, inspiring books from my favorite authors, and candies I loved. I knew he had to be listening to our short conversations to pick up on what interests me. I would text him thank you with him, replying with a smiley face. I considered it a cute way of getting to know someone, but I wanted to make sure he knew we could be friends, but that was it. I didn't want him to get the wrong impression, so I decided to make it clear. I called him one night after finishing up homework to explain how I felt. Ronald understood and said that's what he wants, just a friendship. Before I ended the call, he asked when my birthday was. I let him know my birthday was a week away. On my birthday, he walked into Dunkin Doughnuts while I had my hot chocolate with vanilla and a long vanilla john. He was carrying balloons, flowers, and circular cookies, and cream ice cream cake. I glanced at everyone around, making smiley faces and singing happy birthday. I couldn't stay around long because I had to get to class. But while in class, I still wondered why he was so nice towards me when he didn't know me. Although he said he only wanted to be friends, his actions were speaking differently. I reached out to Ronald and could tell he was surprised I called. I asked how his holidays were and got right to the reason for my call. I let him know the things he was doing for me out of an act of kindness were cool, but he didn't have to do that to keep my attention or build a friendship with me. Before I could go on, he blurted out he wanted more. It had only been a few months since I had first met him at the event, so his response threw me off guard. I ended up saying, you want more of what. With him responding, "I want to be more than your friend." His response shook me because I hadn't been approached by someone who was still a stranger, wanting to be more than friends. Ronald told me that he meant in the long run, once we got to know each other better. I kept how I felt to myself and told him to let us work on becoming good friends. I got off the phone with him, hoping he took in what I said. Ronald sent me a text a few days later, asking if going to the movies would be alright. I didn't have a problem with that because I went to the movies with Tory. But Ronald was not Tory, and I came to terms with realizing this; I even became aware that when we started spending a lot of time around one another at art galleries, plays at our schools, and more speaking events that I was starting to like him. I asked Ronald if he was seeing someone, talking to someone, or thinking about being with someone. I waited for his response, wondering if it would be similar to Craig's experience, but he responded, no, just you. I started opening up to the idea of going from friends to dating. As for a relationship, it would take a while to conquer. Ronald understood and wanted to take his time, as well. I felt like things were looking up for me in the love department. Sometimes, you ever notice when you start being around someone more; you start to see things you didn't see before. I notice Ronald was interested in jumping from the first base of dating, skipping all the other bases, and heading directly into a relationship. But I didn't have the same view or plan as him. I remember the first time he asked me to go to the movies with him, and we had a nice time. But when he asked me a second time around, it was different. I remember being at the movies with him seeing a horror flick, and I realized as soon as the lights dimmed, Ronald started easing closer. I saw nothing wrong with him putting his arms around me, but that is not where his hands went. Ronald kept trying to ease to problematic areas. After moving his hands multiple times, with him still trying to force them back over my way, I got up and left. Ronald texted me later that night saying I was stuck up, and I needed to let loose a little. I was surprised by his words and quickly responded that I made it clear touching in areas you were constantly told not to come near will not happen. He responded, whatever, and I didn't hear or see him after that. Ronald went from a gentleman, kind-hearted friend, to mean in less than six months. I was glad I stood my ground with him. I didn't care what he said; it was not happening. The gifts, sweet text messages, and complimenting how pretty I am, was not going to lure him into my pants. And if he couldn't accept that, then he didn't have good intentions. Nothing was going to keep me sticking around, reaching back out to him, or accepting the disrespectfulness in his words and tone. I was taught never to let someone pressure me into doing what I didn't want to do. So I carried that throughout childhood into my adulthood. I was glad I took things slow with Ronald. I was also glad Ronald taught me to pay close attention to everything. He said swift he wanted us to become more. And I realized fast we were on different levels. From that point on, a rule I made to myself is to be mindful of what people want to do for you; they could be wanting something in return that is not good for you. It set me up for the person I dealt with next.

Chapter 16

Insecure

Insecure

After a year of not dealing with dating, my friend Elise approached me with a plan. She wanted me to go on a date with her friend. Elise had met him through her significant other, and they bonded. And she was aware that he was single and looking. I wasn't fond of being set up on a blind date with someone I didn't know, but I didn't think it could be worse than what I was encountering on my own. So I gave her the green light to set it up during my spring break from school. Elise said she hopes I would enjoy the date. I had hoped so too. From my first impression of Jose, I could tell he was invested in his appearance. And there was nothing wrong with that. I like that he was a dresser, shaved up nice, and had good hygiene. I didn't make a big fuss towards him, not having a car or that he didn't have any money to take us out somewhere to eat. Times were hard for all, so I accepted it. Jose informed me that we would be hanging out at his place with his family. That's when red flags rose for me. I used to meet someone's parents or close family members after six months to a year of dating, not on the first date. When I walked into his house, you would've thought he was hosting a meet and greet party or family reunion. From his great grandmother down to his little cousin born three days before, everyone was there. I acted cordial, spoke to everyone, then found a place to sit while Jose fixed my plate. I couldn't wait to call Elise when I got back home. Jose started discussing his likes and dislikes with me, where he saw himself in twenty years, and what he looked for in a girlfriend. I told him about myself, what I looked for in a guy, and my dislikes and likes. Our communication was stable and I could see myself having and enjoying talks with him. Jose didn't try touching me inappropriately, nor did he speak as if we would be in a relationship then and there. When he had to excuse himself to make his grandmother a plate, I stepped outside for a moment to get some fresh air. I could see us meeting up for a second date, hoping Jose felt the same. When I was getting ready to leave, he gave me a warm hug and said the next time we would go somewhere nice. I told him that I'm going to hold him to it, smiling, and waved goodbye. Elise called me as soon as I walked through my door to ask how the date went. I told her it was nice, but how I did feel awkward about meeting the whole family. She laughed to the point of choking. I told her that I could look past it, though, because overall, the night was great. I became bummed when I didn't get a chance to see Jose during the rest of my spring break because when I was free, he wasn't, and vice versa. And when classes started back up, it was more challenging. We communicated a lot on the phone, laughing at one another jokes, and answering each other questions. He had asked me if him being unemployed for the moment was a problem. I informed him it wasn't as long as he was looking for a job. Jose was relieved by my answer, and we continued our random talks. One day after class, Jose texted to ask if I would come to his house. I told him I had a test to study for so I wouldn't be able to come out that night, but what about tomorrow. He sent back a text saying, don't worry since he was the only one with time on his hands. I decided his attitude was coming from the frustration of job searching, so I left it alone. But Jose needed to realize he stayed in the suburbs while I was in the city. When I got home from school, did my homework, and got out there, it would be late. I also had a part-time job that I worked on the weekends, so it only left the days off from school through the week to be the best time for us to see one another. Jose insisted that if I couldn't come when he wanted me to, he didn't want to see me. I reached out to Elise to see if she was aware of how selfish Jose could be. She let me know she wasn't but will do some digging. I told her not to waste her time; I would call him. It had only been a month in a half since I met Jose, and I didn't like the vibes I was getting from him. I was in school full time, worked part-time, but I will make time to see him at least twice a week to get to know him better. I never told him I was busy, I never said let me call you back, and I never acted like I wasn't interested in him. But Jose started coming off as the type who wanted things his way or else. During our last conversation, he told me that he was interested in someone else. That the woman would drop everything to make sure his needs were met. I told him good luck with that and continued on my journey of discovering myself and my worth. The experiences kept molding me into a stronger woman and made me appreciate my patience with knowing someone. It also made me look further into how I viewed dating versus being in a relationship. I always felt like they were both different. When I decide to be in a relationship with someone, it's a mutual agreement between the person who wants to take it to the next level and make it official. As for dating, I saw it as the time to get to know a person with no title. I realized that I had dated more but made things official less. I was not about to give my all to every person I encounter, with it going wrong, leaving me to regret my decision. I would rather date until I felt like things were going somewhere. Thus far, my only serious relationship was with Shad giving me the platform and observation into how the good and bad works. I wasn't into settling anymore. The guy I decided to be in a relationship with had to be seriously ready for one. I vowed to myself to take time out from dating if the last one didn't get it right. It gave me the time to learn from each failed experience what part I played in it. With Craig, I ignored the signs and shouldn't have given him a second chance after he lied; with Ronald, he made it clear he wanted more after only knowing each other for a short period. This should've made me step away because it was a sign of how fast he would want things to go. And with Jose, I put up with the nagging about the sacrifices he wanted me to make so that he could be happy. Those were my wrongs, but what I did right was never let the person think we were more than we were. I witnessed and was a part of situations where a person wouldn't be fully honest with me. They would rather play around as if we were dating or make me think we were in a relationship. I don't believe anyone should make a person think things are one way, but it isn't. That's how feelings get hurt, and situations get out of hand. Telling the truth from the start to the person you see or want to be with things would be easier. Talk to them and say why you think it won't work or say why it will. The worst thing you could do is have a person standing in front of a door that will never open. If I wanted to become serious with someone, I had to be careful about who I gave my attention to.

Chapter 17
Choose Wisely

. . . .

Choose Wisely

After three years of not being in one, I made sure I stepped in with a clean slate when I walked into my second relationship. I didn't want to bring my past hurts or anger onto a new person. I didn't want to have the thought in my head that I would be done worse than before. I tried to make the relationship work just as much as the person I was seeing was willing too. We both had to realize that a relationship isn't a walk in a park or a bus ride you could just hop back and forth on. If I were spending my time, energy, love, respect, and commitment tending to someone else's needs, it has to be reciprocated. A heart is too precious to be tampered with because you only get one. The guy I decided to spend the next three years of my life with started as the best man a woman could have. But his past and demons caught up with him. Secrets came to the surface, lies were detected, and he made it seem like I was doing the dirt when he was. My intuition had never put in as much overtime as it did in a relationship with Tim. I was down to my last nerve with him. I kept praying to keep us together when the signs were telling me to move on. Timothy wasn't right for me is what all my loved ones said. Did I listen? No. I felt like I could handle him and what he brought to the table. But it is evident to all that I couldn't. Timothy made me realize I was taking my patience for granted. He tried to end our relationship three times, and I kept holding on to it. His mood changed, and he made me feel broken. I was tired of having an unhealthy form of communication with him. I couldn't understand how someone could say they love you but didn't. I didn't know how I could say I loved him when he treated me as if I didn't matter. I started to sink into depression, wondering if I would be able to keep it together. As I neared my college graduation, I realized it was getting harder. I didn't want all my time and energy to invest in the relationship to lose my focus. I felt like something was wrong with me if I decided to go any further. Should I swim to shore or continue to sink with him. Timothy and I met through Tory's cousin at a gathering. We sparked up a conversation about the Isley Brothers; from the music Tory's mother was playing, with both of us saying we had old souls. Tory cousin, Clyde, took notice of us talking from the punch table and came over to introduce Timothy as his best friend. I asked Timothy if I could call him Tim for short with him smiling. Clyde left the table as

Tory approached, looking Tim up and down, being the over protector he has always been. I let Tory know I was okay and that Tim was the perfect gentleman. Tory introduced himself to Tim and let him know he was watching from the DJ table. I laughed while Tim kept his eyes on Tory. When Tory walked away, Tim let out a sigh of relief. "He doesn't play about you," he said, wiping his fingers off on a napkin. I nodded to answer his question. We went back to talking about how the music our parents listened to was better than our generation. Tim and I discussed how ol skool music had a way of making us feel happy, sad, and ready to dance. Clyde and Tory came back to the table to join us in conversation. We started watching the sunset while laughing our butts off at the way ol folks dance, sung along to their songs, and partied. I told the guys I would rather party with the ol folks any day. Tim smiled, turning his attention to the dance floor. Tory mom, my mother, and their friends were stepping to James Brown. It was the perfect way to bring in summer; good barbecue, jazz, dusties, blues, family, friends, and new faces. Tory, Clyde, Tim, and I decided we should keep up the good connection by meeting up throughout the summer. I was looking forward to it, and I could tell Tim was too. We hung out at numerous town spots, from bars, bowling alleys, malls, parks, lakefronts, and beaches. On one of our trips, Tory called to say he couldn't make it, and Clyde declined as well. Tim and I decided to go still since it was a breezy day, and the sky was clear. We walked along the sand, discussing how peaceful the surroundings made things seem. I told him how I would run to the beach during the summer to be one with my thoughts. Tim said he did too and that it gave him a space to write poems. We were so deep into our conversation that I didn't realize our hands were connected. We looked off into the sunset. "What if Clyde and Tory were not coming on purpose," I said, squeezing Tim hand tighter. He said,", it was" leaning his head on mine. Tim and I had a connection right from the start, and we figured why waste time. We started seeing one another when our schedule permitted and even spent summer nights cruising around the city in his car. Our days sitting in front of my house talking about whatever came to mind were most precious. I remember asking him about the tattoo on his arm with him discussing with me it was his child, who was stillborn. I could tell from Tim's face he was still hurting. I held his hand as he asked me a question. He had been wondering what was inside the heart shape locket around my neck, so I told him about Shad and what happened to him. Tim showed concern for me and said he understood my pain. I kept wondering if he would be bothered by me wearing it since Shad was an ex. Tim stated he would never tell me to take it off because of the story and history. Our connection grew for one another after the heart to heart, and we agreed to start a relationship. We spent a lot of time accepting similarities while adjusting to differences. One of the differences I had to adjust to was Tim, and I never talked on the phone. The only time we heard each other voices was in person. I found this to be different. I had texted previous individuals I was dating or in a relationship with, but we also called one another. As for similarities, the little things or moments mattered to us. If Tim just wanted to see me for a few seconds, he would stop by, and I did the same. It was our way of getting some type of time in on our busiest days. Tim didn't care how my hair looked, how quiet I could be at times, or my occasional phone moments. His acceptance made me fall in love with him. I didn't have to change who I was, and neither did he. As the months went on, I tried to focus on all the good times to overlook the bad because it never left when bad came. I remember being on my way out to eat with my family for my mother's birthday when I saw my phone blink with Tim's text. I texted him back, told him I was headed out the door, and asked if everything was alright. He sent me a question back, asking if I would date someone with children. I was hoping he wasn't about to tell me he had a secret child aside from the one I knew about who had passed. So I asked him with him responding no, he just found out that his ex was four months pregnant. She fell pregnant a few weeks before I had met him. He texted back and said, I hope this doesn't stop me from being with him. I told him I had to think about things because it was different from a child already being in the picture to a fresh child in the womb. Tim texted back and said if it was going to be an issue, leave because he would be there for his child. I waited to respond. I didn't want to get myself worked up. The day wasn't about me; it was my mom's day. During the drive to eat with my family, I wondered how things could go from good to confusing just like that? I knew getting used to his child would not be a problem. I loved kids, knew his child would come first, and a child was part of the package deal. Where my concerns stood was him juggling having an expecting ex, a relationship with me, and a child on the way. I didn't think he could juggle all three. I couldn't fully enjoy myself out at dinner, but I tried to hide how I felt because I knew my mom would be concerned. When we returned home, I decided to call Tim. He reached back out, saying that he was sorry for being late getting back to me, but he wanted to know if I thought about our conversation earlier. I texted Tim back and told him I did and was still concerned because many questions ran through my mind. Why did the relationship end with his ex and how was it his child when he told me that he hadn't been intimate with anyone for over a year? I waited for his response. There was none. I went to sleep, wondering if I had gone in too deep, but I wasn't going to hide how I was feeling. I thought we could be honest with one another. The next day I didn't hear from Tim, and that was not normal because we didn't go a day without reaching out. The same night I decided to text him to see how work was and when he would respond to my questions. I received back the message I wasn't expecting, so I sat up in bed for the rest of the night, stressing. Tim texted me back and said it was over with no explanation. I called his phone all night, left him numerous text messages, and begged him to let me know what I did. And the only response I received from Tim was for me to go away, stop calling him, and be happy with someone else. The next morning Tim sent a text saying I shouldn't be questioning him about his business, and if I wanted us to work, I would apologize for it. I quickly apologize and realize I was blinded by the obvious. The months leading up to his unborn arrival, I realize I should've never apologized for the questions I asked. But I wanted so bad to make us work when I should've been walking away and never turning back. Tory would ask how the relationship was going with Tim, and if he was treating me right. It took everything in me to make up a lie. I knew if I told Tory the truth, he would tell me to break things off with him. And I would've said no because, before the newfound information, we were fine. So I should give him the benefit of the doubt and try to work it out with him. I pictured Tory approaching Tim, ending our relationship himself. But before I revealed the truth to Tory, I was hoping Tim and I would get better. A year had passed, and a lot was changing between us. We started having arguments, Tim was in a car accident, so he didn't have a car anymore, and I was spiraling onto an unhappy path with all that was in store. Our date nights faded away; nights we could spend together filled with silence instead of laughter, and I didn't have a sparkle in my eye for him anymore. I begin to feel like he was taking me for granted when I started picking him up from work, when I was available too, and driving him across the city to run errands without a thank you. Tim was not the person I met a year ago and I didn't like the person I was becoming. When I would ask Tim how his unborn child was doing; he would give me quick answers or ignore me. Every time I tried to be supportive about the situation he said he didn't need me to be. Even when I purchased diapers and clothing he yelled saying take it back, Tim would say he felt it was weird that I was concerned and I became offended by this because he knew how sweet, considerate, and supportive of a person I am. And just because it was a struggle for me to adapt to the changes didn't mean I wouldn't be concerned with how his unborn child is doing. When I finally worked up the strength to reach out to Tory about it he didn't like it. He said to me "I know you try to see the good in everyone but this situation is too much. Although I would like for you to end it and be in something healthier I know it's up to you. But I'm tired of seeing you hurt. I'm afraid of where this may lead". While Tory talked with me, I tried to hold back the tears, and rushed him off the phone to recollect myself. I was not looking forward to approaching my mom with the truth. She had been asking me how the relationship was going and I would tell her fine. I decided to write her a letter, place it on her night stand, and head to bed. When I woke up the next morning, before heading to class, I noticed my mother had left a letter on my television stand. Her words were Pumpkin you may have to let this one go. She didn't think I was being told the whole truth which is the reason why he would avoid answering my questions and didn't want to tell me what was going on. She felt that he was probably still seeing her and was keeping me a secret. My mother ended the letter by saying pray on it and it will lead me to my answer. I closed the letter up and meditated on what she said. Have you ever had a moment when your mother or parent told you something wasn't right and you didn't listen? I had a habit of hearing what she said when it came to certain situations but I wouldn't take heed to it. I ended up bottling my feelings inside until they were tearing through me. My mom, Tory, and a few others I confided in said to leave; but I stayed. A month before his unborn arrival Tim started to return back to his old self. I felt like maybe he had finally calmed down and could see that I really wanted to be there for him. I was entering my junior year of college with the hope of keeping things on the path that they were. And even though my loved ones still didn't like that I remained with Tim they didn't stress me with their opinions. I was so busy with school, family, thinking about life after college, and how I would be meeting Tim child soon; it dawned on me that I hadn't met his family. The only thing I knew is that Tim had a younger brother. The closest I got to seeing what his brother looked like was from social media pictures. I had always been inside of Tim house when they weren't home. He lived with his brother and mom. This made me feel really strange because we had been together for a while so why wasn't there a meeting. Tim wanted to take me out on a date since we hadn't been out and I decided to ask him then. While on the date we were talking about when we first met, full of smiles, and a lot of laughter so I decided to wait to ask him. Tim's phone started ringing while we were still talking. He put his finger over his lips signaling for me to be quiet then he answered. I had to have the most distasteful look on my face by the way the waiter approached slowly then quickly walked away. Tim was on the phone saying he would be there in a second then hung up. I must've had the same expression on my face that the waiter had noticed because Tim looked as if he was about to get up from the table and run. He told me it was his mom then tried to return back to the conversation we were having before his phone ranged. I could see the waiter coming back towards the table as I started putting on my coat. I told Tim to pay for the bill and that I will be waiting in the car. He said he hadn't finished eating yet. I said bag it up or get left. The waiter took Tim's credit card and walked away fast. I walked out of the restaurant so mad that I ended up bypassing my car. I stood still for a few seconds to calm down. I would normally let him drive but I was ready to get home so I jumped into the driver seat. Tim approached the car with hesitance and I could still see our waiter looking out the window of the restaurant. When Tim climbed into the passenger seat, sat his left over on the back seat, and turned around to look at me I blurted out "your family don't know about me". Tim looked at me as if I was talking in a language he couldn't quite understand. So I said it again, a little louder. He took his time responding so I took my seat belt off, put the car in park, and waited for my answer. "Martina, my mother and brother are aware that I am dating you but my mom doesn't want to meet you because she wants me to be with my ex". My stomach turned when I heard this and I felt like my food was going to come back up. I kept looking at Tim because I had to hear more. "She feels that my ex needs me". I turned around in my seat, slowly put back on my seat belt, put the car into drive, and dashed out of the parking lot. I kept biting on my bottom lip to try to stop it from shivering. I could feel Tim staring at me. He kept saying my name to get me to talk but my lips felt like they were glued shut. When I arrived at Tim's house to drop him off I put my car into park and waited for him to get out. Tim said he will not move until I said something to him. I turned and said "how do I suppose to continue to be with you. When I'm feeling like this is wrong". Tim's forehead wrinkled up and I took the hint that he wanted me to say more. I exhaled and continued "I don't believe you are telling me the full truth". Before I could finish my thought Tim exploded and said "and to think I was going back and forth with my mom about how I love you and wanted us to work. I even told my child's mother that I was in a relationship so there couldn't be us. But you got the nerve to say I wasn't telling the truth. Man bye" he got out and slammed the door. I watched him walk up to his door, drop his keys twice, opened the door, and slammed it. I didn't feel bad about how I approached Tim because even after he said that I still thought he was hiding something. I went home and prayed. I asked for strength, guidance, and signs and I received what I asked for. A college buddy of mine, Nia, was someone I had become close with and felt like I could talk with her when I didn't want to bring the stresses involving Tim to my mother, the lucky 5 from high school, or Tory. Nia had to stop attending school for personal reasons but we kept in close contact and hung out when we could. I had heard about a new social media site called Facebook but was hesitant about joining. I had taken a long break from any type of social media after Craig but since it had been awhile I said what the heck and joined. Nia added me as a friend and kept me up to date with what she was doing. On Nia's birthday I went to her page and wrote happy birthday. I noticed the comment under me said happy birthday to the best co worker in the world. When I glanced at the profile picture next to the comment I realized was Tim's brother. I thought to myself, wow, small world. The next day I called Nia to see how her birthday went, and I apologized for not attending her festivities, but I had to study for finals. She told me she understood and said she hung out with a few co-workers. I didn't think about asking her my next question; it just floated out of my mouth. Was your co-worker Devin in attendance? I said. Nia quickly responds, yeah, Devin and I are cool, do you know him? I responded sort of, in a hesitant tone. Nia said, wait, that doesn't sound too good, and asked me to discuss more. I told her that Devin was Tim's little brother. I paused and asked could she do me a favor. Nia said yes, so I told her to ask Devin if he knew someone's name, Martina. She said that she could ask him right now since he was at work with her. I said okay with Nia saying she'll call me right back. I was meeting with Tim a few hours later to grab lunch. After our heated argument during our date night, his son being born, and my studies, we tried to make time when it was possible. Nia called me back thirty minutes after I hung up from her. "Tina, I asked Devin. He said no". I put the phone down. I could hear Nia calling my name as I picked it back up. Although I hadn't met his family in person, Tim had told me they knew about me, my name, where I'm from, and what type of person I was. Nia said she went on to ask him if, by any chance, he knew if his brother dated a girl by that name. Devin's response was the same. I was tired of not knowing anyone, unanswered questions, and Tim switching his attitudes. I told Nia to tell Devin who I was and let me know what he said. I didn't know if Devin would come out and tell Nia anything, especially since Tim was his brother. But when Nia called me back, she told me some things that I dreaded. Nia decided to take an early break at work since it was a slow day to tell me all the details. "Martina, Devin said that Tim is still in a relationship with his child mother. Right now, she and the baby live with them". I tried hard to keep from screaming because I wanted to hear the rest. Nia continued, "Devin said she had been staying at their house off and on during her entire pregnancy." No wonder I was never there when the family was. I thank Nia for doing that for me, and I told her that I would talk to her later. I put my studies aside and just sat in the dark. I didn't even notice Tim text me three times. I had an hour to spare before I was meeting up with him. I was angry, emotional, and ready to go off on Tim. I didn't know where the conversation may lead, but I knew arguing would happen. Now I understood why he wanted me to drop him off on the side of his home, come to his house only in the mornings, and kept saying it was over every time he was mad. Tim was lying from the very beginning. When I arrived at Tim's house, he was already standing outside, waiting for me. He climbed into the car and started shouting, "why do you want to play these games with me? If you wanted to know anything, you could've asked me. I've been real with you from the start" he slammed his hand down on the dashboard. I took a moment to observe Tim; he was sweating, panting hard, and turning red. I was hoping I had beat Devin home from work, but maybe it just had to happen like this. I realized from previous experiences that when a person is in the wrong, they will try to take the pressure off themselves and put you at fault. I wasn't going to let that happen. "Why are we still sitting here? Go ahead, and drive off". I didn't move. Tim kept looking at his house door. "You think someone is going to see us?" I said, looking with him. "You are pushing it right now, Martina, let's go" I still didn't move. I never had someone yell at me the way he was hollering as if veins were going to pop out of his head. Three women were walking on the street past his house; Tim slid down but made it appear as if he was adjusting in his seat. "Tim, get out of my car," I screamed. I knew he was doing that because he thought it was his mom or his child's mother. "Martina, I love you," he said, trying to grab my hand. I snatched it away, pointing my finger in the direction of his house window. Devin was in the window, shaking his head. Tim slowly opened my car door "Martina, can we talk about this." My car door wasn't even closed all the way when I decided to drive off. I went home and cried into my mother's arms. I was hurt, confused, angry, and embarrassed. All the signs pointed to Tim hiding something, my loved ones trying to tell me to leave, but I ignored it all and still held on. Regardless of how I felt, I had to find some strength to ignore the situation and end my junior year of college on a good note. Tim called my phone a ton of times, left I miss you messages, and I'm the best man you ever had. I ignored them; I was through. While confiding with Nia about everything, I didn't know she kept Christian up to date with my situation. Christian was Nia, and I mutual friend, attending a different college, but we worked on our schools' projects together. Just like Tory, he was protective of me and honest. I didn't want him to know that he was right when he said Tim was still seeing his child's mother. I wanted to keep it hidden as long as possible. I found out Nia had already briefed Christian on everything. He didn't judge or address that he was right. He listened and let me vent. I had just helped guide Christian through a bad break up of his own, so he knew more than anybody how I was feeling. Like how I was with Craig, I could sense when Christian and I were becoming more than friends. The only difference is; Christian wasn't seeing anyone else. I remember a night he invited me to cook as we tutored one another in a math class. I noticed pretty quickly about Christian that he was the male version of me: quiet around people who didn't know him, sometimes on his phone and experienced having his kindness taken for granted. Due to our many comparisons, we always had a conversation topic. Although we were hanging out more, we both were aware that remaining at a slow pace was best so I could heal from Tim. When I had moments of doubt and wanted to call Tim, he didn't get mad. He said, "Tina just like I had to learn how to deal without my ex, you will. It's baby steps". I would leave from around Christian feeling a little better and able to recognize my strength. Until Tim called one day, and I answered. You ever felt that a situation needed a second chance, although all signs pointing to it said no. But you end up overlooking it to see where things could go. I met with Christian at his house to talk about how I felt. He listened, but I could tell he was hurting from what I revealed. Within three months, I was separated from Tim, and I was happiest with Christian. I was smiling more, returned to my goofy self, and everyone around me could see it. I was engaging more with my peers at school and developing real feelings for Christian. I threw it all away by believing the three months I was away from Tim; had changed him. Ending my dating with Christian was the biggest mistake. He was a good guy, willing to wait for me to heal so we could be together, and he didn't care how long it took. And I messed that up. I finally was in the presence of a good one who held no secrets and did not hide his flaws. I told Christian I was sorry, and I hope that he would forgive me. He kissed my forehead and watched me leave. I left his house, texting Tim to let him know I was on my way home, and asked if I could see him to talk. He texted me back yes, and then I noticed I was getting an incoming call from Christian. When I answered, I could hear Christian on the other end, sniffling. He said if I changed my mind about reuniting with Tim, he would be here. I hung the phone up, not realizing I was digging my own hole for the first time. I couldn't blame anyone but me this time. I regret stepping away from Christian. I couldn't even tell my loved ones about it. I left Christian and me, wanting to be more, to myself, because I didn't want to hear the truth from them. That night I met Tim outside of his house to talk about how we were going to work things out, and he informed me his child's mother was no longer staying with him. Instead of me checking to make sure; I believed him. I tried to put Christian and me in the back of my mind because the guilt was eating me alive. I would find myself in Tim's presence but thinking about Christian instead. I would get phone calls, text messages, and voice mails from Christian but not answer them. One day the calls stopped; I knew he was through. I spent the last year with Tim trying to hold on to what was left of my sanity and hoping my family wouldn't hate me for my decision. They didn't like it, expressed many times to please leave it be, and I continued. From the time I took him back, the good only lasted a few weeks. I decided we should take a five-day vacation from everything. I was a month away from spring break during my senior year of college and felt like a vacation would not only help us but rejuvenate me. I remained in school full time and picked up hours to put extra money aside for the trip. I requested my time off from work and told Tim to make sure he put his in. He told me he did and that he was excited to have some alone time together. Seeing that he was excited started to make me feel like the trip would put us back on the right path. After three years of constant back and forth, I was praying for peace and seeing if this relationship was worth holding on to; the day before our trip, I found out. I remember sitting in the hair shop, getting my hair braided. I had been asking Tim for weeks to check to make sure his days were accepted. He told me yes and said he checked every day. When I texted him while sitting in the salon chair to check again, he delivered the news I dreaded. Tim said his days weren't accepted and that he would have to work. I texted him back, are you serious while panicking in my chair. Tim responded yes and sorry he won't be able to go. I instantly called him and said, "you do know this trip is nonrefundable". I ended up being the only one who paid for the trip because Tim said he had many things to get his son. I understood and said, don't worry, I would take care of it. I sat in silence with Tim saying he would get off the phone because there was nothing he could do about it. After he hung up, I reached out to Nia and told her what happened. She told me she wishes I would see that he was not the man for me. Then said I deserve better and not to be treated like a fool. As my hair stylist finished up, I tried to keep my composure together. When I made it home, I walked into my room with my eye-catching suitcase on the floor. I started crying when my eyes made contact with it. I became numb, the way I always felt when I thought Tim was lying to me. I needed real answers but didn't want to confront him because I didn't feel like arguing. I sat at the edge of the suitcase, wondering if I should still go on the trip and call a few friends to go with me. It was the last minute; no one would take time off. My mother came into my room and could tell what was wrong. She said, "you guys aren't going." I looked up at her, then pressed my chin against my legs and started crying. She kneeled and started saying a prayer I couldn't make out. Then she told me to take a moment to gather myself before she took my sisters and me out to dinner. Tim texted my phone the entire night, and I didn't answer. The next morning he called me and asked could I drop him off at work because he forgot that his boss told him a week before he had to be early for inventory. Tim caught on to what he was revealing to me and said, never mind, he would ask Clyde to drop him off. The truth was there; Tim never put in for his days of requests off. I had not only lost money that could've gone into savings, but I also lost one of the few men I could reach out to about this situation. I knew right then how it felt to be played, and I could only imagine how Christian was feeling. The months after our canceled vacation, I fell into a depression. It was hard for me to concentrate and think. When I would come to Tim about this, he shrugged it off like he didn't care, and it wasn't his problem. Tim turned back into the person I left. He started ignoring my texts, calls and removed me from his Facebook page. For two weeks, I tried to contact him. All of a sudden, Tim reached out to say he was just busy. I had to hit rock bottom and have something meaningful to me, almost taken away to realize it was time to wake up.

Graduation was three weeks away, and I still hadn't finished my senior exit portfolio and paper. Those two were my last contributions to my graduating class, and if they weren't finished, I was not going to be able to walk the stage. My professors were concerned and gave me more time to finish them. Two weeks before graduation, I remember not sleeping, still trying to reach Tim, and only receiving responses when it was convenient for him. I hid my feelings from everyone, and I couldn't eat or think. But something came over me, and I realized I would either stay stuck in the state of depression or do something about it. I could not let a man deteriorate me or deter me from my accomplishments and future. I had made it through everything else, so I knew if I kept the faith, I would make it through and over him. I vented to myself, aloud, how frustrated, sad, angry, tired, guilty, bad, and broken-hearted I felt. I took my portfolio and paper out, diving into them. Before turning my portfolio and paper in, I looked back over them and could see the drive and passion within. My professors told me I did an outstanding job and that they could see and feel the emotion. When they said I was cleared for graduation and told me to go pick up my cap and gown, I cried in front of them. I almost let what Tim was putting me through take away my biggest accomplishment thus far. But when I let go, I did not care about judgments or someone saying I'm flawed; I completed the task I prayed on. I was proud of myself. I was happy for myself. A week later, I walked with Columbia College Chicago graduation class, receiving my bachelor's degree in writing. I remember glancing into the audience seeing my mom, sisters, and Tory smiling, giving me confirmation that I made it. I may have hit rock bottom, but walking across the stage had proven to me and others that I was on the journey of rising again. After graduation, I changed my number, email address and informed Clyde that I would not be associating with Tim in any form. Clyde didn't even know what was going on until Tory briefed him on everything. Clyde had known me just as long as Tory did and said if we would've told him what Tim was putting me through, he would never have let us continue. The truth is, no one could've stopped me from being with him or anyone else but me. It took recovering my truth, worth, self-love, patience, clarity, and strength to understand I deserved better. If I could take any lesson from what I learned from each encounter of dating and relationships that didn't go well is something I've read from Reverend Td Jakes: if a person wants to walk out of your life, let them. His words encourage me to stop begging, crying, or pleading for anyone to stay: I let them go. Because if they were quick to want to leave, play games, fill my head with made-up promises, keep secrets, and lie: they weren't for me. I decided to focus on the path of praying for the better because someday, someone will love me, all of me, and I wouldn't have to second guess.

Chapter 18
Gone Too Far

Gone Too Far

How many people are around you or in your life but are not supposed to be. So it's important to make sure their reasons and actions towards being in your life are built from love, not hidden hate. I was one of those who only saw the good in others; I never thought anyone was bad. Even if it was shown or told that someone should exit my life, I saw differently. It took someone wishing death upon me to realize there is such a thing as bad people. Lidia was kind-hearted, well-liked, and a basketball player. I was introduced to her through Craig because they have been good friends since high school. Even after Craig and I went our separate ways, she remained cool. We would run into one another at events and even talked over the phone a lot about life in general. I started opening up to Lidia about my health and how sometimes it'll go downhill. She told me she understood, and if I needed someone to listen or come around, she'd always be there. When I fell ill with my mystery diagnosis, she was one of the people I would turn to vent. Lidia would listen and always make sure I knew she had my back. Have you ever had someone be there during the beginning of the storm, but when it started to get bad, they ran for cover? I was leaving my mother's office one day and was battling with having a hard time eating, and due to that, I lost a lot of weight. I ran into Lidia like I normally would if I were in the area, but she was with a few of her friends this time. I was excited to see her and call out her name. She turned to look at me and yelled out, "girl, you look bad." Her friends laughed as she continued to walk down the street with them. The night before, I told Lidia how I had gotten small because I was having difficulties with eating. Lidia said, "that is alright; you are still beautiful, and let no one tell you differently." I believed her but seeing how she reacted with her friends was a side of Lidia I never met. I don't know how long I stood in the same spot, wondering why she would say that. I went home and couldn't stop thinking about it. Lidia called and texted me a few times that night, but I didn't answer. She even tried to reach me on social media, and I still didn't respond. How she reacted was not someone I wanted to be connected with, especially when she told me she would be there through thick and thin with no judgment. I didn't want her to think she would be getting off easily, so I worked up the courage to text Lidia to tell her how I felt. Her response back was, "I'm sorry, Martina, for the way I reacted and my friends' responses. I was just shocked to see you like that. It caught me off guard. Hopefully, you could forgive me. But if not, I could understand. Because what I said to you was disrespectful and not something someone should say to anybody." I had an issue with forgiving people and carrying on as if they never did anything to hurt me. So I ended up forgiving Lidia and pretended it never happened. We went back to the normal routine, such as talking on the phone and even meeting up. Lidia would embrace me with a hug and ask how I was. I would tell her that I was trying my best to make it through with her continuously reminding me that she was there if I needed her to be. A few weeks went by; I became sick and rushed to the hospital for a closer examination. I asked Tory to call Lidia to tell her for me, but she didn't answer when he called. My condition worsened. Tory kept calling my family members and close friends to keep them updated while my mother's attention remained on my condition. My sisters stayed at home because Jada was freaking out and was too young to see me in such a bad state. I spent hours being examined, put through a lot of needle pokes and tests. I remembered being very weak and was to a point where it was hard to make out anyone's faces. My eyes had closed and were that way for a few hours until I woke up seeing my mother, Tory, and a few relatives with concerned expressions. My mother scooted closer to me to address that a rumor had spread throughout social media and phones that I had passed away. I thought it was a joke. But her face remained still, so I knew something foul was going on. Tory walked over to the bedpost, took out his phone, and showed me the evidence on my Facebook page. People were writing rest in peace, gone too soon, and sad faces. Tory told me that our mutual friends on the network had pictures and statuses about being shocked that I was gone. My mother started telling me how some people were friends requesting my big sister and messaging her to see if it was true. She ended up calling my mother hysterical, telling her about the rumors, and asking what she should do. I let my mother know what my password was on my network so my sister could log in, but she couldn't. I gave Tory the password to try off his phone; he couldn't. I told my sister to click the retrieved password to my email, but it didn't come to it. I became hysterical and asked where my phone was to try it. No one could find my phone. I remember it being in my purse, so I asked my mother to look through it; it wasn't there. I was sure my phone was with me when we came to the hospital. My mother started going over out loud who had come to see me while I was unconscious, Lidia being one of them. The other people she names were elders of my family; I didn't even think twice about them possibly having my phone. Tory decided to call my phone private; Lidia picked it up after the second ring. He screamed at Lidia with her hanging up. I snatched Tory's phone and called back numerous times. I texted and demanded her to answer. Lidia didn't respond. I was so worked up that my blood pressure started to rise, so my mother and the doctors told me I had to calm down. My mother said she would call my sister, tell her to handle it, and let everyone know through social media, it was a rumor. I couldn't even calm down because I was wondering why Lidia would do something that bizarre. I had my Facebook set in my phone to log in automatically, so my password was already shown, the same as my voicemail, so it was easy for her to access it. My sister had her way with computers and technology, so she took over my page to change the password and email. After informing people that it was a rumor, she called my mom back to let her know and stated that she would call the phone company to shut my phone down temporarily. After she had spoken with the company, they told her they could retrieve messages. My sister went on to tell my mother that Lidia forwarded messages to people in my phone book stating the date of my memorial and funeral arrangements. I was baffled and instantly started to cry because I never thought someone could do that to somebody. I gained a strong dislike for Lidia. Before my sister hung up from the phone company, they told her we should contact the police to inform them and send over the retrieved text messages for evidence. Since I was still in the hospital, my mother made a phone call, and officers came to me. The officers were two heavy-set respectful cops with great knowledge. It's as if they knew what they were dealing with in my situation. We discussed with them what happened and they were shocked. They asked me if she ever showed signs of being intimidated by me or threatened me, and I told them no. They said to think harder; there may be something I didn't pay close attention to. I thought about the recent conversations we were having, and it came to me when she asked over the phone if I thought I would die. I remember telling her my faith was stronger than that, with her responding, "oh." When I told the officers, they looked at one another and said I should get an order of protection against her. They explained that if she comes near me; she would be sent to jail. Lidia had realized my phone wasn't working; she couldn't get into my network or email anymore. She started texting Tory phone, stating that she hated me, and she wished I did die. The officers used that as evidence as well and left the hospital to go track Lidia down. Before they left, I told them I didn't want her to be thrown in jail, but I did believe she may need some emotional help. They stated that they would talk to her, give her a warning, and go back to the station to request my order of protection. When they left, I told my mother and Tory that I couldn't trust anyone. I had many tests with friends, relationships, and life, but this was by far the hardest test of all. I could never fix my mouth or thoughts to wish death upon anyone. I didn't understand how Lidia could come off as genuine but have such a terrible plot in mind. I started wondering if she would try to do bodily harm to me. I felt bothered to be in the hospital, trying to figure out what was wrong with me while she was out there spreading rumors and lies. I wanted to ask Lidia why, but the officers recommended that I shut down all communication. We sat in the hospital, staring at one another while Tory continued to keep an eye on Facebook. He even went looking for Lidia's page and realized it had been deleted. People were messaging Tory to see what was going on and asking who would do something like that.

He informed everyone I was fine, to pray for my speedy recovery, and to respect my privacy at that time. I was in the hospital getting better, gathering my thoughts, and working more on forgiveness. The officers had reached back out to let us know that Lidia was given a warning and was served her papers of stopping all forms of contact. The officers told me to please stay away from her. I left the hospital and returned home with a new look at life. I could've given up and given in to what was going on with me and around me, but I didn't. It may have been hard, and I did have many doubts, but I knew I had to overcome it. And I didn't do it just for myself, but for my family as well. Whenever storms came my way, my mom, my sisters, and Tory were always there. They didn't judge my struggle or knock me down, so they were all who mattered during that moment. I had a few others who were there as well, and I appreciated them. My sister gave me my new password to Facebook and my email. She told me she had cleaned the messages off my page as well. My mother had gone to the police station to retrieve my phone; I sent the phone back to my wireless company and bought a new one. I didn't want any traces of Lidia in my life. When I logged back onto my Facebook page for the first time, I wrote a status telling everyone thanks for their prayers, well wishes, and uplifting messages since the rumors occurred.

I even wrote an inspirational quote that said to be careful who you befriend. In response, I received a large amount of love from people saying they were glad it wasn't true. I started to have visitors come to my house, respecting my wishes not to talk about the rumors. But one friend of mine, Carol, insisted on being mad because she felt like I made everything up. I didn't know what would make her think that, and I didn't bother to figure it out. Especially when I still had my hospital band on, and people who were present with me the whole time could attest to it. I lost not only Lidia but also Carol too. I believe Carol had to be placed in my shoes to know how it felt to be put through it. When I look back, I know Carol would've rather me get worked up about her assumptions, tell her what had happened, and who did it to tell everyone else about it. I wasn't sharing it with anyone until now because I know someone is going through something similar. I feel like I was a victim of emotional bullying because while at my worst, Lidia took advantage of it. I could've reacted negatively to her rumors and even got her thrown in jail, but I decided the best way was to forgive because two wrongs won't make it right. I also decided to pay closer attention to individuals' actions and reasons for being in my life, so I wouldn't have to deal with something so bizarre. I will admit the experience made me paranoid. I started checking my Facebook page every minute to make sure it wasn't hacked and double-clicking to see if I was logged out of it.

I began to feel like my emotional behavior towards social media was becoming unhealthy, so I deleted my page permanently and told people to reach me via phone or in person. When I made that change, I started to regain control of my emotional state, but it took me a while to let people into my life and even longer trust them. A year had passed before Lidia and I came into some type of contact. We were attending a mutual friend's funeral and happened to be right by one another in line to view the body. I was in front of Lidia and didn't even notice until she gasped. I turned around, staring her in the face. She was frightened, and I knew it was because of the order of protection. When we approached the casket, my attention went to our mutual friend's young body lying there from an illness. I couldn't help but think about her parent's and sisters' pain during this. I turned to Lidia and asked, "this is how you wanted me to be. Were the rumors worth it?" Familiar faces surrounding us filled with shock, but they remained silent. Before responding, Lidia stared into the casket. She turned back towards me as I could make out the words sorry coming out of her mouth. I walked off before she could get it all the way out and I didn't run into Lidia after that. If anyone was around me and she came up in the conversation with them saying she was a good friend; I would inform them to be careful. Some wanted to know why but instead of ruining her reputation I insisted that they just pay close attention to her and anyone else to make sure they were around-for them.

After the experience with Lidia I paid attention to everyone and everything on the internet; but, not good enough. Before my college graduation; I started my journey of looking for apartments to build my independence after college. I browsed the internet for apartments in my price range and came across a few places. On one website, I notice an apartment for a reasonable price, great details about the community, pictures, and information about the renter. I sent the renter an email and quickly received one back. The email informed me that there were a few people interested in renting the apartment and, if I was ready I should go ahead and send them a down payment. The woman, Jenny, stated that she was out of the state on business, could only receive the down payment through western union, and upon receiving payment, she would email the keys to me. I felt like the information she was telling me through email was clear and legit. So I agreed to her sending me a contract packet to electronically sign. I cannot stress enough that you have to research things like that. Do not just figure that if it sounds right, it's legit. I quickly became a victim of it. Being eager, I signed the electronic documents with all of my business, sent it back, and went to withdraw the down payment amount out of my savings. When I arrived at the currency exchange to send the money to western union, this bad feeling took over me. I ignored it, figured it was just my nerves, and went along with sending it. When I got home, I emailed Jenny back but didn't receive a response. I emailed her the day after; still no response. A week went past I emailed again; no response. I kept checking for a package with the keys in it; nothing came. I drove by the apartment building a few times and wondered if I should go inside to ask someone about it, but I didn't because I didn't want to go alone. I decided to inform my mother to help me figure out what to do because something was eerie about the situation. After telling her, she instantly went into researching everything, coming upon similar incidents like mine. I became angry, nervous, and panicky with my mother, believing it was a scam. I had heard about scams before but ignored them. I realized we always believe something couldn't happen to us until we're faced with it. Still, in denial, I continued to email the woman, still no response. Desperation and my mother's findings led me to make a fake email account, contact Jenny again about being interested in the apartment, and see what happens. When I emailed her my interest in the place from my fake account, I received the same email in return, worded the same, which I had gotten when I first reached out. I was puzzled, in tears, and my mother was furious. There was no number or address to reach Jenny because the western union I sent was to the phone number of an establishment where it was picked up from. When I called the establishment, I was informed that they didn't have traces of who picked it up because it was a made-up form of identity. I lost all of my savings and was paranoid because the scammers had my personal information. I researched similar situations to see if anyone had luck going to the police. Still, for the people who fell into the same category as me, no form of their scammers' real identity, the police had issues finding leads. My mother and I decided to look up alternative ways to protect my identity from the scammers using it. We ended up coming across a legit site I joined, and it's set up to give you an alert and the police in your district if anyone other than you was trying to use your identification. I remain on the site to make sure nothing ever comes up. Thankfully it hasn't.

The experience made me realize that I had to be mindful of every search engine, website, and person I was browsing when looking for jobs, apartments, and internships. I also started listening and trusting my gut feeling. I may have lost my savings, but what was most important was not being harmed because I had read of scams that could lead to it. I ended up carrying anger around for a while because I didn't understand why someone would want to take something that didn't belong to them. But I had to realize once again; some people carry bad intentions. I started to feel like I was living the events that I would see on the news, making me pray a little harder to stay protected from evil, harm, and bad people. But the unfortunate circumstances that occurred next tested my strength, patience, safety, and faith.

I had started a new job that I was happy about because I brought in a better income to help my household. I started my training a few days before my birthday. In training, I was learning the appropriate skills to become a manager in a popular storage company. I was determined and dedicated to excel within my time there. I was getting along with everyone and enjoying my new chapter. The day before my birthday, I remember leaving training full of excitement to get home to prepare for the celebrations that would take place. I wanted to do something elegant and peaceful, so I decided to have a family gathering instead of going out. My birthday spread of food, made by my mother, was corn, greens, chitterlings, ham, turkey, macaroni, dressing, pasta, buttermilk biscuits, and garlic bread. And a family friend, Jackson, was making my strawberry cake. Since we were waiting for our new stove to arrive, my mother went over to Jackson's house to cook throughout the day. By the time I made it home, my mother had called to tell me she was on her way and to be looking out for her so I could help bring in the food. I parked in the garage and went into the house to wait for her. When she called, I went back to the garage to help her. It was a mild autumn day with little winds, and the sun was shining bright. A vacant house next to mines was getting remodeled, so I could hear the vacant garage workers hammering like they did every afternoon. My mother pulled into the garage, and we started unloading the trays of food into the house. I went into the house first with my mother following behind. We weren't in the house for five minutes yet when we heard our doorbell ringing then banging on the screen door. My mother went to see who it was while I sectioned the food out on top of the kitchen counter. I turned around and could see my mother running past me to the back porch, slamming the screen door behind her. I walked towards the back porch to see what was going on; I could see her standing inside the garage in shock with all of her car doors open and the garage door too. She walked back to the house, opening the door with a flushed look on her face. I asked what was wrong, and she began to tell me that the workers next door saw three guys jump over the back fence. I had to lean against the wall as she continued. My mother said they took everything out of her purse, which was still in the car, and went through her glove compartment. She said the workers let her know that they yelled to scare them off and saw them run down the alley. I couldn't believe it. We were just outside, so how could this happen. I had to rub my mother back to calm her down while my little and big sister looked on. We said a prayer thanking God that we were safe. I told my mother, "maybe I shouldn't have a gathering for my birthday," with her cutting me off, saying she will not let some idiots take me from my celebration. I smiled at her, yet I was frightened and worried. The police arrived, observed the property, made out an incident report, and gave us a number to call them on if we felt uneasy. We cleaned up for my celebration and tried not to think about what happened. On my birthday, I kept it together, enjoyed the music, family, food, and friends. The celebration was exciting, filled with love, jokes, and plenty of laughter. It was as if nothing happened the afternoon before. The next morning was another day off from training, so I decided to spend it with my mom and sisters. We watched old television shows such as Moesha and The Parkers. I remember as a child hoping high school would be like the sitcoms were. I embraced the moment of memories and took in the quality time spent because I worked so much. My sisters, mom, and I ended the night falling asleep on our black living room sofas. The next morning I ate grits, bacon, eggs, and biscuits for breakfast and headed out for work. I told my mother I would call her to check on them like I did every day when I went on my lunch break. She watched me drive off until I was no longer in her sight. My day at work consisted of training programs on the computer and walking through the storage facility to learn the different aspects. I normally would check my phone throughout the day to see if I missed any important calls and text messages, but I couldn't at that particular moment. When I clocked out for lunch, I took my phone out and noticed I had eight missed calls from my mother. I instantly panicked because it was unusual. I excused myself and stepped outside to give her a callback. When she answered, her voice sounded the same as it did when my grandmother passed away. I was hoping nothing had happened to a family member because I couldn't take any more bad news. I was just getting the hang of coping better over the loss of my grandmother and Shad. I asked my mom what was wrong, and she started crying. I could hear my little sister in the background crying as well. I was thinking the worst and asked a little louder what was wrong. She told me someone had burglarized our home. I feel numb and leaned on my office door. My mother told me that she and Jada had just come from dropping my big sister off at work and walked to our door to notice glass was everywhere. They looked up at the window and saw the entire window was shattered. She instantly panicked because our family dog was inside, so she didn't call for help first. My mother said she opened the door and made enough noise keeping Jada far behind her just in case someone was still in the house. She didn't hear anything, so she proceeded through with caution. When she made it up the front door stairs, she turned to our dining room and noticed it was books, papers, and dinette furnishings scattered over the place. My mother also noticed our family computer was missing. She took a turn towards her room and prayed our dog was alright. My mother said the whole time she kept hold of my little sister's hand shivering. She told my little sister to use her free one to call 911 then our family friend Jackson. When she made it inside her room, she noticed our dog was trapped under a dresser drawer. She lifted the drawer, and thankfully our dog was okay but just shaken up. Her room was in disarray with dresser drawers everywhere, her closet torn apart, and her television was missing. Jada let her know that the police and Jackson were on their way. She stepped into Jada's room, which was across from hers; finding out her room was also torn apart with her mattresses flipped over, television missing, as well as her video games. The terrible sights made my little sister scream and tremble. My mother didn't want her to see anymore, so she decided to exit the house until the police arrived. Before walking out, my mother noticed glass covered the wooden kitchen floors. Jada tried to look, but my mother put her hands over her eyes and left out the house. I didn't realize I was shivering, crying, and being consoled by my co-worker. My mother was crying and said, please ask if you could go home. She informed me that the police were there, checking the house thoroughly and dusting for prints. I told her I was coming home then slowly hung up. My co-worker helped me back into the office. I informed my boss, and he quickly told me to go. I drove home with the music off and trying to remain calm. What mattered most to me was that my mother, sisters, and the dog were okay. I didn't care about any material things because they could be replaced, life, on the other hand, couldn't. I shed a few tears while driving home, not even realizing I was halfway there. My big sister phoned me to see if I was headed home, I told her, yes, and she said she would meet me there. Instead of parking in the garage, I pulled into the front of our house, still seeing the police lights flashing and Jackson's car parked crooked. I instantly saw the glass. I breathed and opened our front door. The officers looked with caution, but their faces calmed after realizing I was my mother's daughter. I took a glance around the house and began to shake. Seeing it in person was worse than hearing about it. My house looked as if someone had ransacked it and went about their business. I could see my mother was busy talking to the police officers while Jackson and his friends were standing around with angry faces. So I turned to the living room and went inside to see Jada sitting with her legs tightly together, hands crossed, with her head down, and crying. I could tell the living room hadn't been touched. It was the only place I had stepped in that came with a peaceful feel, neatly organized, while everywhere else in the house was filled with tension, mess, and discomfort. I later found out that our upstairs, where Ta'Rika and I rooms were, hadn't been tampered with either. I walked up to Jada, leaning her head on my chest, and consoled her. Jada whispered, why did this happen to us and that she was confused because we are not bad people; we're good to everyone. Jada continued to shiver while I rubbed her back. Normally we went through tragedies when she was an infant or toddler. Now she was a pre-teen and had to experience someone vandalizing our home. I wish I could take the pain away from her to take her back into the cheerful and goofy person that she would normally be. But I couldn't, and it made me hurt even more. My mother came to join us as Ta'Rika walked through the door. All I could hear my big sister say was, "oh my god, no," with her slamming the door as she walked back out. My mother went outside to console her. Due to our garage's events, the officers stated that our house was burglarized, hoping to arrest some. So they drove around for the rest of the night, circling our area, watching over us and our house. Although they were doing this, my house didn't feel like it belongs to us anymore, and we didn't feel safe. I wished we could go back to the few nights before when everything was normal. I felt like our life changed within moments, and it was about to get worse.

Chapter 19

For Better or For Worse

For Better or For Worse

My mother, sisters, and I woke up the next morning tired but continue to get things back in order around the house. While we cleaned, our conversation geared towards moving forward and possibly relocating. My mother had been up longer than us because Jackson had a friend of his install a new window, and the new window made us relax a little. At 10 am, I decided to get in the shower but not before checking outside. It had become a habit since the garage incident and burglary to check the areas surrounding our house from the windows to see if anything was out of the ordinary. I even went to my room to check our cars parked out front because we didn't think they would be safe overnight in the garage, and we wanted to keep a good eye on them. I noticed my mother was on the phone in the living room. She was repeating Jackson's name in a disturbed tone. Something just didn't feel right, so I walked into the living room to ask if everything was alright. My mother instantly told me to go upstairs and check to see where our cars were. I bypassed Ta'Rika's room, alerting her as I looked out. My mother's car was there, but my car was not. I instantly drop to my knees in tears, screaming, and shaking. I could hear Jackson, my mom, and a few relatives downstairs going back and forth out the door. Someone yelled, dial 911. Another voice stated that they would hop in their car and drive up and down the street. Ta'Rika had run into my room, asking what was wrong, and I told her someone had stolen my car. Jada ran up the stairs, hysterical crying. Why would someone do this? And wondering who was doing this to us? As we got up to make our way down the stairs, I kept yelling my car was just there before I got in the shower. Jackson noticed that there was no glass located outside, so they didn't bust my window. When the officers arrived, they quickly put in a high alert request to locate my car. Then they started to go over the incidents that were on file for the other two days. They asked if we were in disagreement with anyone. And we said no because we didn't have a problem with anyone and kept to ourselves. The officers' attention turned toward their cell phones and scanners, sending out patrol alerts in nearby areas with my license plate number. The officers worked on figuring out what was going on and who was responsible for it. They said it had to be the same people from the burglary and garage incident. I froze, silencing everything going on around me, and just remained staring out the window, hoping I would see my car drive past. Two hours went by when my mom's phone rang, and from the sounds of it, there was good news. She told me that they had located my car with everyone in the living room, breathing a sigh of relief. The sheriff told her that they had arrested a few guys, who were sitting inside my car, with one carrying a firearm. My mother was told to come down to the station to retrieve my car and a set of keys. When she hung up, she went into her room, looked in her walk-in closet, and realized her spare key for my car was missing. We believed they tried her car first, then mine. I was still shaken up but relieved and grateful that they had found them. I had been praying daily for us all to be protected from evil and harm. And I was happy my prayers were delivered. When my mother returned from the police station in my car, she seemed unsettled by how she paced back and forth. After calming her down, she started to tell us about how and where they found them, which I won't disclose for our safety measures. But my mother was able to see their faces from booking shots to see if she knew anyone, but she didn't. My mother said their names to me, and I was puzzled because I didn't know who they were either. She told me she would have to get my car detailed because it shrieks heavy narcotics, which they caught on the individuals inside my car. The sheriff at the booking station let her know that he will keep in touch to inform her of court appearances. My sisters and I didn't attend court appearances due to our mom's wishes, for our safety, which we understood. She attended their court appearances with Jackson, who was a very supportive person during this time. Everyone involved ended up receiving three to six-year sentences as we prayed for our safety and well-being a lot harder from that day forward. Our things that were taken from inside our home were never recovered. But that didn't matter to us, as long as we were safe and in one piece. I remember getting back into my car the first time and it felt different. I felt like my presence was taken from it and replaced with an evil one. I decorated my car with lavender fabric and scents to give it peace again with months passing by before becoming comfortable while driving in it. We stayed in our home, regained control of our sanity, and worked on more safety security measures. I still felt a sense of discomfort at times when I walked around it, especially at night. Every movement I heard outside would send me into a panic. I would have to redirect my thoughts and sit under my mother or sisters to ease my worries. I kept telling myself we were safer now; thankfully, we were. The experiences took a part of my sense of security and made me wonder why there were bad people in the world. When I think back, I still get a panicky feeling, but I pray for closure, awareness, and to move forward. When I think about the experience of the three-day events, Lidia and Jenny, the scammer, I realized if I didn't change my emotional path and attitude, I could've gone downhill. I could've let each experience deter me from believing I couldn't rise from it, but I didn't. It was hard not to ball up, cry, and block out the world, but then I would've let the trials defeat me. I didn't want those experiences to make me bitter, lash out at everyone, stay paranoid, and feel unsafe in my own home. I had to realize my emotional well-being was important. If I decided to let everything that happened consume me, my emotional state would not be healthy. It would shut me down mentally, then physically, leading me towards disaster. I knew how that felt already, and I didn't want to relive it. So the choice was to either take the necessary steps of forgiving, releasing and moving forward or fall deeper into a funk. I never knew how powerful forgiveness was until I made a choice to do it. I don't like staying mad because it takes so much energy from you. I remember always telling myself, "the person you mad at living their life; don't let yours stop" or "don't let this break you down and forget about what matters most, you." It took me falling a few times to realize I wanted to lead a better purpose on the journey of forgiveness, releasing, and moving forward. And I couldn't make that happen if I continued to stay in my own way, so I moved out of it.

Lidia taught me the valuable lesson of realizing everyone comes into your life for a purpose. The main purpose is to teach you something. I remember this poem my mother gave me when I didn't know who was real or not in my friend's circle. The poem talked about how some are in your life for a season, reason, or a lifetime. The poem also stated you'd be surprised what status one would fall in when they show you who they are. Have you ever had a shirt you held on for years? It was like your good luck shirt. No matter how little or worn out it was getting, you didn't want to let go of it because it held so many good memories. That's how I am with people. No matter how much the friendship or relationship is starting to show me that it is unhealthy, I ignore it and keep thinking about the good memories. I never want to believe what's in plain sight. I had to break from that; Lidia being my start of it. She may have started as a sweet, genuine, understanding, and dear to heart person, but the signs revealed more underneath the surface. So just like the favorite shirt that I finally had to let go of because it ran its course, I had to do the same with Lidia. I could no longer be associated with her. Today, I ran into Lidia; but not accompanied by the happy feeling I used to get after not seeing her for a while. I'm more cautious and alert now. Lidia and I still have a few mutual friends who inform me of the difficulties they have with her, such as trust issues, dating their significant others, and borrowing from them but never paying it back. I feel bad for them, wishing they would let go of an unhealthy friendship with her, and hoping she would work on her relationship with herself. When Lidia and I come across one another paths, I'm able to say hello and keep on-going. She always gives me a surprised expression before saying hello back, as if she's shocked that I would even speak to her. I can't say that I blame her if she thinks that way, but my hellos come from the journey of not letting my past situations with her and others define me, not out of spite or to be funny. It's my way of signing my forgiveness to myself and showing her I could be cordial because the negative actions she made no longer held power. Due to Jenny, the scammer, my senses of awareness have fully opened up. I research, check dates, words, images, and logs with clearer eyes. And if I'm still uneasy, I have another pair of eyes to research and look over things for me. I was angry about what happened. I felt I was dumb not to have looked further into it. I realized that I'm human; I will make mistakes and learn from them. I also had to accept and understand that it was not my fault. I was deceived like many others have been. I just have to be more mindful of my decision-making. Most importantly, I had to realize my gut will not steer me wrong. I spent a few nights leading up to discovering the truth about Jenny, tossing, turning, and not accepting that my intuition was speaking to me. I just shrugged it off as if I was overthinking. I've learned in the present not to shrug something off if it is bothering me that much. I try to turn to someone trustworthy for advice. Although I cannot see the person behind Jenny's name to express how I felt having to experience a scam, I emailed her. It was my way of releasing the anger and hurt I felt towards someone I've never met. In the email, I stated how the scamming made me feel and that I have to put it behind me, but I hope they would think twice about doing this to someone again. I also asked them how it would feel if the tables were turned and the scamming was done to them. Of course, I never received a response, but I was happy to have gotten it off my chest. It was my way of closure and starting the healing process. When friends and family would come to me about how they were looking for stuff online: homes, apartments, loans, and jobs, I made sure I told them to proceed with caution. I didn't want scamming to attack anyone else as it had done to me. A friend came to confide in me about this career opportunity they could get and the email they received for it. I was so glad my friend reached out to me as a fresh pair of eyes to look over it. After researching, we found out that it was a scam. The fabricated company was also asking for money to be western union to them. My friend thanked me and still does for looking out for her. It makes the process of healing and moving forward better because I could be of help to others. For the individuals who took the peace and security from my family, our cars, garage, and my sanity, the journey to forgiveness was tougher than the other situations I've mentioned. I not only had to work on forgiving them; but also so-called friends and an ex-boyfriend. As I've stated before, you truly find out who is there for you when you need their love and support the most. The day our house was burglarized, I called and texted friends to vent with only one calling back. Others waited a few days later to respond. It wasn't like I didn't make it clear in the text what had happened. I told them and stated I just needed to vent. When they finally got in touch with me, I was fed excuses for them being occupied, and I started to distance myself from a few people after that. I could understand everyone's life gets busy, but it only takes a few seconds to reach out. They had time to get on social media the same day it happened and the days after but couldn't reach out to me. I didn't try to express myself or get into detail with them about why we could no longer be friends because the reason was obvious. I called my ex-boyfriend, who I was in a relationship with at the time, right after I arrived at home when the burglary happened. I thought he would at least stop by to see me or be concerned for my safety. He told me, "I'm not coming over there; I don't want that happening to me." Our relationship was already on the rocks, but his statement confirmed I needed to let him go. If I was him and he called to tell me something unfortunate like that happened to him, I would've quickly driven to see if he was alright. I loved him, and the thought of him being in danger would weigh heavily on my mind. I ended up texting him back, letting him know we could no longer be together. It hurt texting those words to him, but it was clear he didn't care as much as I thought he did. He lashed back and told me to have a nice life. I didn't respond. I was thankful for the support from the people who mattered. I wrote a letter in my journal as if I would send it to the guys responsible for what had occurred. I wrote down what it did to our family emotionally and how they would feel if it was done to their mother or sisters. I ended it by saying that hopefully, they would get their lives together when they're released. After writing it, I was no longer mad; I closed my journal and thought about how far my family and I had come. I told myself not to let them continue to ruin my train of thought. I took back my peace of mind. The trials and tribulations in life could make one question their purpose and existence. And we also end up asking why bad things happen to good people. You ever just sat around wondering how a particular person's life was going so well for them when they never treated others right, were selfish, or led an illegal life. You always asked yourself how come they seem much happier than you.

Then I started taking the time to realize although they're showing happiness on the outside, they could very well be unhappy on the inside. All I could do was continue to focus on overcoming the storms and hoping for a better tomorrow. I also stopped beating myself up about other's malicious actions.

I realized we don't ask for bad things to happen, but we have to try to think positively for our own sake when they do. And if we have children, raise them to not be like the individuals who have put us in difficult situations. I always shout, why me? Why is this happening? Why can't I live a life with no storms?

Until I opened my eyes to see that I'm not the only one experiencing these things: second-guesses with people's motives, had to experience their home being vandalized, or someone stealing their vehicle. Or someone is wishing death upon them or being scammed.

When I silence myself to internally take in how I've overcome the situations at hand, I realize I'm one step closer to a better understanding of the world around me. Can our world be surrounded and filled with only good people and things? I don't particularly appreciate experiencing or seeing people enduring the cruelty of others. I don't particularly enjoy feeling like I have to live in fear or anxiety.

I had to trust myself to know that it was alright to release the pain of others' wrongdoings. I had to believe that I would be okay, safe, and give a chance to redirect my mind frame back on the good. When I did that, I had a healthier spirit. I didn't look to the next day, thinking I would experience another downfall, roadblock, storm, or trial.

I wanted to do something new and have another day to grow. I hold pep talks with myself all the time when things seem to go wrong, and I tell myself, "it's okay, it will all work itself out." I'm human, learning, growing, and trying to live my life the best way I know-how. I cannot let someone take away my strength.

I always hold on to the thought of life having its way of making the impossible possible. So no matter what I went through during that time, I'm still here. No matter how sad I was, I worked on becoming happy again. When I thought I would be mad forever, I found forgiveness. When I thought about crawling under my covers to hide, I took baby steps to find the strength to stand up again.

The lessons I learned helped me when I came across even more experiences that would make me question more things in life. I'm so thankful that I worked on getting through it. I deserved to be happy and live a life I love. I didn't want to carry around the question in my head of what would happen next. If anything, I was prepared to continue to live and look towards the future.

I wanted to remain the sweet, loving, and kind person I had always been. I didn't want to become defeated by people. I understood that seeing people's true colors and intentions are still hard to accept. I will always hold on to and think about my granny Rosie's words during the times I've mentioned. "You will experience a lot in life; the good, bad, and ugly. But when life gets you down, don't let it keep you down".

I always think of those words when I have bad days. I try not to let situations and circumstances keep me in a bad state. I understand that it's normal to have doubts, worries, fears, and questions about the wrongdoings. I also know it is easy to forget what's going right in life during these periods. I make myself sit down every night and think about the things I should be grateful for, the people who have come into my life for a lifetime, and the storms that turned into sunshine.

I call those moments of thought my check yourself period because I may have been down, but there were many reasons why I should get back up again. I realized for better or for worse, my life has a purpose and meant value to me even if it didn't mean anything to others.

Chapter 20
Altar

Altar

S ince things were getting better for me in my personal life, I wanted
to make sure I took the necessary precautions to stay that way. I
decided to join a college class that wasn't entirely academic-related, but
I would still get credit for, complete a fulfillment towards graduation,
and learn something new. After reading the synopsis, I was captivated
by the internal, external, emotional, and spiritual well-being that would
be the main focus throughout the class. Students also would be engaged
in meditation, becoming one with themselves, realizing their worth,
meeting people whose journey is similar to yours, practicing yoga, and
having a one-on-one with a spiritual advisor. I decided to take the class
during a summer semester when I would have a lesser workload making
it easier for me to be fully engaged. I didn't know what to expect from
the class, but I was open to many opportunities and possibilities to
better my spirit. I was also interested in receiving advice on how to
work on becoming more positive, relaxed, less worried about what
others think, and entirely devoted to working on loving me. I don't
remember the class name because it was a long title, but a few words
that stood out was the importance of identity. The words themselves
brought me into class the first day. The first day of class was similar to
how my other courses started. You get to school pretty early, a little
nervous, and observe everyone around you. You share smiles, glances,
and a few hellos to new faces. Everyone in surrounding classes was
heading into their rooms to get the day started while my classmates
and I were still sitting in the hall waiting on our professor to get there.
Finally, a man walked past us, waving, smiling, giving us the okay to
enter the classroom. He sat his suitcase down and asked us to push all
the tables along the walls. He then introduced himself as Jacob and
said I'm not just a professor; I'm a spiritual advisor and counselor
outside of school grounds. With squinty eyes and jogging-style attire,
a slender woman walked in as he talked. He embraced her as someone
dear to heart the way he hugged and kissed her cheek. She introduced
herself as Mimi, Jacobs's wife, and that she was a yoga spiritual
counselor. They instructed us to push all chairs in a circular style and
place our belongings on top of the tables. My peers and I looked
around at one another and did as told. Mimi and Jacob's chairs were
centered at the circular entrance opening, and they were the first to sit.

My attention turned to Jacob's small grey hairpiece because it was only located in a small section of the front of his scalp. I thought it was unique because the rest of his hair was silky black reminding me of the men in the movie Grease. Jacob was a short, medium built and nicely dressed man. His attention went straight to me because I was sitting in the first chair alongside him. He looks at each student's face. It was an intimate setting because there were only eleven people, including myself. The small-sized environment was one thing I loved about my school because you were seen as an individual. After observing everyone, Jacob opened up the class by telling us to close our eyes, let what's bothering us, come to the surface, and tell the class when we're ready. I believe everyone stopped breathing for a moment and was thinking that Jacob had to be crazy. We didn't know one another to be saying what's really on our minds. Jacob could sense the stalling in the air and shared with us that we will leave class on the first day to better understand the people around us. He also stated that we would be able to come back the following week more open to the exercises he has in mind if we step out of fear. One by one, each student closed their eyes while we listened to a recording of ocean sounds. "Whenever you're ready, open your eyes, and let everyone know what's on your mind," he said in a calm voice. Quietness claimed the classroom, and I could feel a calming sensation come over me. I said, "Jacob, I'm ready to talk," with eyes turning towards me. I told everyone how I wanted to cope better with my past and a few things I was dealing with at that moment. I told them about my unhealthy relationship with Timothy and how I was caught between leaving or working at it. I informed them about how I was losing friends to them backstabbing me, so it was hard for me to trust in making new ones. I got choked up about revealing that I was still coping with losing Shad and how I was blaming myself for all that he put me through. I ended by telling everyone I was in the classroom to become more in tune with getting back on the right path to happiness. I didn't want to cry any longer; I wanted to move forward so I could open my heart to whatever positive places I'm led to. After I was done, I stared at Mimi, who was smiling at me. Everyone else started expressing what was on their minds. Listening to their situations and circumstances, I realized how much I had in common with them. I also became aware of the fact that we were all misunderstood and judged by outside people. It was time for class to wrap up for the day, so we shook hands with Mimi and Jacob while collecting our belongings. As we were dismissed, Jacob told us that he would like our class. He said we were one of the few classes to open up at the first meeting fully. I left out exchanging a few smiles with my peers and was excited for weeks to come. The following week we started our scheduled activities. Opening the class with a quiet moment and music would be the routine until the end of the semester. Then revealing our obstacle from the prior week and how we overcame it would be the spoken word through journaling exercises. Next, Mimi would take over to do stress relief yoga positions that work into a meditation feeling. Afterward, Jacob would break us up into different groups to meditate with one another and work on opening up. We would have a small break and conclude the class by sitting on the floor in a circle going over one thing we learned and addressing anything we wanted to get off our chest before leaving. In the last few minutes, Jacob would ask us to lie down, close our eyes, and just be in the moment. As I look back, I realize how much the structure of activities helped me heal internally, mentally, and reshape my life; especially through journals' spoken words. From my journals, I shared with my peers in detail the struggles I was still battling with, one being Timothy. I would address how hard it was for me to say no to Timothy and how I felt when he would make me feel like the bad guy if I didn't cater to his every need. Jacob's concerned voice would say, "Oh no, that ends today," with him giving me tips of what I could do. I went home with a need to cater more to myself than putting my all into someone else. This understanding brought on the word no to Timothy. If he asked me to take him somewhere, when I already had plans, I would say no. When he wanted to borrow some money, and I had bills to take care of, I would say no. If Timothy would threaten to leave me, I started telling him to go ahead. My change shook him up, but it made me feel better because I was standing up for myself when I thought I would never be able to. I would make Jacob, Mimi, and my peers so happy when I came to class every week discussing how I was becoming one with my word during journal time. They gave me the push to keep at it. I could advise my peers when it came to relationships and returned to class with a newfound strength. Out of all my classes, during the summer, I looked forward to Jacobs. We could get personal and hold nothing back without it being taken the wrong way or spread wrong to someone else. I felt like I found a room full of best friends of different ages, nationalities, and upbringings that I could trust. And thankfully, they felt the same. Mimi introducing us to yoga's art helped shed stress, control our state of mind, and find balance not only physically but mentally. I was concerned about yoga because of my back issues, but Mimi clarified that I could modify how I posed in different positions to accommodate it. My favorite yoga pose is called "the calming child pose." I would lean face down on a yoga mat, knees bent, gently stretching my back, with my hands to the sides. This position helped quiet my mind, ease stress and anxiety. I started doing child poses at home to help relax before I studied for quizzes, final exams, or just to wind down before bedtime. I taught my mother how to do it so she could use it as a stress reliever. Other exercises that stood out in the class were peer builders in which we had to trust the person we were paired up with to guide us through exercises. I remember one exercise being about letting one fall into the arms of a stranger. I stood in front of my partner, relaxed, closed my eyes, fell back, trusting them to catch me. A few of my peers in the class had trouble with doing this. So I would always see people falling onto pillows instead of in their partners' hands. Jacob would tell them to keep trying until they perfect it. He said the exercise was to show how often we try to control everything that is going on instead of trusting people to guide us. I couldn't help but think about how many times my mom tried to guide me away from certain situations and people with me, saying, "I got this." And I would end up crawling into her arms afterward, crying about it. I had to learn the power of having someone there to pick me up, lift me when I needed it most. So accomplishing the exercise of falling into my partner's arms was the first step. Although I had no problem trusting my partner, my partner struggled with trusting me. She kept breaking her fall as she got closer to my hands. Jacob would come over to observe us hearing me saying, "come on, you can trust me. I'm here for you". As I continued to say that, she became calm and fell into my arms. She said thank you, with me later in class learning she never had anyone to cheer her on. I remember Jacob saying to us, "in life, it is always great to have real support when you feel like it's impossible to go on." He was right, and my partner and I were witnesses to it. Each week of the class held its purpose, journey, challenge, and accomplishment. I should've taken the course sooner. But I realize maybe that moment was the right time for me because I could get the best out of it. I hated that the class was only twice a week, but I made sure I embraced every moment. Especially when we meditated at the closure of each day by laying on the floor, with our eyes closed, listening to encouraging words from Jacob's voice, and filling our minds with positive thoughts to collect on. Whatever weight I came into class with disappeared when I left. I started to notice the importance of being me, not being afraid to reveal my flaws, and accepting others for their differences. Classes can introduce you to new faces and new journeys, so it was a wonderful experience to get to bond with Rebecca and Adam. They were the two I instantly connected with during Jacob's class because I could relate to their struggles. Rebecca was dealing with coping with a mental illness, and the reaction people gave her. I opened up to her about the mystery diagnosis and what I learned from it. Adam was experiencing grief from his grandmother's loss, a relationship went bad, and trying to stand on his own two feet again. I discussed my journey of coping with my grandmother's loss, my relationship with Shad, and discovering myself after a few personal struggles. We would talk on the phone in our free time three-way about the things we were learning in class. Rebecca, Adam, and I became one another support system, outside of class, during good times and the bad. It felt like I had known them for years and could tell them anything without being looked at weirdly. I was thankful that Jacob's class introduced me to good people. The weeks flew by, and I was beginning to notice my growth. I smiled more, interacted amongst my peers, and developed the strength to let go of Timothy. Jacob revealed to us that we had a final project to complete by the last day of class. He stated that we had to bring everything we've been working on to the altar.

The altar signified a way of us explaining through visual images and keepsakes what we were working on, what was important to us, how we stand strong, what we carry in our hearts, and what we would be putting behind us to redeem our existence. Jacob stated that everyone would write a message to the student expressing what we like and took from their altar after each student altar. He also wanted us to give them an uplifting comment. Now, if he would've told us about an altar on the first day of class, I would've not been quickly open to it. But since I had time to work on my struggles, learn, grow, and process a few things, I was ready. I knew what to bring for my altar, and I hope everyone would receive it well. It was time to be truthful about everything, even the things I hadn't expressed yet. Ironically the date I did my altar fell on the same day that was supposed to be Timothy and my anniversary. We opened class with our normal exercises then started altars. I was first up and went into the center of the circle to set up my display. I had a blanket that my grandmother made for me when I was a newborn, a family portrait of my mom, sisters, and me. I took out a lavender candle, a picture of Shad, a picture of my granny and me, some white socks with my initials marked in them, two books I had written for a young authors program in elementary school, and a bracelet with footprints. I lit the candle and began my altar. I described how if it weren't for my mom and sisters, I wouldn't still be alive. They made sure night and day I was alright. I explained how if everyone left my life, I knew I could always count on them to be there to lift me when needed. I began to get teary-eyed and explained the importance of family. And that I was thankful to have the bond I got with my sisters and mom. I revealed to them a little about Justice, and from the nods, I knew I answered a question in the air. I moved on to talking about the woman who created my mother to be just like her. I describe how my grandmother made sure we remained on the right path. I discussed how I unexpectedly lost her to illness and the pain I endured for years dealing with it. I told everyone to appreciate their grandparents if they have a bond with them. I told them the story of her making my quilt and how, even as an adult, I still slept with it because it makes me feel like she is near. I picked up Shad's picture and burst into tears. The class went silent as Rebecca came and sat on the floor next to me. They gave me a moment to get myself together. I explained to them how he was my first love, my first serious relationship, and how he died. I informed them that I still carried the weight on my shoulders to believe that I settled for way more than I should have because I loved him so much. I revealed that I was still working on forgiving myself for the things I let happen, but since starting the class, I've been able to forgive him. Everyone commented on how beautiful the candle smelt, and I told them lavender is the stress reliever for me. I let them know that I light a lavender candle in the morning, at night, and while in the bathtub. I informed them that a lavender scent has to be somewhere on me or around to keep my peace. I picked up the socks and told everyone that they were the pair I wore when I was put into a mental institution. The class gasped. I told them I knew I was shocked; then, I explained what led up to it. I could hear one of my peers behind me say, wow, you are a strong woman. I hadn't even revealed that to Rebecca yet; she was still sitting on the side of me, but I turned to her to tell her she will make it through. I put the socks down and picked up the bracelet. I told them the story about my mother giving it to me when I was battling for my life. I let them know the footprints' story, a spiritual story about being carried by a higher power during your worst moments. The bracelet signified that I wasn't alone in my journey of getting through the pain. In the last part of my altar, I picked up two books and informed the class how I was proud of having a love of writing since the age of 4. I began describing the opportunity that came across while in elementary school when a teacher became aware of my writing passion. A program called young authors captured the creativity of writers and displayed the work in their school library. I passed the two books around and told everyone that I knew anything is possible if you believe. I informed them that no matter what I was going through, I wanted to live and love my life from here on out. When I was done, they snapped their fingers poetically and told me they appreciated my altar. As I gathered my things, they wrote down their inspirational messages to me. I was brought to tears when they read them. Even today, on moments when I'm down, I take their messages out of my keepsake box to uplift me and help me realize I've come far.

"Dearest Martina, Thank you for opening your heart fully. That told a lot and encouraged us. We are deeply grateful-Jacob".

"Martina, I admire your strength and honesty. You're such a beautiful and caring person. I can tell that your family and relationships mean so much to you. Thanks so much for everything. P.S. I love and appreciate our talks before class; I'm thankful to call you friend-Cole".

"Dear Martina, You're a strong woman. Conquering through storms and still able to hold your head up. I admire you for your courage to keep living and to keep persevering in life. Always smile; you have a beautiful smile. I hope only the best for you on your life journey. Also, lavender is the bomb-Kim".

"Dear Martina, Your altar was very personal and deep. It takes great courage to talk about the things you discussed; I look up to you and your braveness.-Jillian".

Even today, the messages above, including those not revealed, remind me that I made it. And their heartfelt words keep me motivated. Overall, Jacob wanted us to learn something from one another, love, support, and accept each other. It was the right thing to do, especially since we live in a world where all people do is judge you. You can be doing right, but they will try to find something wrong. You could get your name slandered or looked at with a side-eye by people who once said they love you. All of that happened to me but coming into a class full of positivity helped me realize that there are still some good people. On the last day of the course, I remember glancing around at everyone's faces realizing this was it. I wouldn't walk into class the following week to smiles, hugs, and uplifting spirits. I wouldn't spend time outside of class talking with Jacob and Mimi about forgiveness and overcoming anger. I wouldn't sit in the hallway talking with my peers about journal entries and life struggles. I wouldn't be welcome into class with a hug from Rebecca and Adam. I appreciated Jacob for giving us the foundation and skills to make a better path for ourselves. He had taught me that my past didn't dictate where I was headed. I embrace Jacob and Mimi with a last hug letting them know their spiritual and loving vibes will remain with me. I also had hoped one day to reach back out to them about my new journey. I gave all of my peers hugs and well wishes. We exchanged emails, numbers, and social media names with everyone yelling, please keep in touch. I left the class with my purpose of life intact, and my faith restored. It was unlikely for us to have classes together again because we all were in different majors. I lounge around in the hallway to say another round of goodbyes to my classmates. We talked about our highlights of the class and how much we were going to miss each other. We shared a few laughs and last smiles. We let people from different classes get on the elevator before we did. As we exited the building and went our separate ways, I realized I wasn't the same person who walked into class on the first day. I was looking forward to brighter days.

Chapter 21
Rearview

Rearview

"**O**bjects in the mirror are closer than they appear."

I use that metaphorically towards how I've begun to view things and people. When I used to look at people and situations, I thought the problem at hand was smaller. Then I realized the distance between what they were willing to show me, what they were not showing me, and the signs that passed me by were more significant than I could ever imagine.

Eventually, I began to pay attention to the obvious and accepted things for what they were. I started by trying to figure out a better path for healthier friendships but sidetracked by giving the crew a second chance. The pain, nonexistent bond, and held-in questions towards Justice remain silent, but I could always tell when the thoughts lingered through a room. And let's not forget Travis, whom I thought was the one, appeared into my life with me hoping it was for the long run. The romantic charmer had me head over heels until his closet of skeletons opened a wound.

I had the choice of riding the waves with everyone, getting out, or letting my spirit run on empty. I had learned about not settling for less, stop putting my all into people, trusting cautiously, and developing a healthier outlook on friendships and relationships. Even as I began to accept that a bond with Justice may never be; I realized my sinking or swimming tests were presented.

The crew reached out through social media, stating they wanted to talk. Since years had passed, I had grown and gotten over what they had done to me, and I decided to accept the invitation. I messaged them my phone number, and I received a call a few minutes later. There wasn't tension in the air like I thought it would be.

We talked, reminisced about good times, and caught up with the happenings in one another's lives. They kept telling me how much they missed me, but I couldn't fix my mouth to say it back. I had thought about the beginning of our friendship when we couldn't go days without talking to one another. I even took the time to reflect on the personal relationship I had with each of them. I kept their secrets to myself and held on to my word of being respectful. I realized a part of me did miss them, but I didn't think it deserved to be said to them too soon. I didn't want to regret my words.

For a few weeks, we made calls back and forth to one another, especially Katie and me. Our friendship went beyond the bond I had with a few others because we related so much. Whenever Katie needed to vent or vice versa, we were there for one another. There were times when Katie was going through difficulties with her family and would come out with me just to get her mind off of it. We would sit behind our school and vent. Katie would reveal things to me that were embarrassing, shocking, and painful for her. And I always let her know how I felt and that her secrets were safe between us. No matter how mad I was after we went our separate ways, I never defamed her character. Loyalty and trust stuck with me even in the present. Katie and I were laughing on the phone like we hadn't been apart. She informed me that Sandy was having a housewarming party and would like it if I would come. I message Sandy on social media to get further details. I told her I had to work that day, but I would try to make an appearance when I got off. I was a bit nervous about facing them all after so many years of distance. But I was willing to take the step since we were on good turns to make amends. I spent my entire day at work, trying to erase the bad time between us. But my gut feelings were telling me not to get ahead of myself, to be still cautious of them. Being a lot stronger than I had been in the past, I knew I had to keep my eyes and ears open to everything at Sandy gathering.

As I drove to her house, I listened to the radio, crowded my thoughts with memories of us, and turned my heat on high. It had gotten cold that night, so I pulled my scarf a little tighter as I got out of my car to walk to Sandy's door. From the outside of her place, I could see the shadows of heads letting me know she had a house full. I had rung the doorbell twice with Sandy, quickly opening it. I knew it was her from the crooked smile she made since we were teenagers. "Sandy, you still look the same," I said. She told me likewise and stepped aside so I could enter. Sandy's family members and people that grew up with us faces were full of shock as they embraced me with hugs. People kept saying, "long time, no see," and "you have not changed one bit." I scanned the faces to see if any of them was the crew, but it wasn't. I walked towards Sandy, standing in the kitchen. She told me the others were on their way as I said, "Okay, I will stay around for a few more minutes." I had to get up early the next morning for work so I couldn't stay long. Sandy and I didn't say much inside the kitchen; she just stared at me while I waved to a few more familiar faces in her living room. She broke the silence amongst us by saying, "It is so good to see you." I told her the same here, and I can't wait to see the others too. An hour passed, and I had found a section on the couch next to Sandy's grandfather. "Are you going to take off your coat, pretty lady"? her grandpa said, rubbing his nose. "I'm not staying that long so I didn't want to get too comfortable," I said, watching more people come through the door. I got up to locate Sandy to tell her that I will be heading home. I told her to tell the others that I tried to wait as long as possible but would reschedule for a meet-up soon. We hugged, and I left. I made it home to my mother waiting up for me to see how it went. I told her it was good seeing Sandy and her place. I wished I could've stayed longer to see the others' faces. I fell asleep quickly, thinking maybe letting them back into my life wasn't so bad after all. Until I woke up with an alert on my phone from Katie, texting me to say I need to call her as soon as possible.

You ever was in a good moment, wishing it would last just a little longer, but then everything suddenly shifts. When I called Katie as I was getting ready for work, I couldn't believe what I was hearing. I brushed my teeth in shock, showered, shook my head, and got dressed, huffing, and puffing. I was upset, so I asked my mom if she could drive me to work because I couldn't concentrate. Katie had called to tell me that when she and the others arrived at Sandy's house, a problem was brought to her attention. Sandy had said that I was *talking down* about them. Katie stated that she wanted to call to ask me instead of blowing it out of proportion. She also informed me that she waited until the morning to call me because it was midnight when she made it to Sandy's. I felt like it was déjà vu all over again. I had not said anything bad about anyone. I told Sandy I couldn't wait to see them. Why would she lie and say different things? As Katie kept talking, I could hear the others in the background saying they didn't believe Sandy and that they hoped we could get past it. I told Katie I would call her back after I got off work to finish talking about it. On my break at work, I contemplated giving Sandy a call. When we were younger and approached with something she did, she got loud and obnoxious about it. So I decided to wait to call since I didn't want to make a big scene in the break room. As I ate my subway sandwich, I checked my emails, seeing I had a message on social media from Katie within the time frame before she had texted me. When I logged onto social media, I was displeased with what I read. On the phone, she appeared to be cool and didn't believe what Sandy was saying, but the message I read said differently. She believed what Sandy was saying and accused me of being untruthful. I don't know what happened between the thirty minutes before I called her to make her have a change of heart, but maybe the crew had something to do with it. I spent the rest of the shift working up about it. I had been doing well with the new friends I made. I didn't have a problem trusting them, and there wasn't drama. I wanted to punish myself for thinking they had changed. But I was glad to have proceeded with caution before letting them back in. I believe this was my sign to either keep dealing with them or dismiss myself.

Later on, when I talked with Katie, I expressed how I felt about the message she sent me on social media. Katie responded, "That's why when you called, I changed my tone because I felt like I came off as if I was accusing you." I listened to her apologies, and she stated that we needed to get together with Sandy to squash it. I thought about it, then responded, "No I'm done." Katie got quiet for a moment then asked if she should talk to Sandy for me. I told her no, she didn't have too and we ended the call with me telling Katie to let the others know that I wish them the best in life. She laughed and said, stop talking like this would be the last time we speak. Before getting off the phone, Katie said she would call me the next day. But the next morning, I changed my phone number and deleted them off my social media page. I was not going to make the same mistake twice. I would always love them, but from Sandy's lies and Katie's two reactions; loving them from a distance would work out better. There was no talking me out of the decision I made. And the things I started hearing after I removed myself from a possible reunion was my clarification. I didn't let the others speak to me about the situation with Sandy, but they had still been around one another long enough to take sides already. Our short reunion was a lesson for me to stop trying to fix something that was broken, especially when a mutual friend of ours brought me texts from them defaming my character. I just kept moving on. The move I made by not informing Sandy that I knew she lied to me was an appropriate one. I have always been a believer in killing a person with silence. Sandy had constantly tried to get her family members to reach out to me to see why I deleted her off social media, but they knew why and I knew she did too so there was no reason to entertain it. I learned second chances are not for everyone. And I'm glad I didn't feed into it. Their friendship had brought many twists, turns, and storms making it impossible to see sunshine. I wanted friends who brought out the best in me, not the stress in me. So it was time to remain separated from them forever.

I continue to treasure the personal bonds I have with people close to my heart. I also try to be supportive, loving, kind, and loyal when I receive it in return. Although I decided to look forward and pay more attention to healthier relationships with others, my relationship with Justice was still suffering. We were both hanging from a thin thread, trying to figure out who would break first. It had been years since the abuse, and I could sense his change. I still believe my mom, sisters, and me leaving made the change in him. But I wish he could've worked on a few more changes within his heart to apologize, accept responsibility, and form a pathway towards being involved more.

I was aware guilt can eat a person up, and I knew that was one of the many reasons why Justice had a hard time acknowledging the trust, love, and security he didn't and still is not giving. We would end up around one another due to my little sister Jada being closer with him. But during those moments, it was as if I was around a stranger. The only time we exchanged small conversations were the ones started through Jada. We would even laugh at jokes from television shows I grew up on, but I couldn't remember a good experience from my childhood with him.

My big sister was still having a hard time coming into his presence, so she kept it to a minimum. After we departed from Justice, we wouldn't speak or hear from him until the next time Jada went over. Or he would either call Jada's phone to ask what we were up to. It was the norm for me, but it started to get under my skin during my college graduation. It's amazing how you start to feel things a lot more different from when you were a teenager versus becoming an adult.

When I was a teenager, I put things aside now, as an adult, I was anxious for answers and results. I remember looking out into an audience of parents smiling because of their children's accomplishments during graduation. Justice had never congratulated me on a job well done.

I didn't want him present at the graduation because the way he had treated my feelings over the years made me realize he didn't deserve to be. But at least he could've taken the time out to applaud me for making it through a big journey. My mother made sure her children knew she was proud and excited about our journeys ahead. While Justice made it seem like he couldn't believe we were accomplishing as much as we were.

I would hear through elders or his friends how much he bragged about our accomplishments. And it hurt to know that because I never heard it. When I turned my graduation tassel to the other side of my head, concluding the graduation ceremony, I looked out to my mom in the audience and mouthed a thank you. I proved to myself what I could do while feeling down about the situation with him. I also proved regardless if he was active in my life or not that I could keep going.

I felt as if he thought being there financially sometimes, after grilling one on why it was needed, made everything better. I disagreed; being there meant physically, emotionally, and spiritually because it's most important. I never had a strong foundation of communication with him, so it was hard to express how I felt. I chose not to get upset about the way things continue to be because he would continue to live his life at the end of the day, so I needed to live mine.

I couldn't force what never had been built. A few years later, when I became pregnant with my first child, I knew it was time to communicate with him because I was faced with one of the hardest decisions of my life. The decision was to leave a job due to the environment and high demand not being safe for a high-risk pregnancy.

I kept trying to talk myself out of leaving, but I knew it was best. My child's safety and our health mattered more than anything else. After I resigned from the job, I decided to reach out to him to see if he could help. I was preparing for Justice to say no but was caught off guard with him agreeing that he would do whatever is needed.

Although I was relieved by his generosity, I still couldn't address him like Jada would, or hug him, and tell him he was the best. I couldn't send hearts and hugs through text messages. A bond had to be built over time before any of that could happen. I told him I would come to his place to talk about my plans and what I needed throughout my pregnancy for a healthier state. I didn't know if he was reaching out because he was trying to win my respect and love, but I did appreciate the opportunity to witness him having my back. My mom made sure I was taken care of, but I didn't want her to do it alone. Justice coming aboard to help out when needed was a sign of me being able to pursue more. But that had to be something we mutually agreed on. I had come so far from not wanting to talk with him to be able to. It was baby steps but a start to something new. I reminisce on how much Justice had missed out on in me and my big sister's life. But I was glad Jada had an opportunity to share graduation, birthdays, and a bond with him.

Like I've mentioned before, she was a baby when we left, so there was no reason for her to view him the way we did. So we accepted her bond with him. When my child was born, I had taken the baby over to his house to meet him. He was emotional but wouldn't show it around Jada and me. Justice would tell my mom how much my child resembled me when I was a baby.

My mother would listen while rocking the baby. There was a moment when I observed Justice and my mother staring at my son. And I smiled because I could see how far my mom had come. To stand in the same room with Justice without letting her thoughts go back to the pain he caused. I believed her being wrapped up in her grandson's cuteness during that moment stopped any of it from mattering. As the days go on, Justice reaches out to my mother to ask how my son is doing. I make sure he receives pictures of him to have in his presence.

When I went with Jada to his house, I could see my son's pictures on display in special places. I didn't know if Justice and my bond would ever form, but at least he was putting time and energy into his only grandchild. I was getting somewhere on my path of redemption. But have you ever had a feeling clinging to you, and you couldn't release it? It popped in your mind at the weirdest times, and you could sense an emotional setback coming.

When I was involved with someone, my love and feelings were pure. Then if we broke up, I'd mourn for a while, forgive, become strong, and then remember the past loves as a lesson learned. But when it came to Travis, I couldn't because the wound hadn't closed. Even after moving on, it was still half-open. We didn't have closure, which is why it hurt so much.

I thought since I knew him for so long, we could at least respect one another enough to sit down and express ourselves. But Travis didn't hear it, so I blamed myself. I began to realize the issue revolved around me accepting too much, Travis trying to change me, and plans he had that didn't include us in them. I had known Travis since I was a little girl in pigtails. He viewed my mother as a mom to him. My mother worked inside the schools back then and hosted a program that I would always attend. Travis was a part of the program and others who didn't want to go straight home after school. In the program, they did homework, played board games like monopoly, socialize, and watched movies until it was time to go. Travis was smart, quiet, and had a bubbly personality about him. I had a secret crush on Travis that I wouldn't reveal to him, although it was obvious he couldn't tell. As the years went on and we got older, I would run into him from time to time. We would exchange hellos, hugs, and then kept going. Years flew by again before we saw one another, leading up to the opportunity for us to reconnect as adults. Travis asked me out for a night on the town, and I decided to go with him. We went to a jazz restaurant where they played everything live. I enjoyed the scenery, vibes, and could tell Travis was too. "I see you are still quiet," he said, waiting on a response. I smiled and said, of course, that would never change about me. He laughed a little, and we went into talking about each other's lives. As the music grew louder, we tuned in, finished up our meal, and headed to the movies. We arrived an hour early, so we purchased our tickets and proceeded to the sitting area until the movie started. To pass the time, Travis and I asked one another questions about our favorite color, pet peeve, and favorite foods, then the conversation between us went silent. It didn't bother me because I'm sure we would have more to catch up on, so there was no reason in one night to talk to each other ears off. Luckily we didn't sit in silence for long because it was time for the movie to start. I remember the movie being intriguing but don't recall the title. But I know it had something to do with the snow-white fairy tale. When we departed from the movie theatre, we talked about what scenes stood out from the movie. Caught up in laughing and making valuable points, I didn't even realize we were already at my car. I paused for a moment then clicked the car doors open. Travis and I hugged as if we weren't going to ever see each other again. As I drove off, he observed me, making sure I was out of the parking lot. I glanced out my window at him until he was out of sight. He texted me a week later to meet up again; this time, I knew it was a date. We begin to see one another regularly, but I didn't know where we were going with things. I just wanted to enjoy the time spent after finally ending my relationship with Timothy, so I decided not to discuss it yet. Travis and I quality time went from going out to me spending consecutive nights at his house. We would have a movie night; watch a few basketball games, with him cooking dinner, as we got to know one another more. Although we had a bond since childhood, the transition as adults and possibly being together was a lot to handle. I couldn't believe I was once again taking a leap of faith in dating someone I considered a friend. Travis could sense my hesitation and inform me through a text message that he will be ready when I am. I asked him if he was sure with him telling me, "yes, no need to rush, he'll still be there." I believed him and trusted his word, so I started to open up and develop feelings more. Three months had passed, and it was like we were inseparable. On my off days from work, I spent nights at his house, and I could sense that deeper feelings were starting to become mutual. Since I was letting my guards down, I wanted to know where we were going with dating. I texted him one night while he was out with his friends and asked him. He replied, stating that the only person he was seeing and spending all his time with now was me. I took it as a step in the direction of getting into a relationship. I was blinded by my "knowing him" by us already being friends. But I had to realize it had been years since we had sat in the same room, socialized on a regular, and knew about one another's daily lives. I was aware of Travis having experienced a lot of pain throughout the years that we lost touch. And I informed him of a few things I had endured myself. I remember asking was he sure he was ready. I knew he had a lot to deal with and could want to take his time before becoming more than we were. Travis told me, "no, I can handle it," but then disappeared. I would text him, no response, and then see him on social media out having a good time with friends. When Travis finally reached out to me a week later, he stated that he was busy, which was why he wasn't responding and wasn't getting back to me. My gut started talking to me, and I knew something was off. I started to question whether there was anything I said or did to start this change. Travis disappeared again with me seeing him still out and about with friends through pictures. I texted him and said I didn't like the way I was being treated. Travis said he was busy and needed time to think. I asked him why he didn't say that with him, stating I didn't give him time. I felt like he was feeding me a bunch of crap and decided not to bother him for a few days. Then I found myself thinking about him, so I sent a friendly text message. I received no response, so I called; he didn't answer. Late one night, I was awake wondering what I had gotten myself into because I was starting to feel like he bit off more than he could chew. I told him in the beginning how hesitant I was, but as soon as I started to open up, he disappeared on me. You ever just wanted to get something off your chest, and the person wasn't answering their phone? So you sent numerous text messages to get your point across. While heading to work, I texted him how I felt with him, sending a shocking response back that I wasn't expecting. Travis said he needed to focus on him and couldn't do that trying to focus on us. I was stunned because when he told me, in the beginning, the personal things he was going through, I asked if he wanted me to step away for a while to get himself together. Travis told me no, he could focus on us and what he had going on; I believed him. I texted him back, expressing my anger towards him, especially spending almost four months wrapping me around his finger. As much as he had been trying to dodge me, I told him he could've come out and told me. I didn't get an apology; all I got in return again was Travis saying he had to work on him. Travis stated that I should focus on what I had going on while he goes his way to focus on himself. I was furious and couldn't drive right. I went straight through a red light. I almost collided with a police car that tried to stop me. I could see a police officer pulling up on the side of me. It was a lady cop who took her red sucker out of her mouth to speak. I believe she could see in my face that I was a little stressed and upset. "Sweetheart, go ahead and pull over and take a deep breath. You could've hurt yourself back there".

I didn't know what to thank her for first; caring for me or not giving me a ticket. As I pulled over she drove off down the street. I made a call to my boss to tell her I had to take the day off. I was never one to call off of work so she knew something was wrong. She said to call if I needed anything. I hung up, sat a little while longer, and then drove in silence to my mother's house.

I didn't want to express to her what had happened. I tried to hide it the whole time I was there until she started asking me was I going to Travis's house later. I broke down and expressed to her what he had told me. She was very upset because she had a talk with him and told him if he was trying to take us somewhere then she would send her wishes if not think twice before hurting me; he had told her that he wouldn't.

I told my mom I would handle it the best way I could and that I didn't want their relationship to go sour because of Travis and I. One thing you can't tell a mother is not to be upset, especially when their child is crying and they don't know what to do about it. It could've been a family member that made me upset for all she cares she was mad and ready to strike the target.

But she knew I wanted to handle it myself. I tried to reach out to Travis a month later after time had passed for us to talk. I called this time since he didn't like the fact that I texted him how I was feeling before. Even the phone conversation didn't work because he was not talking to me he was talking at me. Someone talking at you reminds me of a child being scolded.

I felt disrespected because he wanted me to listen to him but he wasn't trying to hear me out. Our phone conversation ended with no healing. I spent months trying to piece together what happened. Was he sure it wasn't my fault? Did I say something wrong? Did I tick him off? I started thinking I was the reason none of my dating and relationships were going right until I received a text into the New Year reassuring me I was doing right.

Travis texted to say hello and that he was sorry if he had hurt me. I felt like it was the opportunity to express how I still felt. I didn't understand what we were doing. He stated he was trying to see if we could work. Before he reached out in the new year I was fed many excuses as to why we couldn't be so how was I supposed to believe what he was saying. He told me I wanted to be what he wanted and not myself.

I told him I was being myself, there for him in all, so what was he talking about. Travis replied telling me that he believes he just didn't know how to be treated. I was relieved that he finally owned up to his part in all of it and not steadily blaming me. He said he didn't know what else to say but sorry. It had been months, I was just getting back to my normal groove, and I had forgiven him, and was moving in a different direction.

I told him I accept his apology with him ending the text with a thank you. I realize that I was once again having to deal with not only ending a time of dating someone but also a possible friendship. That was exactly what I was afraid of but I decided to resume focusing on myself while getting other things in my life in order. Every other month I started to receive random texts from Travis saying hello, just thinking of you, and hoping all is well.

I would respond with a simple text stating I hope everything was fine on his end. He was into poetry so in one text he sent he invited me to see him perform at an event called spoken word. I agreed to go because I didn't think it would be a problem. I asked my cousin Rachel to tag along with me so I would have someone to talk to. We arrived, watched his performance, and observed others as well. After all the performances were over everyone started to socialize and drink. Rachel and I sat towards the door observing the scenery. Travis approached me with a smile saying he was glad to see me. We chatted for a few with some of his friends coming up to see who I was. I remember a few faces he had introduced me to a year before. I let him know that it was good to see him but I was going to head home. He asked if we could meet up for lunch the next day to catch up. I agreed as Rachel and I left. As I drove her home she asked if I should've done that. "Cousin he is probably trying to pick up where you all left off ".

I thought she was just overthinking it so I ignored it. The next day I met up with him at a restaurant. I thought it was going to be lunch with just us but when I arrived he had family members present. His brother and three cousins were in attendance. I hadn't met the cousins in person before but I knew his brother through mutual friends. Travis introduced me by name as I sat slowly at the table. All eyes were on me as if they were trying to figure out who I was and what was my relation to Travis. They started snickering around the table as Travis talked over them. Travis's brother stared at me then resumed his side-bar conversation with the cousins.

I pulled my phone out to text Rachel and tell her I believe she was right. Rachel told me to let her know if I wanted her to come to ease my nerves. I told her to be on standby and that I would call her to let her know. Travis stated, "I see you're still hooked to your phone". I shrugged it off because I was already uncomfortable. I wanted to get up and leave but figured I would try to keep my composure. One of his cousins complimented my hair and said she liked my shoes. Travis asked if I was hungry and I said no. My nerves took my appetite away. They were wrapping up their meals and stated they were about to head to a candy shop within walking distance from the restaurant. He asked if I wanted to join with me responding "sure, why not". I wished I would've said I was going to head home. That day marked the beginning of me letting Travis back into my life in a way that I shouldn't. As soon as I found control again; I lost it.

Chapter 22
What's Left Of Me

What's Left On Me

Travis and I sat in the candy shop, observing his family picking out different treats as I could feel him moving closer to me. He then circled the question about if I was seeing someone new. My attention went to the cry baby bubble gum I use to eat as a child. I didn't even know they still were selling them. I turned to Travis to see that he was impatiently waiting on an answer. I informed him that I was interested in someone, and I discussed how the guy had helped me get over him. He was a close friend of mine who was there to vent, a shoulder to cry on, and advised on dealing with some men. He wasn't forcing himself on me; our feelings just got deeper and transitioned. I wasn't the type of person dating an individual one month, then quickly moving on to the next. I would take time out for myself to get my spirits back up. My friend just so happens to be in town and around when I needed comfort the most. We remained just friends for almost a year because I was still hoping Travis would come back. When Travis didn't bother to reach out, ignoring my calls and texts, I decided to see where things could lead with my friend but on a slow basis. I had a few moments of questioning myself on why suddenly, people who were my friend were becoming more. But a friendship first was the best way to start before it turned into anything more. Travis tuned in to what I was expressing about my path of getting over him, but I couldn't make out if he hated what I was saying or not. I remember a month or two later feeling as if he only heard what he wanted to hear when we were sitting in the candy shop. We instantly were back in each other's arms as if no heartbreak ever happened. I knew that it was a must to sit down with my friend to inform him about being back in Travis's life. I was glad that I took things slow with him and made sure he was aware I wasn't fully over Travis. Because if I didn't, the conversation I planned on having would've taken a turn for the worse. My friend was a little upset with me but told me he understood. He then said, "as your friend, I just want the best for you. And the way he did you, you make me feel like he is not really in it for you. Be careful".

I wish I had taken my friend's advice about being careful, then maybe I wouldn't be back to where I had left off. I believe if Travis and I wanted to be together, we had to take things slow. But we ended up in the fast lane again, leading up to more negative consequences. I started realizing everything between us was one-sided. Then reality set in.

Travis didn't want me as much as I wanted him, and I knew there had to be a reason behind it. He started assuming and accusing me of a lot, which he made up in his mind himself, such as saying I was in a relationship with my male friend behind his back.

I realize that people will believe what they want without checking with you, and you can't keep arguing with them over trying to prove your innocence, especially when they don't have evidence. Travis started to make me feel less than myself. He complained about my hair, my phone habits, silence, not telling him where I wanted to eat, and making me hesitant about everything between us.

It was like Travis was taking my flaws and throwing them in my face. But I wouldn't get on him about what he was doing or flaws of his that were visible to me. I knew how to accept a person, including their flaws, and not address them unless it was harmful to me. Travis couldn't do that, so I had to figure out if what we were doing was worth constantly pursuing.

I started to sense the bad decision I was making as we advanced. Travis was still disappearing at times and only reaching out to me when it was convenient for him. He even continued to question me about my friend that I didn't even see and, at that point, barely held a conversation.

Our time spent together and talking to one another was turning into a migraine. Sometimes I would watch him sleep at night, wondering if I should leave before he wakes. The glow I used to have around him was beginning to fade away, and it sucked. I couldn't deal with Travis being a romantic charmer one day, then turn into having an attitude with every move I make.

Staying at his house was beginning to feel weird, so I spaced out my time over there. I felt like he didn't want to go any further with me, and I believe I was just comfort for him. He didn't talk with me about officially being in a relationship; we just went back to the things we use to do as if a year ago he didn't break my heart. I was seeking signs to let me know if I should stay or go.

I realize that I had to be careful about what I wished. I wanted the truth and found out that the truth with Travis was something I couldn't handle. Have you ever got caught in the middle of a thunderstorm or winter blizzard and didn't know if you should pull over for a second to let it calm down or keep driving through it?

Travis and I were hit with a blizzard that I won't go into detail about because it is sensitive to both of us, and I will continue to respect that. I will say that Travis told me he would be there for me during our trying time. Instead, he left me to deal with everything on my own.

One minute he was at the doctor with me, the next day, we got into an argument over the phone with him hanging up, and then the following day, I logged onto my social media seeing a picture of him out with another woman. Like Shad, Travis had many female friends, but from past experiences, my womanly instincts could now distinguish between who was just a friend and who may be more than one.

I reached out to my friend Elise to vent to her about everything. I also told her about the picture I saw pop up on his social media page. Elise said, "maybe he just met up with a long-lost friend" I ignored what she said, and Elise knew I did.

I had experienced a lot of things being brought to my attention over the years with social media. I started to understand that some people's pages were like open diaries. I told Elise I would figure this out, and I did within a month. Travis hadn't reached back out to me since he had hung up on me. And I was still feeling disrespected from that.

I didn't want to obsess over his page, so I deactivated mine for a while. A day before my birthday, I reopened my page and noticed he was out with his mother and the same girl I had seen a picture of a few weeks earlier. He called them "his girls' with me instantly becoming sick to my stomach. I realize that the woman had to have been around the whole time I let Travis back into my life.

He was trying to have his cake and eat it too, and that's something I didn't like. I would've appreciated it if he just came out and told me instead of disappearing as if he didn't know me. A few months later, my male friend came back into my life after realizing Travis was long gone.

I had heard that Travis was bad mouthing me to his girlfriend and other people. I could've easily lashed out on his case about a few things, but it wasn't like me to lash out on someone, and I wasn't about to start. I decided to keep it to myself, let go of the pain, and work on healing a broken heart.

I was tired of letting my guards down and getting done like this. Why can't I be happy with someone? Why can't a person accept me for me? I was not about to change myself to accommodate someone else. I believe all the signs that were hitting me at once were telling me to exit.

A few months later, Travis texted me, stating that I had been lying to him the whole time because he believes I was still seeing my friend while dealing with him. Do you ever notice when the fire is burning under someone else's behind, they try to burn you too? Travis didn't want to accept responsibility for using me while he had his eyes on someone new.

I informed him that if it were true that I was in a relationship with my friend, we would have never reconnected again. I also let him know that he couldn't be mad that I've decided to turn my attention elsewhere after he played me. I believe he was trying to go through social media to see if I was hiding something from him to make his ego feel better.

He had a habit of paying close attention to my page, my phone, and my conversations. I started realizing the problem was inside of him from personal things he held on to. The first heartache he gave me, he told me he needed that time to focus on not being selfish, getting himself together, working on situations in his life, and didn't have time to focus on a relationship.

A year later, he still was selfish, barely working on himself, not putting all his time and energy into his situations, and had a woman. I started to realize he either wanted to feed me lies to get rid of me, thought I would continue to believe him, make me into what he wanted me to be, or just wasn't that into me. Through text, I let him know that instead of being messy, he could've reached out to me if he had doubts about my intentions with my friend so that the confusion could be cleared up.

Travis went on a rant, saying he wasn't being messy but can be if I kept testing him. While he continued to accuse me of holding back information, I became madder and had to tell myself to calm down and not respond. The conversation was going to continue to be a back and forth thing, and me trying to prove my innocence. I decided to let him continue to argue with himself.

I knew the truth; my worth, intentions, and heart all came from a good place. It was Travis who needed to figure out that the way he treated me was unnecessary. I couldn't believe he was the same guy I was crushing on when I wore pigtails. I had to accept that life changed him, and there wasn't anything I could do about it.

I also had to understand that I deserved way much better. I cried more tears with him than I should have. As I look back now, I think about certain things he used to tell me; how we were made for one another, he liked where we were heading, he loved how god fearing, intelligent, and loving I am. If that were the truth, he wouldn't have tried to change me.

And since he couldn't take me as I am, it was time to close that chapter. Until I could be treated with respect, patience, be loved for who I am, not deceived or misled, single would look good on me. I would not waste my time giving all of my energy, love, and trust to someone who wasn't interested in catching me if I fall.

I remember coming home one night after spending time with my friends. I listened to a collection of music from Keyshia Cole, and out of nowhere, I said, "I refuse to cry any more tears." I remember saying those words before-with the same thing happening. But that night, I sang my heart out and could feel my spirit warming.

I took a different route home to be in the car longer. Her tunes were singing to my soul and were relating to what I was going through. A collage of moments ran through my mind as I sang louder. My professor, Jacob, words came to me saying, "let yourself feel every emotion." In the car, I cried, shouted, and then smiled.

I pulled into my garage, feeling like a different woman. I could hear myself saying, "let it go, leave it right here." I stayed inside the car a few moments longer and began to meditate. I started saying my mantra, "it's time to get rid of what is not best for you to welcome in blessings." Normally, I would repeat the mantra over, but another came to the surface "you are not what people make you out to be, or what they want you to be, you're fine."

The tension in my body started to calm as I said another one "when a person shows you that they can't be there for you, believe them." The garage was getting cold, so I decided to head into the house. As I walked in, my mother called out to me to ask if everything was alright. I could truthfully say, "I was alright." I could feel my mind and spirit stepping into a new chapter.

I didn't want to keep returning to old ones. Every time I did, it was showing me why I shouldn't have. I could feel myself stepping into a new direction. I was afraid, a little shaky, but ready for what was in store for me. I had stumbled throughout this time of growing but what mattered is that I kept going.

I finally was able to tell myself that Travis wasn't right for me when for months, I was working myself up in denial, thinking we were meant to be. When I called out for the higher power to help me, I started to see things for what they were and not for what I wanted them to be.

I didn't want to keep reaching back out to Travis with him showing me more and more why I shouldn't be with him. I didn't want to keep tricking myself into thinking that Sandy and the rest would get themselves together because I was taking my attention off the new friends who were there through the sunny days and stormy weather.

I put in the work, sweat, and tears to close the chapters for good. Even now, I have moments where I think about past situations, but I'm better at focusing my mind on the present time of positive people and things. It's not easy to jump into the pool if you can't swim. That's why a life jacket, swim trainers, and lifeguards are there to help. I view everyone in my life in that manner now because when I'm drowning, they lift me to breathe again.

And even if there is no one around to help me, I knew with practice; I would accomplish getting to humble beginnings. I was ready to take a stand in my life even when the odds were against me. There were constant friend requests on social media from the crew, running into them at events and funerals, glancing at Travis's pages wondering why

I deserved to be sitting in the dust with his woman wearing a smile that he used to put on my face.

However, my loving heart wished him well and I also continue to deal with everyone around me still thinking Justice played a big part in my upbringing when that was far from the truth. Justice watched on the sidelines with everyone else.

Those odds were against me, but the necessary steps, changes, and reconstructing in my life that I was willing to make; made the road ahead of me easier to travel. Also more comfortable to handle and easier to not think of what went wrong but how I could make things right.

I know it's hard getting back up again after wiping your eyes constantly from heartache and lies. But just like everyone else is out there living, you have a reason to live too. Before I knew it, I wasn't checking Travis pages anymore; I was able to reactivate mine to enjoy my family and friends that I couldn't see on a regular daily basis.

I began investing my time and attention into the individuals who showed me what real friends are, wasn't overwhelmed around Justice anymore, and started to pay more attention to myself. Becoming more positive didn't happen overnight. I had to keep myself grounded, disciplined and remind myself that I wanted to enjoy life. I could honestly tell you a smile is so much better than a frown. And I hope someone reading this-frown could disappear too.

Chapter 23
Anybody Listening?

Anybody Listening?

I want to take a moment and vent about some of the heartache happening worldwide from bullying, depression, and lives being taken by bullets. Sometimes I want to turn off the television when I see "Breaking News" flash across the screen in bold red letters. It makes me feel like my generation growing up as a child was the last who could go outside without being hit by a bullet or turn to parents, teachers, and principals who could bring together everyone to get to the bottom of bullying.

And when a kid spirit was screaming for help, people reacted quicker. I don't understand when did the eagerness to help guide children to better go out the window. Where is someone they could trust, without any hidden reasoning? I remember when growing up, the elders in my neighborhood looked out for one another. The elders would be quick to update parents on what was going on if they saw a child doing something wrong. Parents would even give pep talks to children, including ones that weren't their own, with them taking heed to it and doing better. When I look around nowadays, "it takes a village to raise a child" seems to be disappearing.

And I keep wishing that things get better because the generations today are going through it. My little sister Jada was in second grade when, for the first time, she experienced bullying. I remember her coming home crying because a little girl Rhonda was at school pulling her hair, calling her four eyes because she wore glasses, and trying to take things from her. My mother was angry seeing her cry like that, so she called off work the next day and went up to the school early to resolve the problem.

When we sat at the dinner table the same night, anxious to know what happens, my mother went into detail about the little girl who was picking on Jada. Rhonda's mother was someone my mother knew very well because our families had known each other for years. Mrs. Byrd was upset that Rhonda was picking on Jada and screamed at her to apologize. When Mrs. Byrd asked Rhonda why she was mean to her, she said, "because Jada is different."

Jada loved to stay to herself, was smart, had selective friends, was very quiet, and adored by her teachers, which was different in Rhonda's eyes because she was the opposite of that. Rhonda was what we call a class clown, always had parent-teacher conferences, blurted out bad things, and picked on people. When her mother told her it was wrong what she was doing to Jada and others, Rhonda started crying, saying, "well, she needs to be my friend then."

After about a two-hour talk between my mom, Jada, and them; Rhonda finally apologized for what she had been doing. My mother described how she told Rhonda that everyone is different and being different is what made a person unique in their way. Mrs. Byrd thanked my mom for giving Rhonda a pep talk, and they went their separate ways. There was no bullying done to Jada by Rhonda after their meeting.

Shortly after the incident was cleared up, Jada asked if she had to change the way she was so people could stop being mean to her. I talked with her for a long time about good, bad, and mean people. I also let her know that she will encounter people and things that she doesn't understand but know she could reach out to us if she needs help or feels uncomfortable. Jada took my advice and continued to be the unique, smart, sweet, beautiful, and talented young lady she was raised to be. As Jada got older, she made friends with whom related to her; and didn't have any other bullying problems.

From Jada's experience, I became aware of some children who don't know how to tell their parents or someone they are being bullied. And that's when I believe the grounds of open communication with children should be expressed clearly. My mother always told us to come to her about anything with her taking the time to listen. It was never a "get over it' or "this phase a pass." If it was something she could do to help the situation, she did. When I became an adult, there would be friends of mine with younger siblings who would reach out to me expressing that their parents wouldn't listen to them. They would say things like, "my mom said she's busy" or "dad said he's too tired." And that may be true, but children tend to close up when they feel like they can't reach out to you. I was glad they confided in me about it because they saw me as a big sister.

So I would tell my friends, "look, your brother or sister is having a hard time reaching out to your parents; it's time for you to listen so that you can deliver the message." My friends would hear me out and reach out to their younger brothers and sisters. I was happy that my friends stepped up to be there for them, especially when they helped open the door for communication with their parents.

I'm starting to see that teenagers turn to social media to vent, and I would find myself getting emotional about it. When I see young children online doing things or wearing things they are not supposed to, just to be accepted, I can't help but wonder why their parents are not checking their pages. There are times when a beautiful girl or handsome boy on television would be displayed with missing status. And I would pray all the time that they come back home safe.

In this day in age, it's getting harder for children to grow up and be positive. It is a reality that we never know what someone is going through, so we have to be careful about how we treat them. We don't know their living conditions, relationships with their parents, or why they are sleepy, hungry, or not dressing appropriately.

When I see this, I realize how glad and thankful I am that Jada decided to reach out to us and that she knew we would listen. I would be crushed seeing my little sister turning into something that she is not or acting negatively to get our attention.

The bullying of children is happening worldwide, and it could be the beautiful little person inside your home going through it or the one that's doing the bullying. Either way, they both are screaming out for help. And I understand how it feels to scream out when I had to deal with depression. Although my depression path was a mystery diagnosis, I believe the condition goes unnoticed, and I feel like it's not taken seriously until it's too late.

I feel like when it's handle late, it could increase the possibility of more suicide rates. When I was unhappy, I didn't want to live anymore because I felt like pain, misery, and sadness would continue to take over. Thankfully I had my support system to help me get through such a trying time. But I hurt for the ones who don't have that guidance.

When I was in the place that the therapist put me in, I shared a room with a beautiful painter named Lizzie. On her side of the room, she had paintings of happy faces and family. I didn't realize until Lizzie started opening up to me that she was painting what she hopes things could turn out to be. For the three days I was there, she never had visitors and had thoughts of cutting herself.

One night, while attending a group meeting, she asked if everyone would remove the table's pens and pencils. Lizzie was having thoughts of stabbing herself because she didn't believe anyone loved her. I could see the fear in everyone's eyes, including the guidance counselor, and when we got back to the room that night, workers checked on her every hour. I could hear her sniffling in the dark, so I got up to comfort her.

Lizzie told me to be thankful I had a good mother and family because she never knew how it felt. I sat up with her all night and let her vent, and it hurt to hear how much she was going through. Lizzie wanted out of feeling the pain and tried plenty of times to erase herself from the equation. I hated that we couldn't exchange information because of the rules, so I lost contact with her when I left. But there is not a day that goes by that I don't think about her. And I pray that she is doing better.

A few years later, my friend Elise called me one night telling me she wanted to stop her treatments for her illness, which, if she did, would give her a small amount of time to live. Elise had fallen into a deep depression because she felt that the illness she was experiencing had taken over. Elise felt discouraged, stopped living her dream to become a model, and didn't feel beautiful.

When she tried to tell her family how she felt, they would tell her, "beauty is skin deep, stop worrying about your face." But what Elise wanted them to see is how much the illness was changing her physically. Elise was a few pounds lighter, her hair had completely fallen out, her eyeballs were becoming yellow, and she had a permanent frown. Elise was in and out of the hospital. I could sense from the conversation we were having that she was thinking about giving up.

So I drove to her because I was afraid of what might happen. I told her about all the things I had to endure. I felt like a burden on my family because of my situation and health taking a worse turn. But I realize this world needed more sweethearts in it, and that included us. Elise rested her head on my shoulders and told me I had saved her from doing something she would have probably regretted.

I wanted Elise to realize that she wasn't by herself, and if at times she didn't feel like anyone was there, she always had me. In the present, Elise's battle with depression comes and goes, but she is still here fighting for better health, and I'm thankful to witness it. I would not let my friend do anything else other than work on getting through it. Depression is genetic, hormonal, and a variety of names and conditions. And when I see someone giving off signs or expressing the sadness of what they're going through, I take the time to listen, reach out, and be the person they could lean on.

It's hard for a person who hasn't experienced it to handle it. So I learned before wanting to jump down their throat, we have to express it to them. Now, if you come into a moment where you are expressing it, and someone keeps bringing you down or saying "nothing is wrong with you," gradually turn your attention in a different direction to confide in someone who won't be judgmental. I've watched shows, seen articles, and videos of children trying to cope with depression, whether genetic or from their experiences. And I would cringe, witnessing some parents becoming mad at their child or loved one without taking the time to research and reach out for advice on how to make things better. It's quick for some to say that depression would go away on its own, but it's best to figure out what you can do before the condition starts to worsen. From experience, I know how easy it is for the condition to go from something small to bigger overnight. So I believe if we take the time to listen and pay attention to what an individual is trying to reveal or scream out through actions and words, we could help support and love them through it.

I remember a few years ago in Chicago; they had a walk honoring depression survivors. The walk took place in the Chicago downtown area located not too far from Grant Park, which hosts many festivities throughout the year. I could see many faces from different cities and ethnic backgrounds walking to support their loved ones, themselves, and charities surrounding the awareness of depression. People wore shirts with inspirational messages and displayed a tribute to emotional situations. I stopped and hugged strangers as we express to one another our survivor stories. The importance of listening, being there, and loving a person through depression can help give someone the boost they need to make it through.

If we could get people to come together for a friend, loved one, child, or mate when a condition like this first starts taking over, I believe it would be more survivors. Survivors, who could smile, laugh, live, and breathe while telling everyone they will make it or have made it through depression. I didn't want to see tears of sadness anymore from my eyes or others. But as soon as one problem started to be worked out, I started to worry about another.

I could not drive past an area without seeing memorial balloons and cards. There are so many tragic killings happening around the world, from babies to adults. No matter what, I changed the channels too, clicked online to read an article, or even browsed through social media; there was always bad news about someone getting shot or murdered. Innocent lives are being taken and the journeys of others steering onto the wrong path. And I still can't understand why so much of our youth is getting caught in the crossfire.

I have begun losing people close to me to a bullet, making me dread going to funerals. The thought of witnessing a childhood friend I probably ran into a day before giving hugs to lying in a casket was a tough pill to swallow. I started realizing when I left a funeral; I was back at one, a month or two later. It has begun to do something to me emotionally, making me understand that getting through the era of life now is scary.

As I work through my emotions, I stay prayerful and hope things will change. I could sit and talk about what we could do to help our youth, but it's going to take a village of supporters, parents, and love to recapture them. A village that could help guide today's children down the right path, keeping them motivated and believing in themselves. And most importantly, it will take the individual themselves to want to do better, be better, and develop a plan to be something. There are many opportunities and chances that many children think are not there because they aren't willing to see beyond the streets and peer pressure. The saying "you could be anything that you want to be if you put your mind to it" is correct. I know it's possible to redirect your life when you start believing it could happen.

I tell myself all the time that I'm thankful I wanted to strive beyond the statistics and start giving outsiders a reason to see that they're wrong. I also wanted to live a life and accomplish things that I could be proud of for the generations to come that included my child. A light bulb is waiting to be turned on inside everyone, but it needs motivation and drive. I hope in the future, there will be less bullying, a healthier plan on coping with depression, and lives not getting cut short. I know there has to be some way for a better tomorrow and future to come into play in everyone's lives, especially tomorrow's leaders.

If anything, kids should be able to go to school, get to know life, and grow up to do amazing things without their plans, dreams, and goals being interrupted. I look at my sister Jada when she was an 18-year-old graduating from high school with honors. She planned to go straight to college to gain the skills to accomplish her dream of illustration. Jada is the generation, as well as the ones after her, who need our support. They need us to encourage them and keep them focused. The last thing they should be worrying about is bullying or why they are so unhappy.

We have to take our kids by the hand and let them know we will always be there. I have a son now, and I think about what his generation would have to go through. Would my son and his generation be able to enjoy their childhood and go to school without feeling like they are on a battlefield? Will they be able to reach out when needed? Could they come to us and address how they are feeling? I hope that the day comes when the violence, bullying, and depression decrease or leave.

I wish for a lot of positivity to sweep people off of their feet. When I was a little girl playing, learning, exploring, and growing were my only thoughts, and I'm hoping that the feeling I felt can come back into today's attitudes and lives. I know there are times when I feel like "life isn't fair," and I want to ball up and hide from the world. Then I realize there is someone out there wanting someone or something to reach out to them.

I remember going to an event hosted by a former teacher of mine that had an audience of pre-teen and teenagers there, and I talked about how feeling misunderstood meant to me. I glanced around at the audience seeing teary eyes and faces full of questions and worry. When I was done talking, I was supposed to exit off the podium, but instead, I asked if anyone had any questions. The children asked me things that I knew had been on their hearts heavy such as; have you ever felt like everyone hated you? Have you ever taken an inappropriate picture just for likes on social media? Have you ever thought you had to hide your smartness so that someone could like you? Have you ever dated someone who emotionally abused you? I answered every question with some people putting their hands down because I touched them already with my answers. When I finally exit the podium, I leave them with a few words "speak what's on your heart, don't keep it in, because someone out there will listen."

Chapter 24
Grinding

Grinding

Grinding to me is working hard towards doing what you think you can't do. Every day I use it by accomplishing something to get me closer to my dreams and where I would like to be in the future. The littlest goal I make to get there gives me the push to keep on going, and I start to feel like I could accomplish anything. I use a journal for daily goals to remind me of what I've achieved, either big or small. Grinding ranges in all areas to me from emotional, physical, and financial. I remember being a four-year-old with big dreams to become a writer and choreographer. The adrenaline that goes through me when I'm writing or in the past when I danced felt exciting. I never wanted to leave that moment. It was like the happiness I felt about attending a concert. I was able to be lost inside a world I loved and escaped reality for a moment. When I started to get older, I realized the first step to accomplishing your grind is to get started.

As a kid growing up, it was a must for me to grind through education. When you get up for school each day, you are one step closer to living proof that you can make it. I've heard people I was in school with saying, "I don't know why we are learning this; we are not going to use it." But when you get older, you realize how much social studies, science, math, and reading can help you through life. I had a teacher named Mr. Meekins, who had math problems on the chalkboard every morning when we made it to class. Some of my classmates would get tired of it, complain, and talk back. A few friends and I would sit in the front of the class, tuning out the noise, and work on the math problems. If I was struggling, I went straight to Mr. Meekins's desk to ask for help with trying to solve them. He had no problem helping a student when he saw you trying. I went from taking forever on math problems to finishing quicker than I started.

In class, we begin to make study groups to figure out equations with Mr. Meekins observing to see who was working at them. Calculators, using our fingers, and a ton of scratch paper could be seen scattered throughout the classroom. And while we did the math problems, Mr. Meekins would sometimes express knowledge. "When you get out there in the real world, math is just like life; you have to learn how to solve a problem." Some classmates thought he was joking, but in his eyes, you could tell he wanted more for us than to see us outside of school grounds on the streets doing nothing. So I grinded through his class and others to get good grades, get my diploma, and fill out applications for a good high school. When I was in eighth grade, you had to take the constitution, pass it, to be eligible for graduation. Mr. Meekins gave the entire 8th grade the test and gave us study packets to take home during Spring Break. On top of the study packet, he had written, "the day after you all return from Spring Break, be ready for the constitution." I studied hard during Spring Break, making the sacrifice to stay home while all of my friends were out enjoying themselves. Grinding for me then was making sure my priorities were intact so that I could graduate. After we took the test and Mr. Meekins graded them, he told everyone, "you guys should be ashamed of yourselves. The only people who passed are Martina and another female". Everyone else in our 8th-grade classes had to retest. I was so proud of myself for sticking to the goal of making sure I accomplished it. Friends and classmates began asking could I help them study before they had to test again. I agreed because I loved to see people succeed and had faith that they could pass with proper studying. The ones I helped study passed during the retest, and I was happy for them. When teachers or classmates asked how I did it, how was I able to stay focused, I would tell them that it is all about the standards I set for myself and love to see how my hard work pays off. On my last day of 8th grade, Mr. Meekins and I had a heart-to-heart. He told me that he did not doubt that I would go far as long as I hold on to the knowledge I was learning as well as the discipline I had built inside of me.

A couple of years later, Mr. Meekins had passed away, and I went back to cherishing what he said to me on my last day of 8th grade. After finding out he had passed, I opened my eight grade graduation signature book to read his last message. "Martina, keep grinding; you make the word mean more than you would ever know." Every time I read his words, it did something to my soul. It made me feel like someone was paying attention to my determination other than my mom. It felt like someone else realized my potential before I really could understand or knew I had one.

When I started high school, my grind had strengthened, and new people with different learning styles surrounded me. I always share how personal projects in my English class helped me tap into my emotions more when writing. My English teacher, Mr. H, had a driven personality and always pushed you to think outside of the box. I enjoyed assignments when he wanted us to tap into our emotional side. High school was a roller coaster because I dealt with my health, being in and out of the hospital, and grief. Mr. H would say I should write about how angry I was because of the obstacles I was facing. He said not to sugarcoat anything in my project and that I would see why he suggested it in the end. I didn't know he was helping me dig deeper into my thought process. I was glad only Mr. H would be observing our project because I was tapping into areas and situations I wasn't trying to reveal to classmates. By the time senior year came, my project was full circle. Mr. H was shocked when I told him I wanted to reveal it to the classroom. I read about all the things I was going through in high school and how I wanted to graduate with the feeling I could return to normal. My classmates looked on with their eyes, not leaving the visuals I was displaying. As I read my paper, I had visual pictures to describe how I felt, such as a girl crying, gravestones, and hospital photos. After I was done, my classmates started coming up to me saying, "that was good" or "that's how I've been feeling." When class was over, Mr. H had told me that everything I had experienced was my testimony. He told me I would go far as long as I continue to express what was in my heart. I ended my senior year of high school with straight A's, awards, and an acceptance letter to the college of my choice. I graduated knowing that the grind I endured in high school set me up to overcome the odds when my back was against the wall.

Columbia College Chicago was the right fit for me. I learned many skills from professionals who were already in the career structure of where I wanted to be. It was a great experience getting to know creative individuals, seeing how far I could go when writing, and strengthening my skills. Due to Mr. H giving me the push to take a leap of faith when writing real-life situations; it wasn't hard to continue the process in college. A few health roadblocks had me feeling like I was at a standstill; roadblocks consisted of diabetic borderlines, lupus scare, and my hormones acting up. When my health declined, my writing started to feel negatively impacted by it. I had to work on getting my health together so I could make my writing better. I was glad to have professors who understood and could see how passionate I am about what I wanted to be. I had a professor by the name of Sykes going through a similar health crisis like me. He would tell me, "knowing you're struggling is the push you need." When he first said it, he had just returned to class after having surgery. I didn't understand what he meant until he started reaching out to me more. Professor Sykes kept in touch with me throughout my college career. He decided since his health was getting worse, he should go ahead and retire. Sykes told me, "whatever happened, use the drive in you to keep riding through the storm." It amazed me how, through my writings and what I shared with him, he was able to see that I was a person who was determined to keep going. My grind had transitioned over into adulthood, and I realized I was wise enough to accomplish something. I wanted people to understand that nothing will be handed to you. You have to go out, work your butt off, to be blessed with good news. I may have graduated with diplomas and degrees, but the pieces of paper don't define me. What defines me is what's boiling in my spirit, the adrenaline that keeps me itching for more knowledge and dreams, knowing that this world has a lot to offer me. It's so much for me and everyone to grab hold of if we do what's necessary to get there. Education is important because it has gotten me ready for the world in and outside of a career. It has made me more understanding of how things work and how you handle them professionally. Many success stories don't include schooling, but you always hear that they wished they would've gone back to complete it. I don't want to stress anyone going to school or not because we all view education differently. When you feel like you can bring things to the table, invent something creative, start a business, become a lawyer, a nutritionist, and even become president, you are grinding. For the people who have children looking up to them, it gives you the motivation to grind. If you're in between jobs and feel like giving up, look into what you are good at and grind. We are a work in progress, which can become more than what people think we could be. So as you continue to set the foundation for yourself, be mindful that there will be people who come along who discourage or don't believe in you. I use their lack of belief as an opportunity to dive more into what I need to get to where I want to be. You are the one who gets the last say.

I remember having one class with classmates who never responded to my writings, and in their eyes, there was always something wrong with it. My professor started to notice the reaction from them and would respond to my writings himself. During the middle of the semester meeting with my professor, he told me that I was competition. I didn't even understand what he meant because I never encountered it when writing how I felt. My professor was aware of it being times when I would leave the class for a break, and he would overhear some of the students saying that they wished I could be discussing fantasy and not real life. I was stunned by this because I always enjoyed whatever genre someone in class read. I didn't realize me being the odd one out of the bunch was going to cause a problem. My professor said, "do not let what they are saying make me drop the class." I was just glad I knew now why they treated me the way they did. I went home one day and worked on a nonfiction piece, but it sounded like a fantasy. I played with what I was learning throughout the classroom to catch my classmates' attention. When I read the piece aloud a few days later in class, their reaction was priceless. They started talking about how much the piece moves at a clear pace, how the main character showed different phases, and the setting was dreamy. I took a look at my professor, who burst into laughter. I decided to inform them that it was still a nonfiction piece. They gave me a look that was so nasty, but it didn't offend me. I smiled because the point I was trying to make is regardless of how I wrote a piece, I was still getting the same message across just like they were. When I was done with the class, I realized sometimes people try to make you feel bad, hoping it would knock you off your path instead of lifting, supporting, helping one another, and acknowledging one for their craft. I wished them the best on their journeys because I wasn't the type of person jealous of another's strengths. I even remember moments when strangers would see me around the school, ask what I was going to school for, and I respond to be a writer; they laughed. They said I would never get anywhere with writing or get to publish a story. I could've easily run away in tears giving up on my dreams, but I use their negativity to fuel me. If anything, I learned from a person who wanted to shatter your dream that their path is a little clouded. Don't take what they say personally because their reaction or response is bad judgment. I had to realize I can achieve any dream, despite the struggles and nonbelievers. I could grind as much as I could long as I kept bypassing the words "never give up." The next time you sit down and think about where your life is headed, remember; grinding will get you there.

Chapter 25
Footprints

Footprints

"There is a little one in there; listen to your baby's strong heartbeat."

Dr. Colgrove had calmed my worries after a few months before being misdiagnosed with a miscarriage. I sat there, listening to the beautiful sounds of a heartbeat growing stronger every second. I was overwhelmed with so much emotion that I just kept my eye on the ultrasound screen while crying. I didn't understand why the doctor I saw a few months before didn't go back to do a thorough check with an ultrasound. I had spent months depressing, thinking I had lost my child when my baby was still inside of me hanging on. Dr. Colgrove talked with me about the possible reasons behind the bleeding I experienced and informed me that it happens. He told me that he wanted to keep a close watch on things, so he scheduled me for weekly visits. He stated, "when I see that things are moving along well, I will change your appointments to every two to three weeks." Before Dr. Colgrove left the examining room, I told him, thank you. He said I would deliver a healthy baby. As I got dressed, I looked at my mom, who was saying a silent prayer. I believe we were both thinking the same thing about always reaching out for a second opinion. I didn't know what to expect when I came to the doctor's appointment, but I left knowing that the signs of pregnancy I was still showing weren't a form of denial. I had decisions to make. I remember calling my cousin Danielle and telling her the good news. She responded, "I'm glad you went for a follow-up; I'm so happy for you." I got off the phone with her and had a heart-to-heart with my mom in the car. She made me aware that I could end up being at high risk due to my health history. My mother informed me about carrying my big brother and the emotional road she endured while pregnant with him, and after he passed. She wanted to make sure I would try to put my stubbornness to the side, work on getting rid of stress, and focus on my baby and me. I told my mom that I would need her help because we both knew how stressed I could become. My mother let me know that she would be by my side the entire ride and told me not to worry about anything. I couldn't stop staring at the ultrasound in my hand. I kept rubbing my fingers back and forth on the spot where the baby could be seen. I closed my eyes and began to sink in that I was about to become a mother. I didn't care what the sex of the baby would be as long as the baby was healthy. I had a lot to figure out from that moment into the months ahead; decisions, sacrifices, and tough changes.

Before the baby arrived, I wanted to make sure that I was mentally and emotionally in the right space. I realized my life was about to transition into a world I had learned through my mom. I tried not to overwhelm myself with thoughts; instead, I worked on staying at peace. I touched my stomach for a little while, knowing soon I would be feeling feet kicking me. After my doctor's appointment, I had gone to work, receiving a call from my co-worker and friend. She said hello and fell silent, waiting for me to speak. I talked about the doctor's appointment; I had snapped a picture on my phone of the ultrasound to send to her. I was hoping there weren't any customers in her office with her because she screamed out with happiness and said, "God is good." I laughed and smiled at her reaction. We chatted for a little while before customers came into our offices. I told her I would catch up with her later and turn my attention to audits I had to do. I had to have a lot of blood work done at the appointment, so I was anxious to know the results. Dr. Colgrove ended up calling me as I headed home from work. I told him I was shocked that the lab results came back so fast. He stated, "Martina, you are high risk; it's time to start thinking about areas of your life that you can cut out." I knew he was referring to my workload. I didn't believe in taking off work; I was always balancing work inside my office and in the storage area. The storage area work consisted of heavy janitorial duties that Dr. Colgrove told me I would have to stop. On the phone, Dr. Colgrove told me that he would discuss the following week with me in more detail about the decisions I should make. I was thankful to have a doctor who cared about my baby and my well-being, so I considered what he was saying. When I made it home, I told my mother what Dr. Colgrove had told me as she grabbed my hands to say a prayer. Before I took a bubble bath and relaxed a little, I thought about what I could do at work to lighten my load. I talked with my District Manager and informed him of my pregnancy and high-risk measures. Thankfully the next day, he was at my office to check-in, and I sat with him to discuss what was going on. He informed me that I was one of his best workers, so he had no problem accommodating me since I was expecting. I started to work with only men co-workers around my office with me taking care of paperwork and customers while the guys attended to janitorial duties. My district manager also let me come in late when I had doctor's appointments and came to check on me more to see how things were going. I appreciated how concerned and kind he was. It made me realize my hard work didn't go unnoticed. The gentleman I would work with didn't want me to get up from my office chair. Every time I tried to, they yelled, "I'll handle it." I told them how much I appreciated it. The weight of worrying about how I would be able to continue to work full time lifted. And my normal attitude of "I got this "kicked in. But life has a way of telling you it's time to sit down even when you don't want to. My district manager started going through a few personal things of his own and had to step down from his position for a while. Someone else had to take over his responsibilities until we were updated on if he was coming back. I tried to explain to the person in charge what was going on with me. The person in charge said it was understood, but things started changing. Instead of guys coming over to help me out, some females were sitting down doing nothing. I tried to do things throughout the building that my doctor stated weren't safe for me. I started to become stressed because my questions and concerns weren't getting answered. When we finally got an update that my former boss wasn't returning, the person in charge completely took over. It wasn't like I was asking for days off or not coming to work. I was always there, on time, doing my job. I just wanted the person in charge to understand for the next couple of months; I would have to modify the things I did. It became clear the new boss was not in agreeance. During downtime at work, when no customers were coming in, I took the time to contemplate what should be done. I enjoyed my job and the interactions with customers, but I wasn't going to exhaust myself and put my baby's life in jeopardy. I thought about it every day while at work, getting sick during more doctors' appointments, being a little more tired than usual, and my stomach getting bigger. I sent constant emails back and forth to the new boss with no answers with people still being sent to my office, not helping out. I decided to resign.

I had to do what was best, and looking back, I was glad I did. Leaving my job was a very drastic change because I knew it would slice my income in half. I worried about how to pay bills, eat, and keep gas in my car. I had to figure out a plan to keep my savings stored away to prepare for my baby's arrival. I knew I had the support of my loved ones, but the independence in me would stop me from wanting to lean on anybody. I went into full prayer mode and hoped I would be carried through everything. On my last day at my job, it felt like I was ending a relationship. I had made a few close friends with co-workers and developed a bond with some of my customers. A few of my customers came to give me words of encouragement, inspiration, gifts, and cards. And my former boss had come to see me off. I would miss the people I interacted with every day and what my hard work brought to the company. On the last day, there weren't many customers coming in to see storage units, so my coworker and I stayed under the office's heat. I had moments throughout the day when I couldn't believe I was leaving. But sometimes in life, you have to make choices that will guide you in better directions. On the last day, the coworker I worked with was a girl who had taken a liking to our friendship. She told me, "Martina, I'm going to miss the beautiful presence you give. You work hard and keep a smile on everyone's faces". I gave her a big hug because I knew she was going through her situation, and I told her I would keep in touch with her, and please do the same. When it was getting to the last hour of working there, I slowly took all of my personal belongings to my car. I left the key in a safe place for the boss and ensured the office was tidy for whoever would be taken over the store. At times, I caught myself getting emotional, but I was beginning to feel the squirming of my child in remembering my baby matter most. It was finally time to go, and before I left, I had gotten a call from the woman who trained me for the job. She was sad but had wished me the best. I told her I appreciated her for all she had taught me and thanked her for allowing me to trust somebody. We talked for a moment about happy times, and we were always calling one another to vent. She told me not to be a stranger and to reach out to her whenever I needed to. I got off the phone with her and did all the end-of-day paperwork. It began to sink in that it would be my last day preparing the office for the next morning, making sure the computers were off, and the faucets weren't running. It was my last day to see smiles from customers who came in to tell me life stories. My coworker and I closed the doors to the office as I typed in my security code to exit the gates for the last time. Before leaving, my co-worker pulled her car up to mine, jumped out of her car for a hug. I looked in her face, could see her eyes becoming watery, and I told her I would miss her. We got back in our cars and honked at one another as we drove off. I drove home with a smile on my face playing Marvin Sapp never would have made it. A few months before, I was in the office when I began to bleed being told by one doctor I had miscarried. Now I was leaving the same office feeling swirls inside of me. I was always one to believe in miracles, and from past experiences, I always headed for a second opinion with doctors. I was glad I listened to my mother when she told me to take another pregnancy test. She even told me to stand in a mirror and look at myself. My stomach was a bigger size, and I didn't realize it. And that is why I ended up at the doctor again. I had fallen into a depression over the loss of my child, who was still alive and growing inside. It was my time to take in all of the new changes and get used to something I didn't often do, such as resting. Until I went to enough doctors' appointments to make sure everything was remaining okay, I kept my pregnancy a secret amongst a few loved ones. I started prioritizing my life and the people around me a little more than before. I knew carrying a baby, especially high risk, was not a walk in the park. I knew I had to be mindful of everything I did and the choices I made. I knew my problem would center around my emotional state, so I set out to release all negativity and pain through my writing. I started a journal venting out good, bad, happy, or sad moments and thoughts. I reached out to my former teacher, godfather, and Pastor Mr. Spicer. He became my spiritual advisor throughout my pregnancy. I wanted to keep my faith strong through everything that was happening. Mr. Spicer would pray over me and tell me to keep him updated on anything happening emotionally, mentally, or relating to pregnancy. The few friends I knew I could trust checked on me constantly via phone or random pop-ups at my home. I was thankful for the amount of love and support I was getting, especially when I didn't know if I was coming or going. I wasn't used to sitting at home. I had been working before and after graduating from college for so long. It was the adjustment I knew I needed to make, especially when I kept getting good reports from my doctor visits. I was crushed when Dr. Colgrove took his practice back to his hometown, but I knew it was best for him. I found out that he worked with Dr. Davies, who became my doctor and bonded with me. Dr. Davies was my mother's doctor during her earlier health issues in life. I knew since he helped get her to better, I was in good hands. I was excited to see my baby through ultrasound for every doctor's appointment. Dr. Davies could sense that seeing my baby was what I wanted. I was amazed by the kicks, flips, and faces my baby was making. I knew on the outside my child would keep me laughing and on my feet all day. I was getting closer to finding out the sex of my baby, which is when everyone was asking me about what gender I preferred. I kept telling everyone I just wanted for my baby to be healthy, alert, and active. They didn't ask me anymore after that. I remember when I headed to the doctor's appointment that was going to reveal the sex. Like I did with all appointments, I prayed before entering the examining room. Dr. Davies came in and started his journey of finding out. My baby was flipping around, trying to move out of camera sight. As we laughed and talked about my baby being as stubborn as me, Dr. Davies yelled out, "It's A Boy." I sat up a little more so I could see; my doctor zoomed-in, catching it before my little boy closed his legs. I stared at my mom and knew she was happy. It was always just my mom, my sisters, and I after my brother passed away. It was as if we were giving a second chance to have a handsome boy in our lives. I couldn't wait for my sisters to find out. I sent my big sister Ta'Rika a picture of the ultrasound that revealed it was a boy. She was happy and excited, responding "thank god". When my little sister Jada got out of school my mother and I was there to pick her up. All she had been talking about is a boy, a boy, a boy. You would never see her going into a department store to the pink side. When she got into the car she asked what the verdict was. My mother and I burst into laughter because my little sister had a way of being a jokester and making you feel better. When I handed her the ultrasound if she was able to do a backflip in the car she would have. I was in tears watching her eyes get big and her face light up. She was even more excited from that day forward. Having a boy definitely would switch up things in my household. We were used to Barbie dolls, not race cars but I was happy to have a healthy baby boy on board. What was also exciting to have a boy was it giving me a reason to tap back into my tomboyish ways. When I was a kid I had a period where I wanted to jump off bikes, play in the mud, and dress as boys did. Then I got older and started taking a liking to girl fashion and getting my nails and toes done. Even now some people still can't believe I had a moment of being a tomboy. I have to take out one of the rare pictures of me dressed like one. I knew that was something I could share with my son when he grows up with him probably sighing "mom". I was excited and knew that it was time for me to get myself in order. I sent forwarded text messages to my loved ones revealing the gender with them texting back smiling faces, hearts, and the words I love. I went home the same day and opened my journal to pen my first letter to my son. I wanted him to know that I will be there every step of the way and that I will raise him to be a kind, loving, respectful, and educated gentleman. I wrote that he could always come to me about anything and I will always be there. I closed my journal and picked up the picture book I had started of his ultrasounds. I was halfway through my journey getting closer to the moment of meeting him. I had been doing well with balancing my eating and resting. I also was getting the hang of balancing my stresses and worry. I knew if I kept balancing my life in a positive light I will be able to get through a high-risk pregnancy with a blessing. Tears fell as I glanced through my son's development. I had a choice of getting extra tests done through lab work to make sure everything was right with his development. I was thankful that the creation of him was going in a great direction. My doctor had a personality that made you feel happy even when you were down. I couldn't help but have moments of thinking about the doctor who had misdiagnosed me with being quick to say I miscarried. I was upset the doctor didn't go into further examination to check to make sure it could be cleared as that. I had heard of miracles happening within a lot of women's lives who thought, from what was told to them, that what was said had to be right. And from my own experiences, throughout stages of my life, I knew if it wasn't shown to me visually I couldn't just go off of someone's words. But I had forgiven the previous doctor because I didn't want the anger to stop my growth.

I was thankful my son was still alive, and I was thankful my mother had talked me into going to get a second opinion. My stomach got bigger and I started to realize moving around by myself, such as driving, was becoming difficult. I had to be home more and go out when someone was able to drive me. When I was home I had moments of frustration wishing I could still be working and thinking about what the future has in store for me. I knew when I was able to, I was going to branch back into the world to grind. Then while in a moment of frustration I would feel a few kicks, realize I had to focus on the present moment, and put what I was feeling aside. I had someone coming into the world that was going to look up to me, want to always see me happy, and accept me for me because "I'm mommy". Having a baby was already teaching me a lot of things and I knew throughout motherhood there was a lot more to learn. I was glad to have guidance from my mother and the memories of my grandmother. I knew there were going to be questions I would ask and times when I will feel overwhelmed. But I had to take it a day at a time and realize as a mother you will make some mistakes. My doctor's appointments had gone back to weekly as I could see my creation developing into a beautiful baby. I was always full of laughter watching him on ultrasounds as if he was showing me that everything was going to be alright. Loved ones were still reaching out to make sure everything was going well and that I was keeping positive. I decided to start going on walks with my mom and sisters to get my body prepared for labor. We would walk through my old neighborhood revisiting play yards and school grounds. There were moments when we would run into familiar faces with them joining us on our walking trips. I remember picturing the buildings that used to be there and have visions of myself as a child climbing the monkey bars. I would smile because although the buildings weren't there my son would still get to enjoy the area I once occupied. I took a walk through Stanton Park, seeing instructors who I had known since I was a teenager, amazed to see me as an adult with a child. They would give me hugs, ask me to rub my belly, and wish me the best of luck. It was great to have a physical reminder of where I came from. My walks become less when my feet begin to swell. I believe the swelling of my feet was the worst for me because I loved to be moving around even in the house. Since I was dealing with too much swelling I stayed confined to a foot massage or my bed. There were only a few weeks left in my pregnancy but my son was not showing signs that he was ready to come out. He was enjoying his time inside, especially the food I was eating, and kicking me all times of the night. We all started to make a joke about it stating that if it was up to my son I would be pregnant forever. I would have constant talks with him at night while rubbing my belly telling him "come out, mommy's ready". A week before my due date I was hoping to hear that I would be admitted into the hospital. My doctor told me "little guy is still not ready". They checked my amniotic fluid and placenta via ultrasound to make sure it was still healthy. I spent a few weeks at home praying he would come out soon. Now let's fast forward a little and come to the realization that I was overdue. I went to my final doctor's appointment showing no signs of labor. My mother and I went out for breakfast afterward, did a little shopping, and went home so she could braid my hair in cornrows. Before she started on my hair I decided to relax in a bubble bath. I was feeling a little funny, a few aches, but nothing alarming. As soon as I got out of the tub, got dressed, sat down, put my feet up, my mother started on my hair. I turned my attention to the marathon of the criminal minds that was on television. My first sign that I was in labor, came an hour later when sharp pains started attacking my back. The pains kept picking up every time I tried to move. I told my mom there was no way I could sit through another cornrow. I tied a scarf on my head as we got prepared to leave for the hospital. I remained standing up in the bathroom with my little sister holding one of my hands and the other being cradled by the sink. My mother was grabbing my hospital bag while my big sister timed my contractions. The car ride was pretty intense as my mother tried to dodge bumps and potholes. She kept asking if I was okay with my little sister responding for me. My big sister called the hospital so they could alert Dr. Davies that I was on my way. As we drove through the late-night hour I may have squeezed my little sister's hand to the point of her wanting to scream. But she remained calm to comfort me. Jada kept saying "it's okay" with me apologizing for taking the feeling out of her hand for a long period. I'm still apologizing to her today about it with her laughing saying "Sister you were in labor". When we arrived at the hospital the process was long, but helpful, and took twelve hours. When I first saw him I fell in love and knew he was my miracle. I knew my son would be the first guy who would appreciate my love, dedication, and time wholeheartedly. I fed him while he held on tight to my finger. He was just the chubbiest and handsome littlest person ever. I couldn't wait to get home and start my new chapter with him. As he slept during our stay in the hospital I would go over the journey of getting to where we are. There is nothing different I would change about the path of meeting my child. I learned a lot about myself and reconnected with my heart again. The only thing I prayed for when my child arrived for me to unconditionally be happy; and I was. When I brought him home to a room I had been rearranging for him for months; I felt complete. I would come into the room every day before he came and felt uplifted. Bringing him inside, having him to myself, with no doctors coming in and out was the first start to mommyhood. One thing about my son I love is that he has a smile that brightens up everyone's heart and world. His smile has been like that since the day he was born. Every time I wake up in the morning he gives me the biggest smile signifying that it will be a good day. I would take him for his appointments at the doctor with his doctor telling me I look like a natural. He stated I cater to and protect my son with so much love in a world that love is hard to come by. My son gives me another purpose to live my life. I started realizing if I would've given up years before I wouldn't be embracing these moments right now. I wouldn't be waking up knowing that someone held me close to their heart other than my mom and sisters. Being a mommy has given me the courage to make sure my health stays on the right path and that I understand it's not only me I have to think about. Every day I am growing, advancing, and learning to embrace the love I am receiving and giving my son. When he lays on my chest, when he reaches for me when he is sad, and when he touches my face with a smile I know I am doing the best I can. There is no reason for me not to enjoy the unconditional love that is happening between us. While my son slept I had check-in moments with myself. I would tell myself about how I want the best for my son, which I'm willing to go over and beyond with dreams, goals, dedication, and drive to make sure it happens. I had already completed so much in life that I know when he gets older he would be proud of how far his mom has come. My grind was not going to stop; I knew I had a lot more to offer especially for my little one. I would turn my attention back to him and go into thanking the higher power for everything. I knew I wouldn't have made it this far without the constant support of my loved ones, my faith, my dedication, prayer, and belief. I cried silently for being blessed with the opportunity to create a human being who showed in the womb that he was a survivor. I remember my mother sitting me down one night as she rocked my son and told me how proud she was of how I've been handling motherhood so far. She gave me inspirational advice, answered my questions or concerns, and thanked me for staying determined. I knew if anyone could be insightful with me my mother could. I had gotten emotional at that moment because I wished my grandmother was here to see him. But I knew when he laughed and smiled in his sleep she was talking with him. In my own opinion, since we are entitled to one, in this day and age having a child for some is not appreciated the way it should be. I know a few people personally who continue to put themselves and their needs before their children. I would see pictures of a few of my friends in the club every weekend, out and about throughout the week late nights, with their kids fending for themselves. Even after talking to a few of them about slowing down so they could develop better bonds and relationships with their kids; they looked at me like I was talking foreign. I realized all I could do was continue to be a good friend as I expressed my opinion and truth. But I noticed how when I said something to them it would come in one ear and go out the other. I started keeping quiet and just took what they were doing as a message to what I won't do. I believe it's alright to have time for you, to go out and enjoy things as an adult, but not every other day or weekend. It makes me wonder when do some people who act this way go out and do things with their kids? I started learning a lot about my surroundings, people, and their priorities which led me to end friendships. I'm a strong believer that you should surround yourself with people whose path and mindset can relate to your own. I didn't want to be surrounded by individuals who didn't have their morals in order. I was glad I have a few good friends that were parents who knew what came first. I can only speak for myself when I say my son changed me for the better.

I love to spend time with him watching his favorite movie Aladdin. I love to play with him while he kicks on his piano set. Now there are times when my mom relieves me from mommy duties, so I could go outside to get fresh air. I would use that time to catch up with friends for a manicure and pedicure. I also go to one of my favorite spots to eat and even catch a movie. But when I'm away from my son, I miss him so much that I quickly wrap things up to head home. I know my whole world has shifted once again, but at least it's a permanent shift towards happiness. When I lay down at night, I know that I'm beside a person who loves me just as much as I love myself. I don't have to worry about him taking a piece of my identity and running away with it. My son is here to stay with me forever. I cannot wait for the day that I will be able to share with him my experience of being selfless, loving, caring, and my readiness to form a bond together. The poem titled Footprints still hangs in my room because I know for sure a higher power carried me through my pregnancy and blessed me with a little miracle set of footprints that I am thankful to call my son.

Chapter 26
Be Thankful

Be Thankful

There are moments where I felt like nothing was going right in my life. I would get angry and mad, shouting why stuff can't be right. I wanted certain things, people, and situations to work out my way, but it didn't, and I became the why me girl from it. Why do I have to be in this crowded driving lane? Why do I have to feel this pain? Why do I have to toss and turn at night? Why can't I have a real friend by my side? Why can't I be with a man who wants me for me? Why do I keep being deceived? Why the job I wanted didn't come through for me? Why am I struggling? Why are bad things happening to me, and I'm a good person? I have had some why days and nights. And I remember one day telling myself to shut up because of it. I learned a harsh reality when I decided to pay closer attention to what I was doing. Being full of why was making me so unhappy. I kept getting asked why I won't smile. I kept being told that life would get better if I took the time to look closer into the problem. I would turn a song off if it were displaying positive vibes. As I look back, I was not too fond of that period when I couldn't think of anything but why's. I realized that it was so much in my life to be thankful for, including certain things, situations, and people. When I accepted that I was guilty of a why period, I gave myself time to tune into the reasons for being thankful. My whys didn't go away overnight, but I started hearing them less until they completely erased from my mouth. Then I fully appreciated what I had, the people I had, and the things I did in my life. I found myself complaining about not having what I saw others have. I would see them so happy driving their new whip, going on expensive trips, and buying homes that I became blinded by it. I started asking myself why I am putting so much time into trying to make something out of myself and that I may be wasting my time, the reason why I wasn't where I wanted to be. When reality hit me, I was wrong for looking at materialistic things as if they made you who you are; I got myself together. I started appreciating the car I have that is in great condition to get where I needed to be. I may have had it for a few years, but I took good care of it, took it for checkups, and made sure it was safe to drive in. I remember one day during a winter storm driving behind a BMW that broke down at a red light. I realized the outer exterior might be good-looking, but the interior needed work done. I didn't believe the owner of the car was properly taking care of it. So I appreciated my car's outer and interior being in good condition to keep me going. I said aloud, "check yourself, Martina, don't let it happen again." From that check-in to even now in the present, I treat my car like it's my second child by taking good care of it. I would hear co-workers bragging about expensive trips they were going on, and when they get back, I would stare into the pictures wishing it was me in them. I wanted to take a vacation that I wouldn't have to worry about how much it cost or balancing my spending while there. One girl I worked with came back from a vacation with me overhearing her tell my boss that she didn't have money for rent, so she needed to pick up extra hours. It was evident she was living beyond her means. I started taking more appreciation for the trips I took by working hard to save up for a while, still managing my bills. Even the family trips my mom planned for us across the world and how she did it by saving and taking the same steps I did to plan. I realized by putting money to the side when I got paid, saving, and searching for places in my price range, my family and I were able to go to the places my co-worker had gone with wiser results.

A friend of mine called me to come and check out her new home. It was in an upscale neighborhood, with fancy cars and big backyards. As she walked me through the house, I was delighted with what I saw from the chandeliers, furniture, and beautiful art pictures. At that time, I was in a good neighborhood but only had an apartment and the furniture I could afford. I started telling her, "this is nice, wow your carpet looks like it was a million dollars," with my friend responding, "Yeah, I know, right, I work hard for money." At that moment, I came down out of denial and realized my friend didn't have a job. But it wasn't my place to ask how she afforded it, and I was afraid to even to know-how. As she talked with me more, she stated she was involved with a drug dealer. I ran out of that house as if the police were parked outside in front of it. I know you are probably laughing at me right now, but I was out of breath when I got back to my car. I drove off and saw her glancing at me while standing partially in the screen door. She was looking at me crazy and stopped talking to me after that. She told mutual friends of ours that I hated her and couldn't respect her lifestyle. The moral of the story is her boyfriend died, the house, cars, and the big backyard were taken away. My old friend had to find her way back into reality. She made so many enemies that she treated people as if they were beneath her and even burned bridges with her mother. So she didn't have anyone. I sat in my apartment and appreciated it a lot more than I did when I was standing in her house, fantasizing over her carpet and stairs. I knew if I ever wanted something similar to that, I would want to work hard, legally, for it.

After those experiences, I checked myself because I realized the life I led and what I had I needed to appreciate. At the time, I was younger, so I had time to recover and learn from my mistakes. I was ashamed of myself because I was raised to love, accept, and cherish what you have. I didn't like what had gotten into me. But reality set in for me when I looked around and realized the clothes, shoes, food, furniture, and a roof over my head was enough for me. I had to apologize to myself and pray for forgiveness for wanting to have what someone else had. It was a slip-up, but it got me prepared for what I experienced after that and now in the present.

I wasn't raised to be like someone else or to feel like I need expensive things to be fresh. My mother raised me better than that. But I'm human, and I learned a valuable lesson from it.

There was a time when I didn't appreciate my real friends because I was still crying over the ones who had hurt me and showed me their true colors. My real friends showed me they cared, always were there, and had no hidden intentions. It took me talking with my friend Elise to understand the wrong decision I was making. "Martina, there are times when I want you to come out with me, and you say no," she seemed to be upset about it. There was a period when I was telling her I was busy, but I was giving my time and energy to old friends who didn't deserve it. No matter how much they showed me repeatedly why I shouldn't be around them, I kept letting them back in. I started to ask myself why I was always complaining when I'm the one enabling the issue. I felt so bad when Elise brought that to my attention, and when I told her the truth, I felt worse. I thought she would chew my head off but instead told me, "Martina, please stop letting them use you." I couldn't get mad at Elise because what she was saying to me was the truth. When I sat down for my daily check-in with myself, I realized how much I was being used. I started thinking even more about the people who had remained by my side even when I felt I wasn't worth it. I finally cut off all communication from the individuals who shouldn't still be in my circle. I started learning, accepting, and appreciating the true friends in my life. I feel ashamed that it was a moment in time where I was settling for less. But when I realized how much better I've been towards my real friends since I departed from the ones that were not true, I am grateful for the few who have remained here and loyal.

I remember finding out a guy was playing with my heart. I was screaming why he couldn't love me and get himself together so we could be as one, not paying attention to all the signs saying I'm better off without him. There is no telling where my heart or mind would be today if I continued to push for this individual's relationship. I learned slowly but surely to be thankful for all the warning signs I was shown while dating or in a few relationships. I realized I had contributed to my broken hearts, as well. I didn't love myself enough to not settle for less than I was worth. I became infatuated with the wining and dining or someone telling me what I wanted to hear. It was time for me to recheck myself because what I was putting up with wasn't healthy, crushing my identity. When I rewind to now, I stand firm with myself, identity, and beliefs. I'm not wasting my time, energy, or love anymore. I was thankful for my eyes to be washed from what I wanted them to show and made clearer what I needed to see.

I've stated before how I don't particularly appreciate when a person talks at me as if they are scolding a child. I found myself shutting down every time this happens. And I was constantly complaining about why no one would listen. Back then, I didn't realize I had to put my foot down and express that I deserve some respect. Because I realize when you let people say whatever they want to say to you, it allows them to walk all over you. Now I communicate my worries, fears, good times, doubts, and exciting moments with confidence. And if I'm having a disagreement with someone and not being heard, I end the conversation leaving them no chance to continue to talk either. I strongly believe if people want to be heard and respected, they have to give the same in return. If not, then what you dish out comes back to you twice as bad, and no one wants all of that. I reflect on how much the why's of struggling used to be a big problem. I would cry, scream, and yell out, why is this happening to me? I had to realize struggle was showing me valuable lessons while teaching me to stay humble and grounded. I know it was normal to feel mad or sad because of the challenges I was being faced with, but I had to check myself. Some children are not able to eat or have any clothes or shelter. Some children are too sickly and live part-time in hospitals. Children are fighting for their lives and are slated not to make it. Some people had no one to turn to and left out in the cold, praying for lesser storms. I realize I had a million things to be thankful for in the past and present because my life and situations could worsen. For years now, I've been writing down my reasons to be thankful, so when I have those moments when I need to check myself, I could go and read them. I have a lot that I'm thankful, appreciative, and grateful for in my life. I'm glad my past helped me be more mindful and considerate not to start why's in my present.

Chapter 27

Love From A Distance

Love From A Distance

Everything that grandma Rosie taught us had gone down the drain. Cousins became enemies, competition amongst siblings, and disrespect towards parents was becoming too much to handle. I would sit with my mom asking her what is going on with some of our family members. She would shake her head and say, all we can do is keep praying for them because they have erased what was taught. I remember my family members and I being a unit with us getting together, loving one another, and making granny proud. I knew my granny had to have been looking down in tears, wondering what her family had become. I was hurting because I am family-oriented, but the occurring events made me think twice about it. I loved to get together with family and celebrate birthdays, accomplishments, and have dinners. I enjoyed stopping over at family members' houses, checking on them, chatting for a while, and returning a few days later to do it all over again. I appreciated the hugs, encouragement, and support we gave one another. So I was not prepared for half of the family to continue to be on board while the other half was lost, confused, and thinking someone owes them something.

When I look at my family, I wish granny could come back and set some of them straight or, in granny's words, "make them get their act together." When it becomes a habit that when you are surrounded by individual family members and could cut the air with a knife, you know something is wrong with that picture. I would continuously hear how the family was getting into it over things they couldn't control and telling one another business. When it was brought to me, I would say to the messenger to pray for them. Granny Rosie instilled in us a praying family, and I'm a firm believer that prayer does change things. But I had to strengthen my prayer when a person in the family creating conversations and dilemmas started talking negative things about me. If anyone had a problem with one, granny said to "sit down and talk about it until the problem was resolved." But I started to realize that valuable lessons must've gone out the window too. I have a little cousin named Bianca, who is younger than me that always looked up to me and wanted to be around me. I wanted to keep my eye on her and make sure she was not hanging around the wrong crowds, staying focused in school, and was being herself. When she was younger, I would take her to concerts, to the show, shopping, and out to eat with me. When she wanted advice about guys, I told her what I had learned about them from good and bad experiences. When Bianca didn't understand homework assignments, she would call me, and I would finish mine to walk her through it. Bianca is also the only child, so I could understand her wanting to be around someone other than her parents. But when she got into her teenage years, and I had moved across town, we started to become a little distant. I would always tell her that I would stop by, get her, and continue to be present in her life. Bianca would come over to my house; ask if she could be around me for a little while longer, up until she started hanging in the wrong crowd. The girls she was hanging with were older than her, full of drama, and didn't have their minds set to the right things such as education. Bianca started failing in her classes, talking back to her teachers, and even started ditching school. Her mother called me and asked if I would come and talk with her. I came over to their house and expressed to Bianca my concerns. The little girl's hair I used to comb was standing in the mirror, putting lipstick on, and eyeliner. I was hoping I had walked into the wrong house. Bianca said to me, "big cousin, I know what you are saying, but school isn't it right now." I had to catch a breather and call up the disciplinarian of the family who happens to be my mother. Every aunt and uncle called my mother when their children were unreasonable. My mother didn't and still don't care if you're a teenager or adult; she would fix your attitude and train of thought before you could think about saying what Bianca had said to me. After expressing to my mother what was going on; I heard a knock at the door. I said to myself this can't be real, opening the door, with my mother being on the other side of it. She walked past me, asking for Bianca. Bianca had heard my mother's voice and ran to the bathroom, closing the door fast and locking it. She stood outside the bathroom door, talking to Bianca about fixing her mindset, letting go of those so-called friends, and making sure she washed the makeup off her face. My mom told her she needed to be less focused on what a friend is doing and more focused on her books. My mother slammed her hand on the door, and you could hear Bianca scream as if my mother was in the bathroom with her. Bianca had got her act together after that. I hadn't got any calls from my aunt about Bianca going down the wrong road, so I was happy. But I was worried because Bianca would normally call me at least once a week to keep me updated on how things were going. I decided to drive to see her, arriving at my aunt's house, but she wasn't at home. I asked my aunt if she knew where Bianca was with my aunt telling me Bianca had said she was going outside with some friends. I was hoping it wasn't the same friends she was just warned about, but something told me it was. I walked to Bianca neighborhood park, passing familiar faces and exchanging hellos. I had bumped into Bianca's best friend as a toddler, who informed me that she had just seen Bianca walking to the store. I kept walking through the playground, in the direction towards the store, and ended up running into one of my friends who had told me they heard Bianca was fighting. After yelling at my friend, asking why he didn't call me to tell me, he took me to where Bianca was with her not being far from the park. When I got closer, I noticed that Bianca was surrounded by many girls who were holding golf clubs, bats, and socks, which I knew from seeing previous fights contained a can in it. I noticed one of the girls surrounding her was someone I had gone to elementary school with, so I yelled out Cheryl's name with her turning around screaming to the others to stop. Bianca was shaking, crying, and barely dressed. She had on a short black skirt, black heels, and a tank top that had been partially ripped off. I told my friend to grab Bianca, wrap his coat around her, and started walking back to Bianca's house. As they walked off, I yelled that I would catch up with them. I looked at Cheryl as she looked towards her girls, waiting to be told what was going on. Everyone knew Bianca was my little cousin, but it was the clarification I needed to know that Bianca was truly hanging around the wrong crowd. Cheryl and her girls were shocked to see me as much as I was shocked to see them because it had been awhile. Cheryl started telling me how she found out from one of Bianca's friends that Bianca was intimate with Cheryl's boyfriend. I ended up cutting Cheryl off in mid sentence, screaming, "dude is twenty-three, and she is only sixteen." Cheryl smacked her lips and went on to say, "No disrespect Martina but Bianca lucky you saved her life." I was thinking the same thing and was glad I had got there fast enough because there was no telling what more would have happened to Bianca. I knew Cheryl and her crews were known to put females in the hospital. I walked away from them, wondering what Bianca was thinking. As I walked back to Bianca's house, people started running up to me, telling me that her friends ran from the scene. I was upset, angry, and ready to call my mother. When I made it to my auntie's door, I noticed my aunt was hysterical. She asked Bianca why she had on that type of clothing, where the clothes came from, who hit her in the face, and why she had a bloody nose. I stood there staring at Bianca while she tried to turn her face from her mother, who was trying to wipe Bianca's face with a towel. Bianca stood there, looking as if she was big and bad. My friend tapped me on the shoulder and told me he would call me later; I told him I appreciate him bringing her home. When I closed the door after letting him out, I turned around, and I couldn't help but ask Bianca what she was thinking. She shouted out, "everyone can't be like you and your sisters." I was caught off guard by her response. I was about to ask her what she meant until what Cheryl revealed to me popped into my head about Bianca being intimate with a grown man. I had to tell my aunt it was the best thing to do so she could go and get her checked out at the hospital. It seemed like everything I was talking to Bianca about when it came to waiting for intimacy, guys, loving who she was, and real friends; she ignored. I told my aunt what I didn't want to tell her, with Bianca turning to me saying she hated me, she stormed to the back afterward. I was glad I had told her mom because she found out that she had a sexually transmitted disease when she took her to the doctor. My aunt called me to tell me, and I was thankful that she could get rid of it by taking medicine.

After her doctor's appointment, Bianca didn't want anything to do with me, stopped returning my calls, and tried to stay away from me at family functions as much as possible. It stung a bit because I was used to friends turning their back on me but not my own family. I started hearing that she was telling people I was stuck up, hated her, and was always trying to mess her life up. I tried to reach out to her to talk about what I was hearing, but she still didn't want anything to do with me. I knew her wanting to cut off all contact with me was because I told my aunt that she was sexually active. I would've thought she understood that I was thinking about her safety and wanted to make sure she was physically alright. It was shocking seeing her being in the middle of a bunch of older girls who were ready to tear her apart, and if I didn't come over, then what? It wasn't like I stayed on the same side of town as her anymore, so I wouldn't be able to get to her quick enough to save her from any other situations that I hope wouldn't come up.

Still today, my aunt thanks me for telling her even though I felt hesitant about doing so. And I still don't regret telling her because I saved Bianca from dealing with those types of situations for a lot longer. When Bianca turned 18, she started to hang out with another family member, Yana, who was close to me as well. Yana was the messenger who brought things Bianca was saying to my attention. We had enough family member rivalries going on, so I didn't understand what Bianca had against me. She had been holding the grudge of me telling my aunt about her situation for too long. Some girls were around her age; she started to become friends with them, who told her they looked up to me. Yana told me that Bianca was saying to them I was a bad influence, so they better be careful. Bianca was spreading lies and telling Yana things that Yana knew weren't true. She even told Yana to stop coming around me, or their relationship would be through.

From the time Bianca cut me out of her life through 18, she had begun to spiral out of control. My aunt didn't know what way to discipline her, and Bianca became aggressive towards my aunt. Being the family that we were and willing to help out, my mom decided to go over to my aunt's house to do daily checkups. From my mother's presence, in the fear she could give someone through words, Bianca got herself together then fell back down the wrong path. I felt bad for her, but I did not appreciate that Bianca was trying to defame my character. It was a good thing that the girls and their parents knew me well enough not to believe any of it. But I was starting to get more disturbed by Bianca's lies and rumors. Yana pulled out her phone and showed me a text message from Bianca, bashing me as if we weren't even family. The way she talked, by calling me foul names and wishing bad things towards me, you would've thought I had betrayed her or something. I gave Yana back her phone because I couldn't look at the messages anymore. I started saying out loud, "what did I do wrong?" I was a good, supportive, and loving cousin who feared for my little cousin's lifestyle. Yana told me I didn't do anything wrong and that it was right for me to look out for Bianca.

After hearing and seeing Bianca's malicious acts, I decided it was time for me to stop trying to reach out. I contemplated what was best to do because I remember granny Rosie always saying, be there for your family. I was hoping I wouldn't upset my granny with my decision to leave Bianca's lifestyle in her own hands. But I couldn't take my name continuously being dragged through the mud or the lies she would tell. Bianca was not aware of what Cheryl had told me, and I guess she hoped I had never found out. I felt it was best to look out for her health, well-being, and safety. I blame myself for a long time because Bianca didn't want anything else to do with me. "I should've kept my mouth shut," I would say, but then where would that leave me? I would have felt guilty if something awful happens to her, with her being sixteen and engaging in intimate activities. Not to mention how disturbed I was about finding out she was messing around with a grown man. If Bianca was going to continue to ignore me or dislike me for telling on her, then that was something I would have to accept. I remember my mother waking me up late one night to tell me my aunt had called. I knew it was late, and I started freaking out. She said they couldn't find Bianca and had been out looking for her for a while. I told my mom to let my aunt know I would make a few calls to see if anyone knew her whereabouts. That night was when being sweet to others came in handy because when I made the calls to a few people, they helped me track her down. When I was calling people, it had spread to Bianca that I was looking for her. By the time her mom had got to the house she was supposedly at, Bianca was gone. I prayed and prayed that night, hoping Bianca's whereabouts would come up. I got a call telling me where she was, and the person told me that everyone would make sure she didn't leave. I called my aunt back, gave her the address, and let her know the people Bianca was with will keep her there until she arrives. About thirty minutes later, my aunt called my mom to tell her they got her, with Bianca in the background screaming, "why Martina won't just leave me alone." Any other day I probably would've responded to what she had to say, but I was glad that she was safe and left it at that. I didn't try to call Bianca because I knew it wasn't what she wanted, but if my aunt ever needed anything else, I was going to jump right to it. Bianca was scaring everyone, and I felt like she didn't seem to care. My aunt decided to send her away, out of the state, with a few relatives for a while. Bianca needed to be taking away from people and things she was used to. I would call the relatives she was with to check on her to see how she was doing, and they would tell me "better than ever." My aunt's next decision I wish she hadn't made. My aunt went to get Bianca, with her being good for a few weeks, and then she was back to her old ways. My aunt said she was missing her but then started to regret going to get her. The only thing we could do was be there for my auntie when a few family members talked about the bad decision she made of bringing Bianca back. My mother would tell her to ignore what others were saying and focus on getting Bianca the guidance she needed. My aunt reached out to me to see if I would be up for talking with Bianca since I could get through her before. I knew Bianca was still feeling the same way towards me because the rumors and lies started back up again. I told my aunt that I think it was time for Bianca to seek therapy. I was seeing a good therapist, Mrs. Cruz, for a while who was helping me cope through the grief of my granny and Shad. I gave my aunt my therapist information and told her to tell Mrs. Cruz I referred them to her. My aunt said thank you and stated that she wishes her child was like my mother's children. It brought me back to when Bianca commented that she was not like my sisters and me. I said to my aunt," Bianca was her own person and just needed professional guidance." My aunt agreed with me, and when I hung up from her, I decided to have a moment to myself to reflect. I wanted nothing but the best for Bianca and hoped Mrs. Cruz would help her head in the right direction.

Today, Bianca is still out of control as a young adult, but I continue to pray for her. When she sees me now at family functions, she stares or rolls her eyes. And although she does that, I still, out of my love for family, find it in me to say hello to her. While other family members had mended their differences, which were more serious than what Bianca was holding against me. They were able to reconnect with granny values and remember the definition of what a loving family means. I couldn't help but feel a little upset because Bianca wasn't trying to work stuff out. I held granny values close to my heart and just wanted to go back to the way things were. I had to realize family or not; I couldn't live my life worrying and being concerned about who liked me or not. I still love Bianca, because she is my family, but I have learned to love her from a distance. I had a few misunderstandings with relatives from the other side of my family as well.

On the other side of the family, I haven't been close with Tara, Geneva, or anyone else; other than a male cousin of mine whose upbringing my mother was involved in. A bond has never been fully established because of the different ways, revolving around issues and opinions, of one understanding what a family represents. Paying attention to both sides of my family I realized how traditions, morals, and values were viewed differently. So I took in a better appreciation, acceptance, and bond with my mother's side because things were handled better. Although there are times I have wished situations were easier to cope with I know the way things are is healthier for everyone involved. But if I was ever out and ran into the other side I was cordial, respectful, and said my hellos. They did the same in return although things were not right behind closed doors from assumptions, stare-downs, and opinions always taking over. I didn't feel comfortable being around negative energy, not knowing who I could turn to, trust, or lean on. Especially when Tara assumed I didn't come around, thinking I was ashamed of them, because our life paths weren't similar. That was never the case because I know how to be mindful and respectful of one struggle. And I loved my family for who they were regardless of what anyone was going through. I remember Tara's little sister, Geneva, joining the talent show I was in and she was a part of a few dances with kids her age. The kids in the talent show had their attire to go purchase from a list of things the dance instructor wanted. The attire is related to the theme of color for the performance. For that year's talent show the theme of color was black jogging pants, with a hot pink shirt, and black shoes. Everyone had to have the colors on except for anyone coming in to perform who weren't attendees of the gymnasium. I remember Tara's mom having a lot going on and had a hard time getting Geneva her attire for the two-day show. One day their mother approached me after practice and asked if I would be able to help Geneva out. I was very good at saving allowances, worked summer jobs as a teenager, so I knew I had savings to help out. I asked for her clothing size and shoe size so I could purchase her stuff when I went to purchase mines. Tara and Geneva's mom asked why I couldn't give her the money so she could go purchase it on her own time. I thought about the times when my aunts and uncles would loan her money with her spending it on unnecessary things instead of taking care of what was most important. So I responded nicely "it's okay, I'm going to get mine so I will get hers too". Their mom gave me this look as if I said something that offended her. She responded, "you know what you are too much; I don't need your help". Then stormed off telling Geneva she wasn't going to be able to dance. I felt bad for Geneva for her mom acting like that so I went home and thought about what had happened. I didn't say anything out of place so I decided I should try to reach back out again. When I reached back out to Tara and Geneva's mom she ignored all of my calls and told the other side of the family how cruel she thought I was. I was hurt by this and didn't understand why she would go around telling people I was selfish and cold-hearted. I have always been a selfless individual with a kind heart so I didn't know where she was getting that from and I didn't appreciate the made-up story she told everyone as if I was disrespectful towards her. I was raised to be humble about the little things in life and for what I have. And I was also raised to look out for the ones I loved when I could. I decided to vent to my mom and I came to the decision that I couldn't do anything about it. It hurt badly to come to that decision because I could see in Geneva's eyes that she wanted me to help. But to stop any misunderstandings I decided to leave it alone. When the talent show came Geneva showed up with shrunken pants, not so clean shoes, with her hair all over her head. I looked at her mother, wanting to say something, but decided I was going to keep my comments and frustration to myself. It wasn't my position to approach an adult to say what was on my mind if it wasn't respectful. I was taught "if I didn't have anything nice to say then don't say it at all". I stared at Geneva, a little longer at her mom, and walked off. I had to watch people point fingers, make fun of, and laugh at Geneva all night. Even adults were discussing how they thought she looked like a "crazy child". When people saw me looking at them, and knew we were related, they would mouth the words "I'm sorry" and stop talking. I could tell, in Geneva, a little pretty round face, that she wasn't happy. Geneva ended up telling the dance instructor that she would rather sit out for the next two performances.

The misunderstanding I had with their mother was one of many reasons why it was hard to bond with that side. And what I'm about to reveal next is one of the main reasons that I decided to love a lot of family members from a distance. Tara had a crush on Shad and when she was told that we were an item her words were "he could do better". I could've approached her to see if what she had said was true but the above text message that she had sent to another cousin, Lushun, confirmed it for me. The text messages totaled to about six texts and went into detail about how she infatuated herself over him, what she disliked about me, and how she could prove to him that she would be a better choice. I remember handing Lushun back her phone telling her to tell Tara to give me a call. Having a crush was one thing but the bashing about me was not right. I didn't care that we weren't close but I had always respected her and felt like I deserved the same in return. Do you ever realize that when a person doesn't know you on a personal or communication level they start making up their assumption? The assumptions could be their imagination or things they feel like would get you worked up to the point of confrontation. Lushun didn't inform Tara that I wanted to talk with her. I didn't know if she did it because she had shown me evidence or she also had things to say that she would not like if I found out.

My cousin, Germaine, whose upbringing my mom was involved in was somewhat distant from that side of the family; but attended enough events to where I knew he could get me in contact with Tara. I gave Germaine a call and he quickly gave me Tara's number. Before getting off the phone with him he said "what are those girls up to now" and I said "we're going to find out" me hanging up letting him know I would keep him updated. I called Tara with her quickly answering the phone. She must've been waiting on a call, the reason she answered so fast because she never had my number. When I stated who I was she said "oh lord" as if she knew why I was calling. Our conversation was brief and she didn't deny saying the things I read in her messages. She also informed me that Lushun had things to say as well which I had already had a feeling about because of the way Lushun reacted. I decided I would handle approaching Lushun at a later time since Tara was the one who had the issue. I wanted to know why Tara said things about me that weren't true so I asked her before ending the call. Tara responded "I just don't like you" then hung up. I had to take a moment to do a mental, emotional, and physical inspection of myself. I even tried thinking back to conversations I would randomly have if I bumped into Tara or anyone else. I never came off hurtful, untrustworthy, or harmful so why was there always a problem someone had with me. When it was family members against you it hurt twice as much but I couldn't see myself trying to do what I did with Bianca, by reaching out, because it was clear the problem would not be resolved. It was also obvious Tara didn't want anything to do with me from how quickly she ended the call. A few days after Tara hung up on me I remember walking to the store with Shad and we happened to cross the street at the same time as Tara and Lushun. We were going in different directions but our eyes met for a few seconds. Tara looked at Shad and rolled her eyes but she didn't look my way. Lushun's face continued to stare straight ahead towards the playground as Tara continued to mumble under her breath. When Shad and I stepped into the store I asked Shad did he know Tara. He said that he knew Tara was seeing one of his friends, Mitchell, who was off and on with his actual girlfriend. Shad started to tell me about Tara and Blake's girlfriend exchanging words a lot with one another but they never let them fight. Blake's off-and-on girlfriend happens to be my childhood friend Tiffany which I found to be crazy because I didn't know that Tara was who Tiffany would vent to me about.

Shad, Tiffany, nor Blake knew Tara was my cousin. I never told them she was and Tara made sure, if you weren't family, you would never know we were related. I asked Shad if she ever came on to him in any type of way. He said, "no and even if she did he knew she was bad news anyway". Shad added, "just like you girls have a guy code when it comes to dating someone your friend is or have been with, being off-limits, us guys have the same code too". I laughed as Shad put his arms around me and said "and what reason I have to deal with her when I have you". I looked at him and said "don't judge my cousin" in a joking way. If you could've seen the way his mouth hung after I said that you would have sworn I had just told him one of his teeth fell out. I didn't realize Tara was standing at the door, staring at us, with a mean mug on her face. She yelled out "I guess what everyone is saying is true, Blake friend is too head over heels for you" then she slammed the door. Shad said "are you sure you two are related because man" with me laughing about it. After the day in the store, Tara never said anything else to me if we by any chance crossed paths. And I was okay with that.

The three situations with family members I've mentioned have made me realize how much time and negative energy one could put into stuff. If negative emotions and confrontations come up I'm one for talking about it, getting to the root of the problem, making amends, forgiving, and going on together or separate. But some people don't want to do that; they don't want to sit down or make up, they just hold on to bad energy or grudges for the rest of their lives. And that only makes you miserable while the other person is living their life. I honestly don't see how a family can be that way towards one another especially with the way things are in today's society. A family member you could be mad at for whatever reason, big or small, could be here today and gone tomorrow. I understand sometimes there are bigger issues that can't be easily fixed or one party just doesn't want to settle differences; then there is nothing you could do about it. All you can do is forgive so you could be freed from it and wish them well. I see a lot of people go through things with their family that's worse than I had to experience and it ends up resulting in fistfights, revealing secrets, and bashing one another on social media. If my grandma Rosie was here today how she would feel if someone in my family did that. I feel like the only time families around the world come together as one is for a funeral, a crisis, or holidays. The way I was raised to see the family is being able to come around one another at any given time and be able to feel a bond, connection, and love in the air. I know some people who are not close to their own family but they see their co-workers, boyfriend or girlfriend, and friends' family as their own. And I want to say whatever works for you is beautiful because family comes in different forms. We all see family in our way but as long as how we define it is positive that's what matters.

I have recently seen Bianca at a cousin of ours gathering and we shared a moment of laughter. Have we been able to reconnect after that moment? Unfortunately, we haven't. But I will hold the door of opportunity open until she is ready because, at the end of the day, we will always be family. I continue my daily check-in with Bianca's mother to make sure Bianca is safe, breathing, and living. My aunt keeps me informed about Bianca still having a lot going on but I keep her in my prayers and pray that one day soon she will get better. Tara and Geneva's mom runs into my mother a lot and asks how my sisters and I are doing. She tells my mom to send her hellos and well wishes. Geneva is eighteen now and has grown into a beautiful young lady from pictures I've seen. Recently I attended a family member funeral with Geneva walking up to me hugging me. She whispered in my ear "I'm sorry how I treated you" then sat back down next to her mom. I never had a problem with Geneva not even during talent show days. But I understood that she said sorry because she realized her mother's actions were wrong. Tara still doesn't speak or hold conversations with me. When I saw Tara at the same funeral she stared and then walked past me. It was then that I realized every situation will not have a good outcome or beautiful ending. But I had forgiven each person a long time ago so my heart has been cleared of anger.

My grandma Rosie would be proud of her Common Family if she could see how we stick together. Even individuals in my family who may have issues with one another, while staying on opposite sides of the room from each other, manage to bring love, fun, and memories to events, gatherings, or just random drop-ins. My other side of the family I am still estranged from but over time I've been able to find acceptance in that. I can only adore, love, and appreciate the people who are willing to do the same and meet me halfway. I will forever be family-oriented because there's something about seeing family altogether that makes a big difference in a society where we have moments of being against one another. From all of my experiences within the family, I learned that it's okay to walk away from anything or anyone who was not willing or allowing me to reach out. I could only be responsible for myself and held accountable for what I did whether right or wrong. I couldn't continue to feel bad about someone else's wrongdoing, attitude, and the way they handle things. We had to agree that we are going to love one another through good and bad because that's what a supportive and loving family would do.

Chapter 28

Age Is Just A Number

Age Is Just A Number

"You haven't been here long enough, so how do you know what life struggles are"

There is no age to the curve balls life could throw at you. There are babies from infant to eleven in the hospital dealing with illnesses that some people haven't experienced, witnessed, or heard of someone older having. Some teenagers have had to endure what hunger, fighting to survive, and being homeless feel like, and others have always had a roof over their head and support not too far away. So whose opinion was it to say what someone age defined? I've encountered many things that I wish I didn't, and I'm quite sure the beautiful people I've mentioned above feel the same. Life struggles and lessons don't have an age or time; it just happens.

I remember being in a class full of adults when I first started my college career. The adults' ages were between forty and fifty-five, and there I was a nineteen-year-old sitting in a class with them learning African American History. My professor Fatima was impressed by how I held myself together because my classmates would always say, "you're too young to know what our people went through." I didn't become offended, sad, or mad about what they were saying because I knew, learned, researched, and observed enough to know the reason why we were able to be sitting in the classroom expanding on history with a professor who wasn't even our color. Fatima would ask questions about readings she would give; she wanted us to read for the correct answer and have our own opinion about it. So one day, my classmates decided they would answer first because, in their words, "they lived life a lot longer." Fatima observed them with a face revealing no emotion. She didn't shake her head, interrupt, or say I agree, which left them puzzled. She turned to me, giving me the cue to go ahead—the night before, I had taken the reading selection home and read through it slowly. And if I had any confusion about what I was reading, I would stop to search history books and research videos. When I was done, I wrote down a few key points in a notebook and questions for Fatima. In class, I explained what the selection was raising awareness of and my interpretation of it. I looked at Fatima to see if her face still showed no emotion, and I was surprised to see a smile and her nodding to me. My classmates stared at me, raised their eyebrows, and said, "that was a pretty good interpretation." We had been in class for a month already, and it was the first time they had ever complimented me on a good job. I wasn't looking for any compliments, but it sure did make me feel good, especially how cutthroat they could be at times. Fatima asked me to come up to the front of the class and write on the eraser board. After I was done, she told me to look out at everyone, so my eyes scanned the class viewing older women and men writing in their journals what I was thinking. Fatima went on to say, "this nineteen-year-old actually went home, read the selection carefully, and did more research for better understanding. And she is the only one who answered it correctly".

The faces they made were as if they wanted to take back the compliment given earlier. My classmates didn't read the selection and just went off of the "years they have been living." They weren't able to realize the selection covered the past and present. Fatima told them to take the questions I wrote on the board and do their research to understand better. Class ended with them leaving out, mumbling to one another, saying, "a young lady does know something." I know there are times when young people go through similar situations that I've experienced, and I'm going to tell you a little secret, "don't let it get to you." Regardless of age, background, or race, everyone knows a little something. I worked with an older woman who started having back pains. She couldn't stand for an extended period without having to take breaks sitting down. I was concerned about her because of the symptoms she would tell my coworkers, and it sounded very similar to Scoliosis. After years of having it, I had researched a thing or two about how it could attack elders. I told her to make a doctor's appointment to check on things and ask the doctor to check for a condition called Scoliosis. She wanted to know what it was, and after I explained to her a few things that were happening with me, she said, "girl, your body not going through that; you too young for that." I started to wonder if it was just that some older people who felt like teenagers and young adults' bodies were in better shape didn't believe we couldn't have anything wrong with it. I had wished I didn't have problems with my back because I would still be dancing if I didn't. I could tell she wasn't hearing me, so I left it alone. A week later, she approached me in our break room to say to me, "thank you for informing me about that. I made sure my doctor ran tests to look at it". I smiled and gave her a soft hug while rubbing her back a little. She looked at me and said, "I didn't mean any harm when I said that silly stuff to you." Two weeks later, she came into the break room again to tell me her results were in and that she found out that she does have a mild case of Scoliosis. She said, "my doctor told me to thank you for making me aware of it and that yes, it is a condition a child could have." I informed my co-worker on things that help me when my back has its moments of feeling bad. I told her when her back acts up to take bubble baths, get massages, and use extra pillows when resting. I left the break room, telling her to take care as she yelled out another thank you. In my sophomore year in college, I wanted to start seeing a therapist on campus, and I remember registering for it. My therapist asked if I wanted to sit in on a group meeting about getting through depression and grief. Since I was trying to turn things around in my life for the better, I agreed to attend. I was a twenty-year-old walking inside the group area, sensing confusion. The group of individuals was twice my age. When my therapist first introduced me, they asked her, "Is she your daughter?" I knew then I was in for a rude awakening. That old soul of mine started speaking, saying, "you got this." I turned my attention to the plants sitting near windows around the room, which I learned from my mother signified peace for people going through things. The door opens, and I was relieved to see a guy my age, who I knew from a few of my classes, walk-in as I took a seat. My therapist told everyone to introduce themselves, state why they were there, and what they hope to get out of group therapy. The adults didn't respond while the guy and I looked at each other. One woman expressed that she didn't feel right talking about her business in front of kids, while the others co-signed on what she said. I could see the guy getting ready to get up to leave as my therapist told him to sit back down. She yelled, "Everyone is here for the same reasons, just different experiences. And if you want help, then talk; if not, there's the door" I could tell my therapist was agitated by the woman's remark the way her nose turned red, and her forehead wrinkled up. I decided to start by saying my information, and as I talked, others chimed in saying, "I know the pain" or "girl, I've been there." This was coming from the same ones who wanted the guy and me out of there. Everyone started to express why they were there with my therapist getting up to pass out brochures. The brochures showed two people shaking hands with the quote "together we stand" printed at the top of the brochure in bold letters. The tension left the room, and everyone forgot what age the guy and I were. We were just a room full of people trying to receive help, get support, and listen to one another. After the group session ended, we talked with the woman coming up to the guy and me to apologize for what she said. The guy and I looked at one another, then back at the lady and said, "no hard feelings." We couldn't wait to return the following week and continue our journey of listening and expressing the pain we were trying to overcome. In group therapy, I learned never to judge a person by age because everyone is going through something. When I'm asked randomly, "what have you been through," I tell a person: life. Even when we don't want to realize that we could learn something younger or older, reality always comes to us. One of my friend's children lived in the ICU for the first couple of months of her life. When I went to see her, I was afraid because I walked past more babies, just like her, battling for survival. It took me to a moment where I would complain about not feeling good; then I realized these babies can't take care of themselves as I could. My friend's daughter was resting in the machine, and I watched her little fingers snatch at the cords that were applied to her. She kept pulling, pulling until she heard her mom's voice. I watched her calm down, and when her mom stopped talking, she was at the cords again. In the present, she's older, beautiful, full of life, and still the fighter she was when she was firstborn. I would never forget that moment.

As an adult, I take moments to remember when people felt and still feel like I haven't lived long enough to have experienced, witnessed, endured, or learned anything. Then I wonder what older people would be saying to her when she got my age. Before even knowing her story, they would be quick to tell her, "You're too young." I picture her showing them pictures and saying, "let me show you my testimony," with them being silent. That's how people are when I show them pictures of the days when I was sick or I tell them the stories of the reason why some days I felt like giving up. They get silent and want to take back the words of "you are too young." All the time people say to me they apologize, they hope I'm not offended, or girl you have been through it. Even today, I still don't let others' opinions about my life and the trials I've experienced deter me from expressing myself. I learned a lot over the years by observing how people view, see, and assume things. Age to me is just that: an age. Every birthday I am thankful to turn another age for a chapter of more to this here life. I want you to know never to let someone think they could tell you your life for you; because only you walked the ages and miles in your shoes.

Chapter 29

Found My Way

Found My Way

I'm spiritually, emotionally, and mentally blessed. I can shout and say, I'm blessed. I am blessed to be still living, pushing forward, dreaming, releasing, and the blessing of all being a mother to my miracle son. I want to repeat it: I am blessed. Being blessed has nothing to do with material things or what someone can do for you. Being blessed has everything to do with being able to wake up. I'm going to repeat that being blessed has everything to do with waking up and being able to start a new chapter, journey, dream, and purpose. So I do it. I spend less time worrying about yesterday while I prepare for my present and future.

I humble myself more when I see all the heartache taking over the world. I stand in the mirror more because I realize that I am beautiful. I appreciate my mother even more because I'm a parent now, and I understand, respect, and cherish, all the sacrifices she has made to pave the way for my sisters and me. I hug my two sisters a little tighter now because I appreciate their friendship and sisterhood. I laugh a little more now because laughter does soothe the soul. I do all of these things that might not seem like much to others but means everything to me. I just read my first short essay from when I was six years old. The topic of the article was, what do I want to be when I grow up? I read my answer now with emotion because I set out to do what I said as a little girl I wanted to be, becoming a writer and an author. I remember people saying, "your dream would change," and I would tell them, "no, it won't; I know what I want to be." And here I am living proof of it. When I was six, I didn't know what path I would have to travel to get here, but I knew what I wanted, and I wasn't going to let anything stop me from getting here. I remember when I slipped on something in my first-grade school lunchroom in the Cafeteria and had to be on crutches for two weeks. I thought my life was over. I had to modify how I got dressed, bathe myself, and navigate through school or home. I didn't realize that was how life was going to be: a navigation system. But good or bad, I had to find a way to navigate through it.

Like how I felt back then, I've experienced that same feeling about my life being over. But I'm here. Sometimes I look back and think about all of the articles I read that said children from the projects were not going to amount to anything. Children from the projects were going to drop out of school and be on the streets. Children from the projects had no drive, dedication, and determination in them. And you know what I say now; speak for yourself. The statistics I would read fueled me to work hard because I knew I could as long as I put my mind to it. I was determined to surpass the negative comments that others were stamping on children from the projects. I let my being born and raised in the projects guide me to becoming a smarter person. And since I used to hear the negative remarks about being from the projects, I decided to give people something positive. I wanted to encourage people to reach for their dreams and know they could. And what I'm about to say is taken from a living example. When I'm in a room with people and everyone is talking about where they come from, I get excited. I get excited because I'm waiting on my turn to reveal to them my start in life. I start by saying I was raised near the gold coast area while watching their eyes light up. They ask in Lincoln Park? I say not too far from it while they wait to hear more. Soon I find the conversation turning into a road map being looked at for a destination. They'll keep asking until they get closer to the landmark where I reveal where I'm from Cabrini Green. The room goes quiet while they wait for me to say I'm joking. But I don't. I could see in their eyes they are trying to figure out how am I even in a room with them celebrating college life's successes. They wonder how I talk with so much manners, professionalism, and respect. They wonder how I can share a secret with them that some would keep hidden forever. I wasn't ashamed, and I would never be because I learned that no matter where you are from, the door to making yourself a better person and creating a life you love was opened to everyone. All you needed was to reveal the drive to do what people think is impossible for you.

On a more emotional note, those who feel like they can't go on after someone's passing, take your time. Take your time to feel anger, frustration, and sadness. You need that time to release your stresses, fears, and anxiety. It took years before I was better able to cope with losing my grandmother and Shad. And after a while, my coping got better because I didn't rush it. What has always helped me is writing letters to them and then going out to the cemetery to read them. The letters can be about anything from how you were feeling, a pet you just bought, accomplishment, and a type of food just ate, or something you didn't get a chance to tell them. If you are a little stronger, try going out there alone, and you would feel just how close you are to them. If it's still hard for you to go alone, take someone you trust who would be able to comfort you when it gets hard. My time at the cemetery on random days, holidays, and birthdays has helped guide me through grieving better. If someone tells you, "it's been a long time you should be better," or if you were in a relationship with someone and people say "move on, it's time." Don't listen. No one can force the grieving process because when you try to, destruction within yourself can happen. Take it a day at a time, and then you will realize how the weight gets a little more bearable as the years go on. Pray on it. The signs I received and the strength in me to move on doubled when I prayed on it. And in my time, I took steps to move from it. Yes, it is normal to have doubts and say, "I don't think I could be without them." I had moments like that all the time, but I knew I deserved better in the back of my mind. Until I realized I deserved better, I continued to cry, be deceived, lied to, and cheated on. I wanted my sense of worth back, and I did everything possible, with time, to get it. If you are a person who observes every moment, feeling, and though I know you have times when you're thinking about if the friends you have are worth being around. I spent years questioning that and years receiving the answers to it. I cherish the real friends I have now and thank myself for finally letting go of those who weren't. I knew friends would be there through thick and thin, not leave you when things get harder. So I'm glad I took time and reflected on the decisions I made for a healthier start. There are many things I could say I learned so far in life, but one that sticks out is to always go for a second opinion with anything that could be critical to your physical and mental existence. I'm sure you know where I'm going with this, so when you receive news that you have an illness after numerous tests, check for another opinion. See a different doctor for another set of results, then make the changes needed. I want to see more people getting through health issues and fewer people sitting around wondering what's wrong. When you get the moment of relief from finding out the reason for a situation, the solution is not too far behind. Please make sure you have people in your life from family to supportive mates and good listeners who won't leave if things get worse. As I say to myself all the time, when I fell, who was there to lift me is what matters.

I want you to do one thing for me right now; put the book down, and look in the mirror. Say out loud "I am handsome" or "I am beautiful" and then smile. I want you to keep repeating it and remembering you are a unique gift given to this world; don't let anyone make you feel different. If someone is complaining to you about the way you dress, act, look, or how you style your hair, and it makes you feel low on the inside, they don't deserve you. When a few of your flaws are revealed, big or small, and they make rude comments or demand you change, they don't deserve you. We live in a world where even the people who seem to be perfect on the televisions screens are also carrying flaws we know nothing about. But we wish we had their hair, style, career, and happiness without knowing what's under the surface and how they got there. You can be one thing to the world but see yourself differently, either good or bad. I remember feeling like I was being forced to look like, dress, act, or wear my hair the way people wanted just to be accepted. I sat down and realized that if I changed myself to accommodate someone else, I'm not accepted. When you accept yourself, you love yourself for who you are and expect others to do the same. And if they are trying to fix their mouths to make you into what they want you to be, take a moment, and look in the mirror and say you deserve better. Only you can build the confidence, strength, and understanding inside to know you are human; you will have flaws, but you are you. Remember that.

One thing that was and still is a work in progress for me is learning how not to blame myself for someone else's decisions or actions. The friend who crossed me would say maybe if I were around more, our friendship deteriorating wouldn't have happened. The relationship that went sour because of how I was treated, I would say maybe if I did more of what he wanted, we still would be together. The job I worked so hard to get but ended up having to leave because higher-ups didn't understand my situation at hand; I would say maybe if I would've stayed, they could've taken the time to work with me. I played the blame game through many situations out of my control, but I realized it wasn't my fault. I can't control what someone does; I could only worry and control how I react and learn from it. I had to stop taking ownership of someone else's issues because that freed them from dealing with them. I've noticed when I free myself from the guilt of what's done by others; I relieve myself of a lot of stress. Unfortunately, situations that have happened in my life, such as scamming, have made me become an alert person in the present. I'm mindful of things I purchase, get involved in, and read thoroughly over contracts. Even being a victim of burglary has made me more aware of everything and everyone around me. I know some things we aren't able to control, such as burglary, but it gives us another reason to be thankful for security measures that can be taken. I just ran into one of my former classmates that attended the inspirational class with me at Columbia that revolved around an altar, and we caught up on how we are dealing with things in the present. For the most part, we both are finally coming into our sense of peace inside from our past, and we exchanged numbers so we could keep in contact. It's something about seeing a person down and then seeing them up that shows we can get through our most trying times. It just takes us opening up our hearts to receive the support that's needed to guide us.

I dislike watching the news and seeing youth being killed. I continue to pray that violence will decrease and unity will increase. I know a guy who is a role model to a few teenage boys from his old neighborhood. I remember him telling me how in his old neighborhood, you would be lucky if you saw the front porch or the age of sixteen. When he told me the different experiences he witnessed from crossfire and friends lying in the middle of the street, I couldn't do anything but cry. My friend is a thirty-year-old, in his career, and being a role model to the generations of now. I watch him in action, trying to guide, mold, and lift the boys' spirits who want out of the lifestyle they encountered. And when I ask the boys what made them change their life around, they look at me, smile, and say, "wanting to live for a long time." If you are in situations or locations where you feel like there is no way out, research boys and girls centers, volunteers who have changed their lives around, could guide you on a new path, and reach out to good teachers. Some beautiful teachers treat their students as if they are their own. Teachers who have no problem staying after school with you to help with homework, taking you home, or getting you to help with personal problems.

In third grade, I knew a girl, Lonnie, who was having a hard time at home. She never slept, barely ate, and had turned to sell drugs for family members to try to make a living for her sister and mom. I would bring her things to eat in the morning at school and ask my mom if it was okay to give away clothes or shoes we couldn't fit for Lonnie and her sister. Lonnie would always cry when she saw my mom and me bringing bags to her house as she fell into my arms, saying thank you. When she felt very sad during times in school, she would confide in me, as I wiped her tears, with her emotions catching my teacher, Ms. Cain, attention.

One day we headed home from school, and Ms. Cain stopped us before we walked out of the school building. She asked Lonnie if she could talk with her, wanting me to come along. We went back into the school, inside a conference room, overwhelmed by the clothes, shoes, and food sitting on top of tables. There was a card in the center of one table that read Lonnie's name. Lonnie started crying, and I did too while Ms. Cain's adult children continued to come in with more things. My teacher was always a sweetheart who wanted us to succeed, but she also wanted her students to be happy. Lonnie fell into our teacher's arms sobbing with tears of joy, and Ms. Cain told her to promise that she would stop selling drugs. Thankfully Lonnie kept her promise, and in return, my teacher helped pay rent at Lonnie's home for an entire year. She also helped Lonnie's mom get a job at a local restaurant. Someone is willing to help, and you would be surprised by who is observing your pain. But it's all about reaching out and wanting the positive help that comes. I pray more people will understand that there is so much more in the world to turn to when you struggle instead of your corner streets. You could travel and learn so much about people, things, or possible careers to get you to where you're destined to be. I've seen lawyers, doctors, sports players, actors, and entertainers talk about how they have changed their life around, but I believe only a certain amount of youth is taking in the message they are trying to get out. I want to see more people becoming something and knowing that they could get there if they grind. Grind starts with you being willing to work towards a better life and position for you instead of crime. Today, I take a moment to reflect on everything. And I can tell you getting to where you want to be or are can result in a little struggle. The struggle has awakened my identity, passion, and drive with people looking at me crazy because I say, "I wouldn't want to change the struggle I went through to get to where I am now." I would have loved to go through life just happy, but then I wouldn't be as appreciative as I am when I know things being shaken up helped me realize my direction. Many people didn't believe I could rise again after tragic situations, and at one time, I didn't think I could either. But I always had that hidden strength in saying, "get back up and try it again." I didn't want to live my life full of "what if's" because I knew it wouldn't lead me on the path I have always dreamed about since a little kid. I look at my son and realize I used to be just like him; alive, alert, excited, and full of happiness. I wasn't thinking about becoming older; I enjoyed living freely where I was fed bottles, catered to, and loved on. I think about my son taking his first walks, and I envision how scary that was. When I watch babies try to walk, I see them stumble and get back up to try it again. They work on it daily until they can walk everywhere. I define that as how I've lived my life by taking a few walks, stumbling, getting back up, and continuing. I want you to try to do that the next time any situation occurs with a mantra saying, "I'm a keep on moving on." I look around me at family members who are a little off the path, and I want to help them, but they are quick to say, "I don't need any help." Since I'm doing what I love to do and am very grateful for it, they feel like I come off as if I'm better than somebody. Remember how I talked about not letting what others are saying get to you, especially when it's not true. I've taken my advice and put it to good use. That's why it's safe to love those who think and assume things like that from a distance. Think about the people you have in your life. Next, please draw a line down a piece of paper with each side reading season or lifetime. We never realize how much the energy from others could positively or negatively affect our personal growth. When you are finished writing, people from family, friends, co-workers, and significant others sit back to meditate on your next action. I did this same technique in the past and present, realizing a few people I was still trying to hold hands with that didn't serve a good purpose. I had wondered why I was still feeling weird around them, noticing their attitude switches, and witnessing bad energy. I took what I found through meditation, internal thinking, and gradually began to move forward without them. I hope the technique works out for you because it can help you get to new stages in life without having to worry about who is down for you or there to just take from you. Take your time writing down the seasons and lifetimes so you can see clearly how to change the atmosphere around you. My life changed in many ways with the most important change being when I became a mother. I've made sacrifices, changed my decision-making, and developed a better understanding of my responsibility, role, and purpose as a parent. I also love on a level that I didn't know existed until I became a mother. I also realize how much of a multitasked individual I've turned into when balancing motherhood and my dreams. I want you to understand if you have children and believe you can't accomplish your dreams pray about it. Pray that you can take time while your children are sleeping and research your interests. If you're at work at break time do a little more digging. And when you feel a little discouraged look at your beautiful children and realize you are doing it for you and them. I go to my goal book every night after I put my son to sleep and I start writing more things I would like to conquer. Then I look over goals with a smile, big or small, that I have accomplished. Each day we can accomplish something if we stop putting it off. Let this moment be yours to think about your future. I realize every day I'm given to breathe, laugh, smile, talk, learn, and spend time with my son is a gift and I won't take advantage of it. I also spend my days being thankful that mentally and spiritually I'm in a better place than I was a few years ago. Past experiences have helped mold me into the woman I am and made me realize I didn't know my strength. "I'm not going to make it through" doesn't exist in my vocabulary any longer because I have myself and a child to live for. Yes, I could've easily let all the storms that came my way, snatch me up, and take me away but my faith and power of prayer wouldn't let me. I've been at the bottom and the road to get up and stay up has not been an easy one but with time it's doable. You see the world differently when you are at rock bottom and I wouldn't wish that type of pain on anyone. I found out who loved me and I realized who never did. I experienced how far I could go and realize it was going to take time to get there. I found out releasing tears is a way to cleanse your soul. And I found out that when I loved myself a little more my spirit had grown. I'm spending my days being a lot more grateful for my health, son, and loved ones. And I take time out to tune into my present because right now is the only moment that I'm promised. I take so much pride in knowing that in the present I'm continuing my path of working on forgiveness. Forgiveness is the hardest thing for any of us to do but it's what's needed so no one could hold the power of you. There are people in my past that took a part of me when they left; leaving me feeling alone, done wrong, wanting to scream, and taking my anger out on everyone. But then I realized how much I deserved to live a life I love. I've forgiven so that I could free myself of the things that were pulling me back from exploring better areas of my life and within myself. I recently took out the keepsake boxes that remind me of where I've been, the people I've encountered, as well as memories. I remember I used to be angry when I looked inside at pictures and cards with the faces of people who once played a major part in my life. Now I can glance through them with a smile and be thankful for the lessons I was taught. But when I got to the keepsake box of myself I looked at the pictures and realized visually how clear it was I was ready to give up. I stared closely at my face and examined how sad, depressed, fed up, angry, and exhausted I had to be. And it takes me to a moment that I haven't shared yet but I would like to because I'm feeling like someone needs to read it. When I was sick and had passed out I was told I didn't gain consciousness as quickly as I normally would. I was told everyone was going crazy and praying in tongues. The doctors didn't think I would recover so they prepared my mom for the worse. In the present when my mother talks about the situation tears still fill her eyes and I get choked up hearing it. During that time I remember having many moments of my life flash before me. A vision of seeing my grandma for the last time, Shad's voice saying I love you before hanging up the phone, standing at the window hearing my friends degrade me, and visioning my mom holding one hand throughout it all when Justice should've been holding the other one. When I woke up my mom was holding my hand, crying, and told me "she lost one child and she is not trying to lose two". I still remember her saying it and how I had let it go in one ear and out the other. I ended up at the hospital again only a short time after. I didn't feel like I had any fight in me left and wish my eyes had never opened back. I was tired of being hurt. I was tired of heartache. I was just tired. But the second close call made me realize I had way too much to live for. So once again my mom whispered, "I lost one child and I don't want to lose another one". I understood it that time and realized how losing my brother deeply affected her and I didn't want her to feel that pain again. So I couldn't give up the fight of surviving. I had to find my way. I decided from that moment on that I would not let my life slip away from me again. I took what she said and let it sink deep within my spirits. And I realize I had to live, I had to overcome it, I had to forgive, and I had to keep the drama and heartache in the past so I could get back up again. I took a long hiatus from the world to work on me and was surrounded by my mom, sisters, spiritual advisors, lavender candles, pictures of my angels up above, and inspirational messages from friends and loved ones. When I took the time to fully reconnect and find myself I came out of hiatus a better me.

Read On for an exclusive excerpt from my second memoir Reset 11:22

Code Red

If there's such a thing as hell on earth, I resided there. Deadly health scares consumed every waking moment, insecurities altered my appearance, and foreclosure signs rested on my front entrance. I instantly became head of the household while having difficulty accepting my reality: I had always been a single parent. I remained devoted to a man that didn't love me back; old wombs resurfaced from past hardships while closets released dark secrets I could no longer hold back. My friendships were hanging by a thread, and I became the person who had to borrow money without a deadline for returning it. I put my career on hold and lived paycheck to paycheck as I developed a deep hatred for myself. I spent months thinking that I was hiding my pain from my son, who all along could sense something was wrong.

My son was overwhelmed and confused by my daily breakdowns at four years old.

"Don't cry, momma!" he said, staring, misty-eyed, with his little hands shivering as he touched my face.I couldn't explain to him why his mommy was upset. I couldn't explain to anybody that I wanted out of this thing called life. I remember riding home from work in a 2-hour commute when bad flashbacks, doubts, fears, anger, sadness, shame, and hatred consumed my thoughts. I was sweating, tearing up, and biting on my lip, not wanting to confess to what I had done too-myself.

Who am I?

Why am I so helpful to people who are not showing me kindness?

Why do I have to sacrifice everything for everyone?

Why am I putting my career on hold?

Why am I raising my child by myself?

Why am I not using my voice?

Why am I not losing weight?

Why is everyone turning their backs on me?

Why am I not at peace?

Why am I not happy?

Why am I here?

www.ingramcontent.com/pod-product-compliance
Lightning Source LLC
Chambersburg PA
CBHW062322120626
46553CB00015B/236